D1135312

Crop Circles

CROP CIRCLES

A Mystery Solved

Jenny Randles
and Paul Fuller

ROBERT HALE · LONDON

Copyright © Jenny Randles and Paul Fuller 1990
First published in Great Britain 1990

ISBN 0 7090 4127 6

Robert Hale Limited
Clerkenwell House
Clerkenwell Green
London EC1R 0HT

The views expressed in this book
are those of the authors
and should not be associated
with Paul Fuller's employer,
Hampshire County Council,

Photoset in Ehrhardt by
Derek Doyle & Associates, Mold, Clwyd.
Printed in Great Britain by
St Edmundsbury Press, Bury St Edmunds, Suffolk.
Bound by WBC Bookbinders Limited.

Contents

Plates

PICTURE CREDITS

Figures

'Crop circles look artificial ... They have a symmetry and a neatness which make it difficult not to believe some form of intelligence is behind them. However, I am afraid the cause comes from inner – not outer – space.' (Dr Terence Meaden, quoted in *The Observer* (London), 4 June 1988)

'The extensive data now gathered at our base in Andover, Hampshire, indicates some form of intelligence is involved, probably working in tandem with the magnetic field around our planet – and could be an aerial entity of some kind.' (Colin Andrews in *Mutual UFO Network Journal* (USA), July 1988)

'Serious and responsible ufologists must learn to persuade other investigators to adopt a more critical approach ... Too many reports are still being promoted as inexplicable in our literature when they are, in fact, clearly identifiable ... Ufologists must seek explanations.' (Paul Fuller in *International UFO Reporter* (USA), May/June 1988)

'We must be honest and true to the facts. We are not investigating the UFO or circles phenomenon to prove that men from Mars have landed. We are enquiring into fascinating questions that could be of future scientific interest. Frankly, anyone not motivated in such a manner does not deserve to call himself a ufologist.' (Jenny Randles in *BUFORA*'s 1989 status report)

'If the top scientists who have been helping us can't produce the answers through conventional science – where are we going to look to? ... The paranormal or the spirit world ...?' (Pat Delgado, on BBC1 *Daytime Live*, 3 November 1989)

These are just some of the differing views that are being expressed about this fascinating issue. Are you now thoroughly confused about who holds the answer to the baffling crop circle controversy? If you are, read on, for we think we may have the solution.

Introduction: An Alien Delusion

> A group of Extraterrestrial sympathisers plan to set up
> a special embassy for aliens after reports of strange
> circular marks in Devon. Psychic experts believe the 9
> feet rings found near Bovey Tracey are a sign that
> creatures from outer space are about to land ...
>
> *Exeter Express and Echo,* 7 August 1989

This rather startling news story could only date from the latter half
of the twentiety century. It is symptomatic of an alien delusion that
has swept across the planet since World War II – the idea that the
human race is not alone in the cosmos and that beings from
another solar system are actually coming here to establish contact.

Just what makes our society so certain that 'ET' is real and not a
Steven Spielberg fairy tale? Why do we seem to have an almost
desperate need for the intergalactic cavalry to ride to the rescue of
a stricken Earth? And why should some peculiar circular crop
marks in a British field be seized upon as 'proof' that we are facing
alien invasion? These are some of the questions which this book
will address as we face up to a fascinating scientific challenge. But
there is an even more unexpected consequence of having *solved*
the riddle of the crop circles ... which we are now claiming this
research *has* done.

For here – almost by accident – is the answer to another great
mystery of the modern age: the truth about UFOs – unidentified
flying objects.

After all, a crop circle is nothing more nor less than an oddly
uniform depression seemingly cut into free-standing cereal.
Usually there is a swirl pattern inside the flattened centre and quite
sharply delineated edges. It does look strange at first glance, but
why should we immediately presume it has anything to do with
UFOs?

There is no doubt that the crop circles are a puzzle. Here is the full, unabridged story of how they came to be discovered, initially in ones and twos and then in astonishing abundance, growing from a local fad into a national debate and becoming by 1990 a topic under discussion from Wall Street to Fleet Street and from the Meteorological Office to the House of Commons.

Crop circles may be 'new', but UFOs and aliens have always captured the public imagination. As officers of the British UFO Research Association (BUFORA), both authors are very familiar with the facts and the fantasies that pepper this field. Ideas that are paraded as scientific truths concerning spaceships are often nothing more than wild speculation.

Jenny Randles receives press cuttjngs on behalf of BUFORA through a respected national agency: this enables her to distribute promising cases for full investigation by trained and cautious researchers, people who fully admit – up front – that they can explain away as many as ninety-five per cent of these sightings. Prior to 1987 a typical year's stock of cuttings, culled from national and local newspapers and magazines, averaged out at between 250 and 350. But suddenly there has been a huge escalation: 1987 brought 520, 1988 led to 885 and 1989 reached 900! Just what is going on? Do these figures prove that we are being invaded by aliens? Or do they reflect a change within society on a more subtle level? Certainly recent surveys by the Gallup poll show that in Britain as many as one in five educated people believes alien UFOs to be a fact, whereas in the USA the total of believers climbs to a staggering near one in two! '

Serious ufologists have never been so busy attempting to stem this tide. In 1989 Jenny Randles found herself appearing on all four national TV networks in Britain (BBC, ITV, Channel 4 and SKY satellite channel) as well as stations in the USA. The Ministry of Defence (which receives reports of UFOs from police stations, coastguards and military bases) had a record time of it during the last three years of the decade – receiving over 2,000 cases. In just one week during late October 1989, Jenny was asked to evaluate more than a dozen reports from north-west England which were received by the Jodrell Bank radio astronomy centre in Cheshire. Of course, the fact that so many people choose a space centre as the correct place to take reports of UFOs shows the strength of the alien myth. All we have are reports of strange phenomena perceived in our skies, so why do these witnesses report them to a space centre?

This trend is global. All over the world UFOs are taking hold of the imagination – and now, with the great new wonder of the crop circles dangled before us, we *seem* for some to be heading toward a fabulous revelation.

Understandably, many intelligent people, especially scientists, scoff and demand proof – although the proof they request is of spaceships. They presume that the phenomenon must be alien in order for it to exist. Yet such proof is impossible to offer, because UFOs are not spaceships. So the entire subject is dismissed as an irrelevancy through circular logic.

Reviewing Jenny's book *Abduction* for the *Daily Telegraph* (11 November 1989), respected science writer Adrian Berry makes that point. Whilst Jenny rejected the spaceships solution in her work (for many cogent reasons inherent within the data), she suggested that the reports do require consideration by professional scientists, because something (even if it be only psychological in origin) *must* be taking place. Yet Berry says (without justification in our opinion) that it is an 'obvious fact' that witnesses are 'either lunatics or hoaxers or are of extremely low intelligence … [she] castigates us for rejecting UFOs "without proper study". But this, until there is proof, is exactly what we must do. One must reject it because there is nothing to study.'

This view is sadly typical but fails to represent the reality of the dilemma. Mr Berry, like so many others within the scientific community, assumes that UFOs are supposed to be products of an alien intelligence, rightly says there is no acceptable evidence for that and so erroneously concludes that there is 'nothing to study'. But just because we can prove that the moon is not made of green cheese hardly makes the moon unworthy of scientific exploration. In our view the same is true of UFOs. There is good evidence of value to accepted fields such as perceptual psychology, sociology, atmospheric physics and geophysics. As ufologists we have striven for years to persuade the scientific community to reject false logic that has now become a creed. It is no longer acceptable to argue that UFOs must be spaceships or they cannot exist.

If we applied Adrian Berry's opinion in general, it would stifle all scientific progress. The history of science is the result of mysteries and puzzles that required answers, and so answers were duly and rigorously sought. True those answers when postulated are sometimes absurd, but modern atomic chemistry exists and benefits all our lives, whereas, had we denied the very existence of chemical changes simply because we could not believe in magic or alchemy, presumably we would not now have nuclear reactors or effective medicines. Science has to understand that its dogma on such contentious issues filters through to the thinking individual and causes some to rebel. If there is no common sense or moderation offered by science, it is inevitable that humanity will be driven toward extremes.

Take one instance. In his local newspaper (*Basingstoke Gazette*, 28 July 1989) 'alien hunter John McShane' typifies the many amateur UFO buffs springing up as pundits in the wake of the circles mania – eager to find answers when science runs away. We are told that, 'He plans to spend nights on Salisbury Plain hoping for a glimpse of a flying saucer and trying to make contact with its occupants.' Why should an intelligent man want to forsake the comfort of his sofa and TV in search of such improbable activity? The paper reports that he tells us that UFOs are appearing in great abundance because, 'The environment is under threat ... they are worried we will destroy the planet and put the whole solar system out of kilter.' As for the circles, there seems to be no doubt: 'Aliens have landed and are taking soil samples to find out what chemicals we are using on earth.'

Well, maybe he is right. His theory is no stranger than many others which these baffling crop marks have generated. But it is just speculation, even if it does masquerade quite successfully as something more.

Phil Shaw, in a letter to the *Bournemouth Advertiser* (28 September 1989) says that the patterns may be 'the ghosts of prehistoric round barrows'. Ancient fertility rites at such spots may have left an imprint in the 'tape recorder' of the earth which is coming back to haunt our troubled species and to remind us of 'our responsibility to keep our planet clean and fertile and free from "meanness and greed"'. Maybe he has got it right?

Not so, claims one lady from London (in a letter to Jenny Randles dated 13 October 1989). She argues that the power of collective human thought is manifesting the spirit of ancient crop goddesses to spell out dire warnings of ecological catastrophe. 'See here – this is what will happen to your food if you do not pay heed,' seems to be the motto from the cosmic supermind.

Peter Froude (again in the *Bournemouth Advertiser*, but on 14 September 1989) has yet another source for these danger signals. These are 'spiritual minds, that we once called Elohim'. He elaborates: '... we live in a greedy, materialist world that is rapidly destroying itself through industrial pollution and the burning of the rain forests ... these circles are an indication of a concern that emanates from far beyond our planet ...' Apparently these universal masters (which we may sometimes call 'gods') are beaming thoughts instantaneously across dimensional space and flattening the crops with psychic powers, like super-efficient Uri Gellers.

Why do these people feel so strongly that both circles and UFOs have an exotic answer? How many people have familiarized themselves with the data or spent time researching circle sites first hand? Probably very few. It is just that the human thirst for exciting explanations for mysteries has overpowered the need to be rational. But (as Adrian Berry and many others show so well) it is just as easy to be *too* rational and conclude that, *because* an anomaly generates exotic solutions, the anomaly itself has no substance. True objectivity requires that you reach conclusions from the full range of facts, not choose sides through prejudice about extremes.

Such esoteric ideas have joined the ranks of the mundane (for example, foxes, demented hedgehogs and the mating habits of deer!) as postulated causes for over 800 documented crop circles – of all shapes, sizes and patterns. These have turned up in fields all round Britain (and to a lesser extent in Australia, Canada, the USA and many other nations) throughout the 1980s seemingly arriving in ever-increasing profusion.

But it is undoubtedly the mystique of the alien that is so attractive to most people. These patterns *look* disturbingly artificial. We cast aside appreciation that nature can and does work sometimes in order and beautiful intricacy and yearn for someone 'out there' giving us 'a sign'. Yet think about snowflakes under a microscope or the precise geometric patterns in the Giant's Causeway rock formation of Ireland: you are forced into sudden recognition that nature can – and does – sometimes work in a manner that *seems* artificial. However, even if we know this at one level, most of us prefer to wonder and grasp at any opportunity to ascribe these circles to a non-earthly power.

Here is that point graphically portrayed: 'I was enthralled by the recent pictures of the mysterious circles that have appeared in English corn fields,' BBC personality Gloria Hunniford told the 325,000 readers of *Weekend* magazine on 9 September 1989. 'They are huge, isolated rings where something heavy would seem to have landed ... Maybe the circles were made by the wind generated by rotating helicopter blades. But there's part of me which would prefer to believe in a more colourful explanation.'

Ms Hunniford is honest about a feeling we all share. And, of course, her opinions are persuasive to millions who read her articles, listen to her on radio and watch her on TV. In this way they reinforce a widely held (if subconscious) desire. It is a desire which can easily go too far.

'The circles are indeed the result of a UFO landing to probe the crops. There is no other explanation ...' says Ken Rogers of the Unexplained Society, with admirable assurance and conviction. His voice is amplified by others: 'The formations suggest some kind of aerial machinery,' warns Richard Lawrence of the Aetherius Society – which claims telepathic rapport with aliens (*Today*, 6 July 1989). He adds: 'Of course, the main problem is UFOs are capable of being invisible.'

Such strong viewpoints do not reflect the attitude of all ufologists but are the ones that attract most media attention (because they are dramatic and newsworthy). In this way the alien delusion is strengthened, and it is hardly surprising that sober commentators such as Adrian Berry conclude that UFOs and crop circles have got to be utter nonsense, if they are supported by a group of individuals whom they more than likely consider to be preaching pseudo-science.

Even the erudite and normally quite practical *Wall Street Journal* has discussed the circles (28 August 1989), reporting an allegation that the Queen was personally interested and that they '...could be a cry for help. It could mean – if you destroy this food your planet is finished.'

This last quote is now helping to conquer new heights, spreading the alien delusion around the United States. You see this in the December 1989 edition of *Fate*, the large-circulation paranormal magazine found on the world's news-stands and issued from Minnesota. Donald Michael Kraig commented: 'There is something strange going on in the fields of England; so strange in fact that Queen Elizabeth has been studying the problem.' That is a contentious statement. Has anybody *asked* the Queen and established the facts? Even if the Queen was sent a copy of the book described below, that does not mean that she asked for the book (many are sent to her unsolicited) or that she read it.

Nevertheless, *Fate* continues: 'Nobody knows what [these circles] are ... One debunker claims it is a whirlwind, but farmers who own the land where the circles are discount this ...' Kraig then lists ideas proposed: 'An unknown intelligence, a Star Wars type defence system gone amok, a crazed hedgehog, too much or too little fertilization and alien ships – UFOs'. He even adds of UFOs that, 'Near some of the circles a mysterious white substance has been found. So far laboratories haven't been able to identify it.' Similar ideas were later featured in the top-rated NBC television show 'Unsolved Mysteries'.

You will see as you progress through this book that several of these opinions (now influencing millions of people – particularly in the USA) are open to very serious doubt. But the problem stems from the media snowball: taking dubious sources, rewriting what was said, translating this into other words and crossing oceans. In the end it becomes like the legendary army message which began its life as 'The enemy is going to advance: send reinforcements' which was passed down the front line of soldiers in whispered voices and finally reached the last man as 'The enemy has gone to a dance: send three-and-four pence'!

Where did the story of the crop circles suddenly achieve such international proportions? The *Wall Street Journal* quote comes from British engineer Pat Delgado, consultant to a wonderful magazine of sincere yet delightfully odd anecdotes, the *Flying Saucer Review* (usually abbreviated to *FSR*). Never one to balk at the unusual, this journal (which apparently circulates in some influential places) has debated how UFO-orientated library books might be spirited away in order to condition the populace into patterns of thought, how Jinns (i.e. genies) may be piloting UFOs and how AIDS could be a plague sent here by the aliens.

Along with his colleague Colin Andrews (who also spent several years as a *Flying Saucer Review* consultant), Pat Delgado published 'Circular Evidence', which in 1989 was almost single-handedly responsible for ensuring that the circles became an international topic of major debate. It tried very hard to be analytical and does contain some excellent photographs (thanks greatly to private pilot 'Busty' Taylor, whose tireless work is regrettably unsung), but the book also unfortunately has what we believe to be serious deficiencies which prevent the reader's reaching a full conclusion about the crop circles. We shall try to compensate for this in our text.

Nonetheless, the furore generated by publication of *Circular Evidence* has a special part to play in this study, for it highlights how large sections of the general public believe what they want to believe and disregard facts if they seem on the surface to be unpalatable, and just how many folk can be led all to easily into what we are calling 'the alien delusion' – presumably because society is of the view that both UFOs and crop circles must have exotic explanations in order to be interesting.

This is a view that we intend to challenge.

Throughout the summer of 1989 we inevitably saw many media appearances by Andrews and Delgado as they promoted the exotic views about the circles that can be found in some parts of their book. The 4 million readers of *The Sun* (11 July 1989) were told: 'There must be some force field manipulated by unexplained intelligence.' This was reputedly a quote from Pat Delgado, which (as we appreciate) may not be wholly accurate or fully in context. However, it seems to match what he has been quoted as saying in many other places, even if the book itself wisely draws back from saying it too explicitly. Yet in the joint conclusions we find both Andrews and Delgado saying: 'Each new formation strengthens the current feeling of many people that we are dealing with something that hints at some form of manipulated force.'[1] And elsewhere phrases such as 'unknown powers or forces'[2] and, 'We may be looking for an unrecognised force ... perhaps a transportable force used at will by some controlling power.'[3]

It is not hard to understand why journalists tended to translate such obscure comments into what they *thought* Andrews and Delgado had meant – that is, that 'unknown intelligence' equals 'aliens', and 'transportable force' equals 'spaceships'. It may well not have been what the authors intended, but they have to forgive others for thinking so, given the ambiguity of their words and the frequent references to UFOs in the concluding section of the book (indeed, all bar three of their seventeen cited references are actually UFO books or magazines – and even the other three are for a book called *Life in Space*).

In *FSR* in 1987 Pat Delgado discussed the discovery of the letters 'WEARENOTALONE' (all mixed together like this), found marked out in crops in a field beside the 1986 Cheesefoot Head (Hampshire) circles.[4] The photographs of this were not published in *Circular Evidence*. To us, this incident is one of the clearest indications that hoaxing sometimes complicates the circles issue.

Andrews and Delgado have said that they are not fooled by hoaxing, but of what looks to us to be a quite blatant example by some unknown source, Delgado told *FSR* readers: 'At first sight it was an obvious hoax, but prolonged study makes me wonder.' He adds that the circles appear 'strongly symbolistic ... in the form of a challenge to de-code'. He suggests cell structures and planets or asteroids circling the Earth as possibilities, then adds: 'Maybe these circles are created by alien beings using a force-field unknown to us. They may be manipulating existing Earth energy.' Yet when the authors appeared on BBC television in November 1989 and it was suggested that such claims as these mean that they regard 'little green men' as likely agents of the circles, the idea was vehemently denied. This inevitably creates confusion as to what they *do* mean.

It may appear that we are out to discredit UFOs, crop circles and those who connect them, but that is not our intention. We have been personally involved in the crop-circle mystery for some years and have worked with professional scientists – notably physicist Terence Meaden, who has studied it for longer than anybody else. Jenny Randles first spoke out for a natural scientific appraisal of the circles in the national press during 1983 and appeared on national TV debating the circles with a scientist before (we think) any of the other parties now involved. Paul Fuller has conducted in-field and original research since 1986 that has not been duplicated or reported to the general public as yet.

We believe we have something important to contribute to the ongoing debate and that Dr Meaden's work needs to be better and more widely read. Also there are some aspects of his research that we do not entirely agree with, so that, whilst we contend that he is on the right lines, it is important to make clear that we are not his mouthpiece and have reached our own independent conclusions with much original data. These conclusions do differ in part from those expressed by the atmospheric physicist.

It is really a fascinating story, full of the stuff that makes a good spy thriller. It also happens to be a wonderful testament to the human spirit's innermost needs, and a fine example of how science can triumph over magic. More important than that, this is a factual drama of how a fight to disprove what seemed to be the superstitious myth of funny circular marks led, almost by chance, to a breakthrough in earth sciences which may provoke technological revolutions.

1 The Arrival of the Circles

UFOs have been a popular issue for many years, but strange circular marks in fields are apparently something new. That is why they provoke such interest. According to most sources, they arrived in the summer of 1980. Since then they have rapidly become something of an epidemic, with fields in southern England regularly coming out in 'extraterrestrial' rashes every year between May and September.

In *Circular Evidence*, Andrews and Delgado assert that it was a triple formation (three single circles in a line) which appeared at Cheesefoot Head, near Winchester, in 1981 that had 'the honour of starting the flood of interest and exchange of information about this phenomenon'.[1] That passage is said to have been written by Colin Andrews, but he was not reportedly involved in circles research until about 1985, so it presumably must be Pat Delgado who wrote that, 'The impact they had on me was sensational'. In the book's introduction he uses other emotive words, such as 'profound', to tell how he decided to alert the world to this new-found mystery, immediately contacting national newspapers, the BBC and ITN. He should not have been surprised when they carried features interpreting the marks as evidence of alien spaceship landings.

However, this honorary status afforded the 1981 circles is a little unjustified. Delgado did not appear to know of the precedent for the Winchester circles that was set in 1980, when similar marks first attracted national attention. However, these were still not the first to be reported locally or in UFO records. It is surprising that Delgado seems to ignore them in his book's historical overview. Here is what occurred.

On 15 August 1980 the *Wiltshire Times* had a small item referring to the discovery of some unexplained circular marks in a field of oats owned by John Scull at Westbury in Wiltshire. The field was overlooked by the spectacular White Horse carved onto the hillside[2] and is in the vicinity of the town of Warminster – which during the sixties was the centre of the UFO universe, drawing spotters from all over the world to watch 'the thing', as the glowing lights seen frequently in the area became affectionately known. Books were written on the topic, especially by local journalist Arthur Shuttlewood.[3] Today Warminster's UFO heritage lives on through graffiti on the local barns and through a number of esoteric societies which in the actions of regional mystics and UFO-enthusiasts periodically seek (with little success) to resurrect the importance of this 'place of power'.

Such a significant social context for the arrival of the circles ought not to be overlooked, but few commentators spotted the clue. Fortunately the area supported serious ufologists, such as Ian Mrzyglod and Mike Seager from the local group PROBE. Ian soon became a director of BUFORA and reported soberly on his investigations with much skill.

The two ufologists saw the press cutting and decided to look into the matter. They visited the site as early as 16 August and took photographs (see Plate 2). Unfortunately the first circle (a single one), found in May, had not been reported by Mr Scull and by 16 August the field in which it sat had been harvested. When he discovered two more, on 13 August, Scull reported them as a curious anomaly – nothing more.

The circles were 135 metres apart. One measured almost nineteen metres in diameter, and the other was just under eighteen metres. As Ian Mrzyglod quickly noted in *Probe Report*, the journal which he edited, 'Neither of the depressions were exactly circular, but about 90–95% so. The beds of the nests consisted of flattened corn (oats) although in [the larger circle] there were small patches where this was still standing at varying heights (between 1 foot 6 inches and 3 feet 6 inches) (i.e. 50–100 cm), but in general the corn was totally flattened at ground level creating a spiral effect in each circle that extended from the centre in a clockwise direction ...'[4] The larger of the two circles (both of which had sharply delineated edges where the crop stood up straight) was less well defined. One side of the circle had an inward spur at about four o'clock and an outward spur at one o'clock. The inward spur had non-flattened crop but did show a slight tendency to bend in a clockwise manner.

Thus even the very 'first' reported circles had features that were rather complex and which some researchers have falsely ascribed only to much later examples as evidence suggesting ongoing alien messages.

The *Probe* report, very sensibly, concluded: 'This would indicate that the corn was flattened by air pressure or pressure of a similar nature. There are no tracks leading to or from the depression except for the small tracks made by Mr Scull and ourselves ... There are several irregular marks in the same field which bend the corn to a certain extent and these may be connected.'

Later research showed that the circles probably first appeared overnight on 21 July and 31 July 1980. Soil samples and other readings were taken by *Probe* in an admirably scientific attempt to seek an explanation. In no way did they try to link them with UFOs – Ken Rogers was the first to do so, on behalf of the UFO community. He was one of the leaders of the ufological 'New Age' movement and endorsed the UFO nature of the 'landing nests' in *NOW!*, a national news magazine which picked up on the local press item and alone promoted these strange marks during that first summer.

The 1981 circles at Cheesefoot which so entranced Pat Delgado were in most senses similar to those the year before at Westbury. However, they were all in a line, with a large central circle and two smaller satellites, somewhat more 'perfect' than those at Westbury and also suspiciously 'artificial' rather than random. This caused many ufologists to wonder if Ken Rogers might not be right about the origin of these marks.

Nevertheless, *Probe* had continued their first-class research and had joined forces with physicist Dr Terence Meaden, editor of the *Journal of Meteorology* (abbreviated to *J Met*). In this journal he had already published his views on the 1980 Westbury circles, based on his joint evaluation with Mrzyglod. He suggested that a rare species of 'whirlwind' was to blame.[5]

The ufologist and atmospheric physicist collaborated again in *Probe Report* to lay to rest the spectre of artificiality besetting the 1981 circles. They pointed out that both sites (Westbury and Cheesefoot) were adjacent to steep hill slopes and that meteorological factors were too similar at times of formation for there not to be an apparent causal link. A weather-based theory seemed not only plausible but probable, given the accumulating data, and they suggested a monitor of the sites in mid-summer

1982, when both the weather and the growing season of the crops combined to make recording of the vortex most likely.[6]

Pat Delgado told *Flying Saucer Review* about the Cheesefoot circles as soon as possible.[7] He recorded how he had instantly alerted all major media sources, who promptly tried to wish it away. He noted that one of the landowners, Mr Rowsell, called the views of UFO-spotters such as Ken Rogers 'a load of tripe' but that in his own view no solution fitted, causing him to ask *FSR* readers: '... what are we left with? The UFO society's load of tripe?' He further noted that a famous (if rather curious) UFO abduction story had occurred in 1975 (in fact, it was actually November 1976) just a few miles from Cheesefoot. Thus it was evident from the very start that Pat Delgado was considering the exotic UFO explanation.

At the time, *FSR* was a much respected magazine edited by the late Charles Bowen, a highly responsible diplomat at a state office. (Jenny Randles was in 1982 secretarial assistant to Mr Bowen and to *FSR*.) To his credit, he allowed Ian Mrzyglod space to comment on Delgado's piece in a letter published two months later.[8]

Mrzyglod pointed out that he and Dr Meaden had studied the circles and had concluded that there was a natural explanation. He closed: 'What now concerns me is that ... people in the four corners of the world may now be under the impression that UFO activity caused mysterious circles in a Hampshire field ...'

1982 turned out to be a poor summer weatherwise, and this was probably not unconnected with the fact that the fairly small-scale monitors by *Probe* and Dr Meaden at Westbury and Cheesefoot failed to find any circles.

Ian Mrzyglod took the chance to try to demystify the events along the lines of his *FSR* letter. In *J Met* he wrote of the 1980 and 1981 circles: 'At first we were at a loss to find a rational and realistic explanation for their occurrence, but eventually help came from Dr G. T. Meaden of the Tornado and Storm Research Organisation ... [who] studied photographs supplied by ourselves, together with this information, site measurements, general topographical details and prevailing weather conditions [and] arrived at the theory that whirlwinds were responsible for creating them. This explanation was treated with some scepticism, especially by members of the *Probe* team who actually stood in the centres of these circles. It seemed inconceivable that mere weather could cause such precise and massive damage ...'[9]

Of course, as those of us involved in the saga were all coming to realize, 'mere weather' was very much an understatement of what was involved, and the term 'whirlwind' was slightly misleading, as we were not dealing with an ordinary species of wind vortex such as commonly happens in many places. This was clearly something interesting and different. It seemed to represent a novel and potentially unrecognized atmospheric mechanism.

Another magazine for which Ian Mrzyglod wrote was *The Unexplained*. In this he had an article which argued that circles were not supernatural, and it reached all serious students of the paranormal and many members of the public. After that there was no longer any excuse for ignorance amongst ufologists of at least the basic facts as then understood.

This liaison with *The Unexplained* had an unexpected benefit. Their London offices called Mrzyglod to say that a member of the public had sent photographs of a fifteen metre diameter circle which he had found on 10 August 1982. This man claimed not to know of any media publicity for the 1980 and 1981 patterns and had merely submitted what he saw as an 'anomaly'. This circle was at a new site – yet again in the lee of a hill, but a quite remarkable hill: Cley Hill, Warminster, one of the key sites from which tens of thousands had watched for UFOs over the previous two decades! PROBE went to the site, found the circle and indeed saw another (even larger) single circle in another field in the lee of the hill. This field had been harvested by the time of the visit (late in August), but from the high vantage-point the remains of that second eighteen-metre diameter circle were still clearly visible.

As you can imagine, this discovery was important for several reasons. It tended to suggest that many sites might be generating circles and that most were going undiscovered. From ground-level the Cley Hill circles would have been almost impossible to spot unless you walked right into the middle of the fields containing them. Quite what the very direct connection with the UFO capital of Warminster said about the developing situation was another matter, and sensibly Ian Mrzyglod did *not* go running to the media or to *FSR* with this story but reported it factually through meteorological sources.

The lack of activity in 1982 had also given PROBE the chance to seek out historical data. It was already becoming clear to Dr Meaden that circles *had* been found before 1980 and had often been interpreted as 'UFO nests'. 1976 (a hot summer) had

generated several and also offered a series of photographs of a
whirlwind that had attacked a cereal field between Braintree and
Halstead in Essex on 18 August. These photographs, taken by
witness Roy Williamson, were used by PROBE to try to pacify
ufologists still arguing about how a whirlwind could stay still and
create circular damage.

Unfortunately no circles were left in this Essex field, because the
crop was already harvested. But Ian Mrzyglod discovered from
extensive local inquiries with farmers in and around Warminster
that they accepted the whirlwind solution to the circles because,

> They had seen them on many occasions causing similar damage,
> in some cases ripping the corn out from the ground ... They also
> informed the author that four smaller circles were seen dotted
> about the [Cley Hill] field we were standing in, and luckily the
> remains of one, measuring roughly 15 feet (4.5 metres), were
> still visible. But this circle was not quite the same as the others;
> the corn had not been totally flattened, just angled over, giving
> the impression that a lesser force had been responsible. When
> looking closer at this circle, which incidentally was placed
> several hundred yards away from the base of Cley Hill and thus
> was not in a position to suffer the full effects of a stationary
> whirlwind, it was not really circular, but oval in shape. This
> indicated that the whirlwind was moving as it flattened the corn
> until it died seconds after birth.[10]

You can perhaps see why BUFORA associates, fully aware of
the work of Ian Mrzyglod and Terence Meaden, had concluded
that the case for the meteorological solution was too solid to be in
doubt. We were amazed at the apparent myth-making desires of
some ufologists (who either ignored or did not know of these
matters but who frankly should have found out before speaking
publicly about the issue). Presenting circles as alien and exotic was
discrediting serious UFO research, let alone hampering Dr
Meaden's attempts to prove his case before the scientific court.
This is why BUFORA fought hard to clean up the image of the
circles, despite what was then our (incorrect) view that there was
no direct relevance to the UFO phenomenon.

By now Pat Delgado's discovery of more 'odd' things in
Cheesefoot was sufficient to persuade him, as he told his *FSR*
readers, that, 'These circles are formed by some force unknown to
us.'[11] Again, Delgado explains that he took his discoveries to the

media and was this time much more successful in whipping up national attention.

The events of summer 1983 must be emphasized, because they turned the circles from something that for three years was barely mentioned outside local media in Hampshire and Wiltshire (plus UFO and meteorological journals) into what was now a national 'silly season' hype that lasted several days and even achieved brief attention outside Britain. The American tabloid newspaper *Weekly World News* announced on 16 August 1983 that a giant UFO had landed and created great consternation amongst mythical farmers. The story appears to have had little (if any) substance but was symptomatic of the depths this relatively innocuous mystery had begun to plumb. The intervention of the media hailing UFOs as the source of the circles was the last thing we needed at this stage.

On 8 July 1983 the *Wiltshire Times* first reported the matter, with the news that circles had turned up at Westbury. Unlike the initial ones in 1980 or the 1981 Cheesefoot triple, these were in a formation of five. Whilst at the time this seemed like a dramatic new escalation of the mystery, it was later found by examination of the best aerial shots of the 1980 circles at the same spot, as taken by *NOW!* magazine, that these too had faint outer satellites. There were only three of them, not four as in the new 1983 formation, but the fourth one would have been precisely where a hedgerow sat, and so this presumably prevented the final satellite's forming. Indeed, subsequent reports indicated that a quintuplet may also have formed even earlier, at Headbourne Worthy, near Winchester, Hampshire. So the increase in complexity seems to have been an accident of reporting, not a true factor.

The *Wiltshire Times* trotted out the usual mass of conflicting explanations, saying that 'UFO-believers' reckoned they looked like 'the landing pads of a giant flying saucer'. But BUFORA and Dr Meaden were trying to accommodate the new pattern into the weather theory. July 1983 was the hottest for 300 years, which was possibly a reason for the increased number of circles, and the quintuplets that became quite common that summer.

The media loved the spaceship theory. The *Western Daily Press* said on 9 July, 'Watch out! Martians are back' and explained how locals were 'keeping an eye out for little green men'. Ken Rogers was happy to reinforce this view, suggesting that the circles indicated that a new wave of sightings was due.

By now terminology such as 'the famous Warminster triangle' was being invented by the press (*Daily Express*, 11 July 1983). With TV news bulletins and several national newspapers in on the act, a whole new series of possible explanations had to be contemplated for what was taking place.

No longer could we be sure we were dealing with a phenomenon that was occurring without the intervention of social factors. There was a much wider awareness throughout the nation that the phenomenon existed, meaning that people went out and actively looked for circles in fields. Copycat hoaxing was also likely to be incited by all this attention. Overnight the entire circles phenomenon had become vastly more complicated by the involvement of the media in such a big way.

The main national press attention was in the *Daily Express*, which carried stories on 11, 12 and 15 July. The movie *ET* was popular at the time and the Space Age angle for the circles was the one this normally middle-of-the-road newspaper adopted, giving a pin-up of the Spielberg 'alien' alongside a circle formation and a headline reading 'ET – Phone the Express'.

After extensive involvement within it, Jenny commented on a very interesting consequence of all this media attention, which did produce more reports of circles than ever before and further new sites of manifestation. She pointed out that, 'A media hype of the most extreme kind did not create masses of spurious [UFO] sightings. Not even one sighting ... nobody [has] seen a UFO anywhere near [the circles], either before or since their appearance.'[12] Hardly proof of a UFO link.

Another result of the summer's massive publicity was the arrival of the first *proven* hoax: a 'discovery' of the most complex type of circle yet seen (the quintuplet formation). That it was seen, reported and apparently only discovered to be a hoax weeks later by diligent work from Ian Mrzyglod argues against the claims of some circles researchers that hoaxing is never capable of fooling anybody with a knowledge of the phenomenon. (See Chapter 5 for a fuller account of this important hoax.)

Needless to say, some ufologists were far from happy with Jenny Randles' public support for Ian Mrzyglod and Terence Meaden's natural solution. The reaction from some quarters might fairly be termed hostile.

Paul Fuller had now joined the ranks, and we fought within BUFORA to justify time and expense on circles research. We believed it was important to speak out at every opportunity to correct false impressions and dubious speculations filling the media and linking alien powers with this intriguing phenomenon. Those discoveries were not what many subscribers to UFO societies appeared to want, but scientific integrity dictated that keeping believers happy had to take second place to sober reporting of the facts. Luckily BUFORA responded well, and the membership generally applauded the thankless task the group took on. There were some who did not.

Things were never less than eventful. In July 1985 Jenny had a fascinating conversation with one Fleet Street newspaper. They were looking into more tales about a circle in Findon, Sussex, where a witness had seen vaporous smoke rising at dawn. Jenny tried to suggest that the smoke might just be normal dawn mist rising from the field; and she was curious as to why, if spaceship landing marks were to blame, these were never the same size or even circular. The newspaper indicated that the mist was probably 'exhaust fumes' and that the changes in shape and size were explicable if the UFO tended to skid on impact!

In summer 1988 Dr Terence Meaden came into the firing-line. He began to talk publicly about his work, clearly dispelling the alien intelligence media hype as nonsense and strongly demonstrating that a novel but natural phenomenon was to blame.

Some circles appeared in Leicestershire that year, and the *Leicester Mercury* aired the gathering debate. On 8 July 1988 Pat Delgado insisted: 'A natural force could not create such intriguing patterns', whereas Dr Meaden countered (13 July) that (in his interpretation), '[Some people] believe these circles were formed by UFOs. That is nothing but pie in the sky which is wasting a lot of people's time ...'

Not surprisingly, Colin Andrews disputed these words. He is quoted as considering the weather-based theory as 'far too simplistic ... it is ridiculous to keep harping on about it. We now have the data to prove these circles are intelligently locating themselves. And there are even more bizarre facts that we dare not release. It is chilling ...'

By 21 July Delgado was telling the *Winchester Extra*: 'We are so disgusted' with Dr Meaden and his theory. Furthermore, '...we don't want anything to do with him.' Dr Meaden had just addressed a meteorology conference in Oxford, had papers in the major weather publications upcoming and within a year was asked to give a keynote speech at a conference on atmospheric physics in Tokyo. This hardly suggests that the meteorological community was openly ridiculing his work. Yet according to published quotes from Delgado, the meteorological office in Bracknell 'fell on the floor laughing' when asked about Meaden's ideas.

2   The Intergalactic Cavalry

It is important to evaluate the social context of the subject, so in order to see why crop circles are treated as a paranormal dilemma (and usually one involving UFOs) we need to assess the people and the data from which such presumptions arise.

By the end of this section we will be ready to tackle the issue of the crop circles with surprising new insights to bring to bear on the matter.

A Magical Deception

Most major powers take at least a routine interest in UFOs. The French, for example, have a small team of scientists based at the official space centre in Toulouse and trained *gendarmerie* who investigate cases in the field.[1] Documentation available shows that the French government does accept that scientific puzzles remain within ufology and that it has carried out in-depth inquiries, even into curious circular traces on the ground.[2]

The British defence ministry does acknowledge that (as they phrased it in a letter to Jenny Randles), 'Many puzzling things are seen in the skies.' But this is very different from an acceptance that *any* of those 'puzzling things' is a spaceship from another world. Nevertheless, any official admission that UFOs were 'real' would undoubtedly be misinterpreted as an admission that the aliens have landed. So the authorities (who may consider UFOs to be interesting 'natural' phenomena) are really forced to show caution when they relate in public to the issue.

One internal memo from early in the life of the French team tells how the scientists and government officials debated release of any news that their investigation was providing positive scientific data. They concluded that 'great vigilance' was the order of the day when speaking out on such matters.

31

The British Ministry of Defence (MoD) has often stated that they collect data and don't dismiss its relevance. Unfortunately the media market-place inevitably sensationalizes what is being claimed into talk of cover-ups and confrontations. More 'responsible' journalistic outlets shy away from debating the situation altogether, which only further reinforces the image of crackpot crusaders fighting to prove that 'the great truth' is being hidden from us all.

In fact, just about the one conclusion we have been able to reach with any certainty is that (in our view) no huge secrets are being kept. Frankly, in this day and age how would it be possible to prevent leaks or death-bed confessions filtering out through totally conclusive evidence?

No – the so-called 'cover-up', such as it is, surely exists for sensible, precautionary reasons because of the alien delusion that accompanies the UFO subject. It is also in force to hide the important fact that unexplained phenomena *do* occur. They are in the archives of every major government – as we know from nations which openly publish such material.

It is very probable (indeed, given conversations we have had with ministry sources, we would say 'certain') that within the MoD data there are baffling cases that appear to represent novel scientific phenomena. It is not the task of any defence unit to research the nature of these phenomena. The MoD merely filters out any cases that might represent enemy aircraft or foreign technology. That is, after all, what we pay it to do.

But there is more to it than that. Such data may be of potential use to science. We have copies of several of these MoD 'UFO' reports given to us by ministry sources since 1983. Some of them include distribution lists demonstrating that the only recipient of two copies of all such cases is the Department of Scientific and Technical Intelligence (DSTI), where MoD scientists and RAF intelligence officers can presumably check them over for any clues about novel science. One has to remember that weapons systems *are* of interest to the MoD, even if UFOs (strictly) are not, and it pays to monitor the data just in case they represent information about unusual energy forces amenable to useful technological development.

Many *thousands* of files have emerged from nations with freedom-of-information laws, especially the USA. Sources as diverse as the armed forces, CIA, FBI and electronic-monitor and satellite surveillance outfit, the National Security Agency, have poured out a stream of paper dating from 1947 (when the modern UFO mystery was born) right up to more recent times.

Naturally enough, this mass of paperwork (much of which the present authors have studied or possess) is interpreted rather like pictures in tea-leaves: you can read into the words just about anything you want to read. What is beyond question is that such groups as the CIA collate data on UFOs for reasons of defence potential, and there are obvious signs in some of the documents that research projects are ongoing which are seeking to develop energy sources and propulsion systems based on some of the (almost certainly natural) phenomena now being reported as UFOs.

The cover-up, if you like, exists to hide ignorance, rather than amazing truths obscured for the good of the world. Answers are still being sought.

By late 1989 parts of the American UFO community had developed an entire extra-terrestrial anthropology and sociology from these papers, typified by an extraordinary twenty-seven page 'secret' dossier widely circulating amongst the UFO community and containing yet more 'high-level' leaks.

Reputedly, *dozens* of spaceships have crashed in the past forty years, and countless alien bodies and survivors have been recovered. By 1952 the United States was desperately trying to save the last remaining live alien (who was none too well) and started beaming out intergalactic 999 calls around the universe. Within a year a fleet of giant spaceships headed for Earth, and the 'large-nosed Grays' (just one of a whole tourist industry of alien races visiting us by then) landed at Holloman Air Force Base in Texas after flying there from Betelgeuse in the Orion nebula.

President Eisenhower, ever one to court new allies, apparently struck up a treaty with the 'Grays', and Krill (actually spelt Krlll!) became Earth's first ambassador from another world. In exchange for UFOs that the Americans could fly themselves on secret bases, and for other magical technology, a quota system was agreed for how many people the 'Grays' could kidnap in any one year. Such abductions began in earnest in the late fifties, and the USA was given a regular list of all humans chosen by the aliens (since the humans did not normally remember the kidnaps for themselves).

Unfortunately the Grays were not to be trusted, and Earth soon found out that they were carrying out a double-cross. Terrible genetic experiments had begun, siphoning off body fluids and other bits of homo sapiens, apparently necessary because the aliens were a dying breed. The aliens admitted to stage-managing all the world's religions and showed a hologram made at the time of the crucifixion of Jesus as 'proof' of this.

We should stress that we are not in any sense claiming these things to be true. Our point is that this is the climate of opinion developing within some sections of the ufology community – out of which emerge their highly esoteric views on crop circles.

Sex Monsters From Outer Space

Ever since UFOs were recognized as a phenomenon worthy of their own name, the belief that they are from another world has been widespread.

A former US marine, Donald Keyhoe, was initially responsible for persuading the millions with his *True* magazine article 'Flying Saucers are Real', (a book of the same title soon followed, during early 1950.)[3] This was reputedly one of the widest-read magazine stories ever. It caught the mood of a society emerging out of World War II and looking towards space as a 'new frontier' for conquest during peacetime.

Ever since then, ufology has been fighting a constant losing battle, and before long such entrepreneurs as Californian hamburger-stand man George Adamski and London chauffeur George King became overnight celebrities. Adamski's books became best-sellers; he lectured all over the world and even had an audience with the pope. Many other so-called 'contactees' followed with further tales of alien contact.[4] The fact that many of these stories had no real scientific credibility is largely irrelevant. This was a pre-Sputnik age, when flights to the planets were the dream of a society. Adamski fulfilled that dream for many who would never see it happen in real life and further drove serious ufology away from science and into the arms of self-deception. Whether as a natural consequence of human yearnings or a partially engineered official smear tactic (as some documentation from the time vaguely hints), it changed the face of the entire UFO question for a generation. The next cycle of activity was the development of 'the abduction'.

The incredibly complex questions posed by these alleged 'alien kidnaps' is fully documented elsewhere.[5] Suffice it to say that there are numerous – and seemingly overwhelming – reasons why it is almost impossible to take them literally. Many of the witnesses, it should be stressed, do not personally contend that they have been picked up in a spaceship by little green men and whisked off to some alien laboratory. In the main, this imposition is placed upon their experience by outsiders.

Legitimate research into these so-called 'close encounters of the fourth kind' will be examined later in the book, as it impinges directly and dramatically on the mystery circles. You will see then that it is not imperative – in fact, not even sensible – to evaluate such matters as proof of an alien intelligence.

Again this has important lessons to teach about crop circles.

If we have a dream that sees us fly out of the window and float to the ground below, and if we then find that dozens of other people have had similar dreams, do we conclude that people truly can fly through windows? No – we only conclude that this was the form that this experience took, and we seek to understand how and why it came about. The same applies to the alien abduction. In UFO terms, appearances are nearly always deceptive.

Observers of innocuous lights now tend to visit a doctor or psychiatrist specializing in hypnotic regression (probably at the behest of a ufologist). The idea is that by reliving the incident the missing 'memory' will be coaxed out. Unfortunately, because hypnosis can provoke fantasy just as much as it can facilitate recall, the often confusing, conflicting and imperfect tale that emerges is of very doubtful value. This is a prime example of what science calls 'the experimenter effect', with the outcome being compromised (unconsciously) by the strong beliefs of the analysts.

Nevertheless, some fascinating research into this phenomenon has been carried out and documented, notably in the New York area by artist-turned-ufologist and hypnotist Budd Hopkins.[6] Since the mid 1980s Hopkins has become a folk-hero of American ufology. He has been voted 'ufologist of the year' and praised for his breakthrough research.

But it is wise to ponder just what his sincere efforts have actually established. Certainly, the many memories (or pseudo-memories) that pour forth from his studies share a thematic stereotype. During the 'time-lapse' the witness recalls being magically floated into a strange room where a medical examination is conducted by beings assumed to be aliens (normally the small, large-headed 'Grays' of crashed-spaceship lore). After their possibly 'implanting' something (although no implants have been publicly recovered from witnesses), the person is placed back in the situation from whence they were taken and the memory usually (although not always) disappears.

This vastly oversimplifies what is actually a terribly complicated business with no straightforward answers. It also has fascinating parallels and overlaps with other altered states of consciousness of a bizarre nature still subject to contention amongst psychologists. Cases from other countries often show the same pattern, almost theme for theme, but there are also tendencies for cultural differences. 'British' aliens, for example, tend to be tall, blond and akin to a Nordic god, rather than the American version of mean and cynical 'Grays' – conveniently similar, note, to the beings from the crashed-spaceship folklore prevalent throughout the United States.

Sex has reared its head now, and at times close-encounter reports need pornography warnings stamped onto them! Some American researchers contend that aliens are performing genetic experiments, impregnating nubile young women and then re-abducting them to extract the foetus and 'grow' it in an extraterrestrial laboratory with certain cellular 'modifications'.

Of course, this sort of association between sex monsters, aliens and UFO abductions has guaranteed an escalating level of interest and ensured that the subject has retained a high public profile. Inevitably the debunkers use such imagery to reject the whole subject.[7]

In a recent issue of *FSR*, editor Gordon Creighton discusses why the US and other major powers keep searching for radio signals from other worlds when they know that 'the aliens are here in huge numbers'.[8] He concludes that they will soon release news – in a form to mislead us – as dictated and distorted by our friendly neighbourhood monsters, who have 'run this place, and owned us, from time immemorial, but who don't see why we should know this'.

We say all this because we both care about what it implies.

In the same issue of *FSR* Colin Andrews first commented about a causal link that he claims may exist between the tragic crash of an RAF Harrier jet on 22 October 1987 and some circles that turned up near where the Harrier's parachute and dinghy landed (we think by pure coincidence). This was, of course, months after the crops were all harvested! This article is first class as speculation and may or may not be justified, according to your viewpoint. It led Andrews to argue: 'It is evident that the people in charge of our national defence and those who operate as pilots in our skies are quite sure that the answers to all these big questions are not to be found in some meteorological manual ... The truth of the matter is probably a great deal more worrying than that.'

We agree that the truth of this crop-circle phenomenon is indeed worrying, but the worry has to stem from the way in which such extreme, if sincere, ideas now rub shoulders with the alien delusion and are rapidly spreading around the globe. As ufologist Andy Roberts said when discussing crop circles and referring to nobody-in-particular, there are times when an 'open' mind can risk becoming 'so empty that the contents had dribbled out'.[9]

It is probably not too hard to see why the British newspaper the *Daily Mirror* announced to its three million readers on 9 September 1989 that the TV soap opera *Emmerdale*, set amidst the beautiful Yorkshire Dales, was to feature nothing less than the mysterious crop circles mixed up in the plot. It was inevitable what direction this would take. To quote the *Mirror*: 'Visitors from outer space get the blame ... Amos [one of the soap's main characters] goes out at midnight to investigate the circles and is overcome, according to Yorkshire TV, by a "strange and powerful lethargy" ...' The TV company insisted that, 'The introduction of UFOs is not frivolous. They are a subject that fascinates people.' In fact, according to the plot, the character in the series who discovered the circles had been hoaxed by jokers intent on using his role as a local newspaper columnist. Being a gullible chap, the fictional journalist had not sought explanations but had imagined the marks to be alien in origin. This occurs in real life all too often.

Emmerdale is a TV show viewed by twelve million people in Britain alone, and its treatment of the question of crop circles probably effected the average person's viewpoint far more than anything we might say or do. That it helped to reinforce the idea that these circles are created by UFOs and that UFOs are, of course, spaceships serves only to illustrate why we felt it essential to write this book. Not all ufologists are this dogmatic.

If you take a strange human experience – for which no obvious cause is apparent but which the facts show to be overwhelmingly subjective in nature – and then turn this into a science-fiction nightmare, in our view, whether it be intentional or not, you are guilty of myth-making.

Hocus-pocus Focus

The final strand of evidence from the annals of the believers touches most closely upon the crop circles' effect.

Here, as with the circles, we have a visible result produced by some quite definite cause, and we are interested in why anybody should seek to explain this as the result of a power from the beyond, particularly when there are other, more rational possibilities to choose from. To give some clues about the mental processes involved in this decision, we can examine the way in which those who promote UFOs as the product of an alien intelligence research photographs of their reputed craft.

There is a curious anomaly here that is rarely, if ever, noted by ufologists. There are far more pictures dating to the very start of the four decades of UFO research than come from the past thirty years or so. By 1990, when almost everybody owns, or at least uses, a camera, and with increasingly sophisticated film and equipment on offer, we ought by all application of logic to expect more and far better UFO photos. In fact, nearly all the classic photographic cases date way back, and there are few recent 'classics' at all.

Unfortunately, experience based on the *hundreds* of cases that we at BUFORA have evaluated since 1962 shows beyond doubt that almost every photograph is the result of one of two principal causes. Either some minor event in the camera work or processing has left a smudge or mark on the negative and when developed this looks like a UFO by pure coincidence, or else something mundane such as a bird has flown through the shot whilst the picture was being taken. Of course, the bird was ignored (and probably not even consciously 'seen' by the photographer) because birds are such a natural part of the environment, but when the fast shutter speed of a modern camera freezes one in flight, it may subsequently appear very deceptive.

So far as we know, *none* of the very few still baffling photographs depicts an obvious spaceship. *None* shows a UFO on the ground. *None* offers any unambiguous evidence of alien pilots or unknown intelligences. These are hard and cruel facts that ufology in the main is sweeping under the rug.[10]

It is because of a social belief system; exactly the same process which allowed columnist Philip Cuff in the 11 August 1989 issue of the *Solent Reporter*, discussing crop circles, to say the following: 'The human race thrives on mysteries. True, we would like to know the reasons behind the Bermuda Triangle and what happened to the crew of the *Marie Celeste*. But if we did, we would have nothing to wonder about. And not only would bar room talk dry up but Arthur C. Clarke would be out of a job.'

Perhaps he is right, but this little note excellently demonstrates the problem we must face up to. Cuff reports two other modern myths and has perpetuated them in his story. There is no such thing as the Bermuda Triangle – it is nothing but the natural result of so many ships being lost in mid-Atlantic because so many ships sail along that stormy route. And the *Marie Celeste* was actually called the *Mary Celeste* – only myth and legend have made almost everybody believe that the former name applied.

Whilst Philip Cuff can be forgiven for bemoaning the disappointment that demystification can bring, there has to be a balance between doing that and allowing false information to enter the history books. If similar myths were promulgated about political figures, a journalist would rightly be chastised for making such a hash of his research. In the world of the unexplained it seems to be considered fair comment to let slipshod thinking and unchecked, or 'light-hearted' reporting be allowed. We would like to see that situation end.

3   The Nature of the Circles

Many people in over a dozen nations have by now seen photographs of cornfield circles on television and in the press. Articles and books have graphically detailed the mysterious patterns that are appearing in our cereal fields. Such is the fascination surrounding the markings that by now there can be few people left in Britain who are unaware of the problem or the bizarre variety of formations that are appearing all over the landscape.

This chapter attempts to describe the circles so that you can begin to appreciate why they are unusual and have attracted so much attention.

They are not rough patches of ordinary crop damage, such as might result from many causes. These markings are stunningly beautiful creations which at first glance immediately seem to be artificial or man-made. A look at any photograph will demonstrate that impression right away.

Yet, whilst their unexpected appearance and complexity provoke thoughts that some kind of 'intelligence' must lie behind them, it has also been no surprise that the phenomenon has attracted many sensational and often wild explanations for their existence. For most people mere forces of nature seem utterly inadequate to account for the dramatic impact of these circles. Indeed, a whole section of the population has already become conditioned to accept that no mundane solution can possibly exist. Instead, a series of increasingly esoteric concepts has attempted to account for the variety of formations that are regularly manifesting themselves in our troubled environment.

Throughout this chapter we will be examining the cornfield circles and trying to emphasize what complex, intriguing anomalies they are. Although BUFORA has been investigating the phenomenon for a decade, much of the evidence in this chapter is based upon Dr Meaden's study of nearly 800 circles, which forms the National Archive and Register – the largest scientific collection of circles reports anywhere in the world.

We list the nature of the circles in three sections: characteristics of the affected zone, characteristics of the circles' geometry, and characteristics of the sighting locations.

Characteristics of the Affected Zones

PRECISE DEFINITION
The first thing that people notice when they visit a circle site is the way in which the affected crop has been laid down in a precisely defined area (see Plate 1). The cut-off between the affected corn and the surrounding area is very sharp. There is little or no gradation between affected and unaffected crop: the boundary is precise and sudden. This characteristic extends to all parts of the affected areas and seems to apply to the vast majority of circles. The only exceptions have been a handful which displayed a regularly spaced and peculiar 'spiking' effect and formations where the crop appears to be only partially affected.

SWIRL PATTERNS, SWIRL DIRECTIONS AND SPIRAL CENTRES
Take a good look at Plate 4. Notice how the affected crop has been carefully laid down in what circles researchers describe as a 'swirl pattern' which emanates out from a spiral centre as if the circle was really some kind of giant 'catherine wheel'. A plan of this circle is shown in Figure 1, with distances from the spiral centre. Note that, because all these radii differ in length, the so-called circles are actually ellipses, not real circles! The spiral centre is usually not positioned at the precise centre of the affected zone. Instead the spiral focus in this circle is offset from the geometrical centre by almost a metre. This means that any mythical alien spaceship causing *this* circle would actually have to be lopsided instead of being a streamlined version of the 'starship Enterprise'!

Although most crop circles display only one spiral centre, some display two, which normally lie less than a metre or so apart. Furthermore, whilst the majority of crop circles display a fairly tight swirl pattern, some feature that has been described as a 'starburst' whereby the spiral effect is restricted to only the very centre of the circle and/or the outer circumference of the affected zone. Many observers comment that the overwhelming impression created by this spectacular pattern is that whatever created the circle descended onto the crop and then shot out in all directions into the surrounding corn, where it dissipated suddenly.

CONTRA-ROTATIONAL SWIRL PATTERNS

Single circles display both clockwise and anti-clockwise swirl patterns in roughly equal proportions. However, some circles even display *mixtures* of swirl patterns within the same affected area. The existence of contra-rotational swirl patterns was first documented in 1986, when Cheesefoot Head no. 1 circle and ring displayed a clockwise inner swirl and an anti-clockwise outer swirl. A few weeks later another single circle was discovered in a field of barley at nearby Headbourne Worthy. This circle also displayed contra-rotational effects – with the inner zone swirling in towards the spiral centre in an anti-clockwise manner, whilst the outer zone swirled away from the centre in an anti-clockwise manner.

Although contra-rotational swirl patterns had not been reported before 1986, it seems likely that this is merely because no one was systemmatically documenting such differences prior to 1980. This assumption would be proved if someone were to find a photograph of a circle discovered prior to 1986 which showed contra-rotational swirl patterns.

Some commentators have suggested that the existence of contra-rotational swirl patterns represents the influence of some kind of alien 'intelligence'. Pat Delgado comments: 'One of our major problems is trying to understand close-proximity contra-rotation, that is a circle with a contra-rotated flattened swirl and no gradation between the opposing lays. This seems unnatural and, on the face of it, a deliberate attempt to display intelligent manipulation.'[1]

Why should a circle with opposing swirl patterns suggest the presence of some kind of 'intelligent manipulation'? In later chapters we examine some of the more esoteric claims being made about the circles, and describe a 'non-intelligent' mechanism that may create contra-rotational swirl patterns.

SWIRL DIRECTIONS

In the more complex circle formations, no rule has yet been discovered which governs the direction of spin in the outer satellites, as these can swirl in either direction regardless of the direction of the central circle. For example, the 1988 Beckhampton quintuplet displayed clockwise swirls in both the central circle and three of the outer satellites; the remaining satellite displayed an anti-clockwise swirl.

Although no rule has been discovered to account for the spin direction in the more complex circle patterns, circles with outer rings normally contra-rotate with each other and the central (parent) circle. For example, the 1988 Cheesefoot Head double-ringed single displayed a clockwise swirl in the inner circle, followed by an anti-clockwise swirl in the inner ring, then a clockwise swirl in the outermost ring.

During 1989 three ringed circles were discovered which displayed rings that flowed in the same direction as the circle. This characteristic had never been reported before and led one commentator to note that, 'The circles display a sense of humour,' since three publications were in print and ready to point out how ringed circles always contra-rotate between circle and ring! This ability of the phenomenon suddenly to produce new, previously unreported characteristics 'in response' to research has led many people to consider the possibility that the circles are the result of some kind of 'unknown intelligence'.

CIRCLES WITH VERY THIN OUTER RINGS
Some circle formations display very thin outer rings which are almost invisible except from the air. These outer rings are only a few centimetres thick and normally pass through the centre of the outer satellites of the more complex formations. Sometimes these thin outer rings are so faint that they appear to pass through only two or three of the outer circles (e.g. in the August 1987 quintuplet at Cheesefoot Head), but this may merely reflect minor variations in topography and stem density rather than a real effect from the 'thing' that caused the circle.

These thin outer rings have frequently been mistaken by casual observers for tracks allegedly left by animals or human sightseers. However, they have now been observed so rapidly and often that their existence seems to be a part of the genuine phenomenon rather than an effect left by subsequent visitors.

THE EXISTENCE OF BANDING AND LAYERING EFFECTS
Although the circles seem very attractive from a distance, members of the public are largely unfamiliar with the fascinating features that are displayed within them. Two of the most

important characteristics are shown here in Plate 4, in which readers will see that groups of stems have been compressed together to form identifiable 'ribs' or 'whirls', as if the corn had been forced to follow a spiral pattern by rotating a giant comb with teeth unevenly placed through the crop. This rib-like effect is frequently accompanied by the presence of lone 'arcs' or 'tufts' of corn remaining upright within the affected zone whilst surrounding corn is laid flat in the normal manner. These arcs are normally curved and tend to be found near the perimeter of the circle.

Not only are bundles of crop stems twisted into fantastic shapes and unusual patterns; closer examination reveals that the crop is often laid down in distinctive *layers* which all tend to point in different, highly divergent directions.

In one circle, the 1987 Pepperbox Hill formation, there were three such layers, with two pointing in almost opposite directions. Any explanation for the phenomenon must be able to account for these important characteristics.

THE LACK OF DAMAGE TO THE AFFECTED CROP

Surprisingly there is normally little or no damage to the affected crop. Stems are simply sharply kinked just above the ground surface, and the rest of the stem is either bent gently or (more often) very firmly against the ground surface, as if the crop had been pushed down from above. The heads and stems of the affected crop are nearly always fully intact, and perversely the crop normally continues growing after being depressed.

Occasionally a small proportion of the crop stems has been snapped off. In these cases it is difficult to determine whether this is a genuine effect or whether the damage has been created by subsequent visitors arriving at the scene after the circle has been formed. The Littleton single (1986) may have been damaged due to abnormally high numbers of visitors trampling across the site which was well publicized and in close proximity to a major road and a housing estate.

A great deal of effort has been expended trying to create cornfield circles using poles, chains and ropes by people who claim that all the circles must be hoaxes and who rush to demonstrate the simplicity of the hoaxing process. (Some of these attempts are described in more detail in Chapter 5.) Unfortunately it has been conclusively shown that these attempts necessarily damage the crop, and their effects can be recognized with little trouble. If a hoax *is* to blame for any of these circles, a more interesting and novel method must presumably have been used.

The surprising lack of damage also negates another popular theory – that physically real (but conveniently invisible) alien spaceships are descending onto crops to produce the circles. Regretfully, if this *were* occurring, damaged corn would be evident across the entire zone of every circle being discovered.

The lack of damage – and the uncanny way in which the affected crop continues growing despite being permanently deformed – clearly demonstrates that mechanical pressure is not the effect that causes the circles.

THE LACK OF DAMAGE TO THE SURROUNDING CROP

It is important to recognize that, in addition to the lack of damage to the affected crop, the surrounding crop (that outside the circle) is also normally unaffected by whatever causes these patterns. Plate 6, which was taken soon after discovery, shows no sign that someone has walked into the field to hoax the circle. Extensive attempts to walk into a mature arable crop during daylight leave very obvious tell-tale signs, yet even in rain-sodden fields newly discovered circles fail to display footprints or trails that might have been left by hypothetical tricksters.

Photographs taken immediately on discovery show no sign of tracks between the cornfield circles and adjacent 'tramlines' (the marks left by tractors spraying the crop with pesticides). Photographs of circles appearing away from the tramlines also show no connecting tracks between the affected areas and the tramline such as would be expected if someone walked through the crop at night.

TYPE OF CROP

Although the majority of British circles have been discovered in mature, near-ripe cereals, such as wheat and barley, it seems that virtually *any* arable crop can record the presence of the causal force, providing the stems are of sufficient pliability to deform permanently. For British cereal fields this means that the crop is usually nearing a metre or so in height before circles form. Circles have been discovered in wheat, barley, rye, oats, oilseed rape, mustard, runner beans, soya beans, grass, spinach, tobacco, sugarbeet, maize and rice – and in sand, dirt and snow. Some circles have also been discovered in long grass, but these tend to be blown out quickly by ordinary wind currents.

Foreign circles have also been reported in savanna and swampland (as in the Tully, Australia, case), but it is not always clear whether these are identical to the phenomenon at work in southern England, and in some cases different explanations may well be more feasible.

The implication of the wide variety of crops and vegetation known to display circle-type phenomena is that some kind of 'natural' mechanism exists which normally goes unnoticed unless a mature arable crop or some similar agent is present and so can permanently record the presence of the causal mechanism. This has important implications for the geographical distribution of circle formations and for the number of formations appearing in historical times – issues which we deal with in chapter 8.

THE DOWSING TRICK

As if these characteristics were not complex enough, research initiated by Richard Andrews and the Circles Phenomenon Research group (CPR) has demonstrated another bizarre feature of these delightful circles. Dowsers walking into a circle with a pair of divining rods consistently claim that they detect some kind of 'field' which causes the rods to point in the direction of the swirl pattern noted above. When they are walking across the site, the swirl pattern alternates, causing the diviner's rods to turn first one way then the other. Even first-time diviners discover this little party trick and watch with astonishment as their rods twist backwards and forwards, responding to some 'unknown force' which some claim is controlled by an 'unknown intelligence'.

Returning to sites where circles are known to have appeared, diviners have supposedly demonstrated that they can detect circle's precise location, even two years after the event. Furthermore, compasses taken into circles have occasionally been reputed to spin near the centre of the circle, whilst tape recorders and camera equipment sometimes fail to work.[2] These odd effects are prime reasons why some commentators seem so keen to promote esoteric explanations for the existence of these phenomena.

Another commonly reported and associated 'clue' consists of the alleged effects on animals taken into circle sites, seemingly responding to a 'force'.

Figure 1: A typical circle and ring formation discovered by Paul Fuller at Chilcomb, near Cheesefoot Head, Hampshire, on 15 August 1987. This formation exhibited a classic 'starburst' effect, whereby the spiral outflow is restricted to the outer zone of the parent circle.

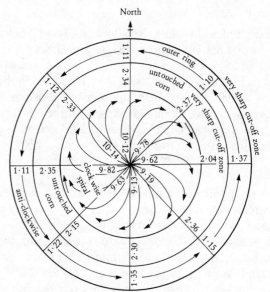

Figure 2 shows the same crop circle and illustrates that it is in fact oval in shape. Note the difference between the geometric and spiral centres, and the unequal diameters.

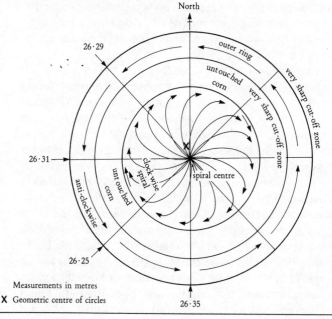

Measurements in metres

X Geometric centre of circles

Characteristics of the Circles' Geometry

SHAPE

Take a second look at Figure 1. Now look at Figure 2 below. This is the same formation. If we add up the diagonals, we discover that they are all of different lengths. This is typical, showing how virtually all our 'circles' are really oval or elliptical. Perhaps this characteristic is unpopular with pundits, because nowhere have we seen articles dealing with 'cornfield ellipses' or 'the mystery ovals'. Is that because the term 'circle' implies order, perfection and the sort of artificiality expected from a constructed 'machine'?

SIZE

A wide variety of patterns of all sizes is being discovered, ranging from mini-circles only a metre or so in diameter to enormous ones with diameters of more than thirty-two metres. The largest formations measure up to forty-five metres in diameter, whilst the majority lie between ten and twenty metres diameter. The sheer size of the circle formations tends to argue against the possibility that they are all hoaxes, because tricksters run the risk of being caught and prosecuted for damaging farmers' fields. We might presume that the time taken to create a hoax is somehow related to the size of the circle being formed. For this reason, the larger the circle, the greater the risk would be for any potential hoaxer.

THE LARGE VARIETY OF DIFFERENT FORMATION TYPES

Increased searching has resulted in the discovery of many different formation types. It is difficult to determine how many different types exist, because sometimes formations overlap the edge of fields or adjacent roads and tracks, where part of the pattern may not be recorded. Under these circumstances the existence of outer satellites can only be inferred. Also no account has been taken of variations in the dimensions between the component parts of each formation, and no attempt made to account for the varieties in spin direction or the contra-rotations within the same circle.

Each summer researchers have discovered new formation types, and our knowledge of the phenomenon is continually being revised. During 1987 BUFORA and TORRO carried out a survey of cereal farms in Hampshire to demonstrate that knowledge was inaccurate and that exotic speculation was both premature and unwise. The survey produced accounts of two previously unknown formation types (a regular quadruplet and a triangular triplet) from only eleven farms reporting then-unrecorded older circles. This seems to imply that further searching will uncover further formation types that *have* occurred but are yet to be discovered.

The existence of so many different formation types suggests that a single, very complex causal mechanism may be a less realistic explanation for the phenomenon than several similar causal mechanisms.

THE EXISTENCE OF MEASURABLE DIFFERENCES BETWEEN THE DIFFERENT COMPONENTS PARTS OF EACH FORMATION

Contrary to newspaper reports, circles are not all the same size, and the outer parts of the more complex circle formations are not precisely laid out in geometrical patterns. Typical quintuplet patterns have varying distances between the spiral centre of the parent circle and the outer satellites. Again, this factor rather tends to negate the popular theory that giant spaceships with retractable legs create the circles.

THE LINEAR SPURS

Several circles display curious features that have become known as 'linear spurs' (Plate 1). These can extend out into the surrounding crop and on several occasions have been very noticeable. The one depicted is perhaps the best-documented spurred circle investigated by BUFORA. This was the Whiteparish formation, which was reported by Ken Douglas in September 1987, some weeks after the formation first appeared. In this example the spur was more than fourteen metres in length and extended between two adjacent tramlines in a down-slope direction. This proves that the force that creates the circles pursued the lines of weakness induced by the presence of tramlines – grooves cut into fields by machinery and constantly used by farm-workers during future operations. However, in other known examples the spurs did not follow tramlines and simply extended into ordinary areas of unaffected corn.

Because so few circles have displayed these intriguing features, it is difficult to generalize. However, the Childrey (July 1986) formation exhibited a spur which ended in a distinct arrow-shape beyond which was a small circular hole in the ground. This unique pattern led one researcher to compare the formation to the symbol for the human male (another indication of some 'alien intelligence', no doubt). In both formations, the join between the ring and the spur is sharp and sudden, a characteristic that is consistent with the sharp cut-off between affected and unaffected corn in the ordinary circles.

Characteristics of the Circles' Locations

THE CLUSTERING EFFECT

Although circles appear all over Britain, the media's attention has been particularly focused on those that form in Hampshire and Wiltshire in central southern England (often called Wessex, after the ancient kingdom). This has attracted undue concern for a phenomenon restricted to a small geographical area – an impression that we believe to be both misleading and erroneous. Sensible circles researchers have known for some years that circles appear all over Britain, but for various reasons formations appearing away from this area receive little publicity and go unreported outside their local media.

Due to the increasing attention being paid to the circles, a number of locations have been discovered which seem capable of generating circles year after year, and it may not be just a coincidence that three of these sites lay in this allegedly 'haunted' Wessex, a region long known for its mystical past. Three of these sites are discussed below and their existence as such major foci is crucially important to our understanding of the circles mystery.

The Cheesefoot Head 'Punchbowl', near Winchester, Hampshire
Pronounced 'Chez-Foot', this enormous natural amphitheatre is perhaps the most famous site yet discovered for producing circles. A well-known beauty spot with two conveniently sited car-parks and good local walks. Cheesefoot's southernmost perimeter is an extensive, steep hill slope some fifty metres in height (which is populated largely by rabbits). This was the site of 'Operation Whitecrow', an eight-day exercise involving (according to various media sources) '60 of the country's leading scientists', which failed to see any circles being formed during June 1989. Circles appear here most years and can be clearly seen by passing motorists using the busy A272 Winchester to Petersfield road that sweeps across the southern rim of the punchbowl. Prior to the D-Day Normandy landings, Eisenhower addressed thousands of Allied troops in the 'punchbowl' itself (see Figure 3)

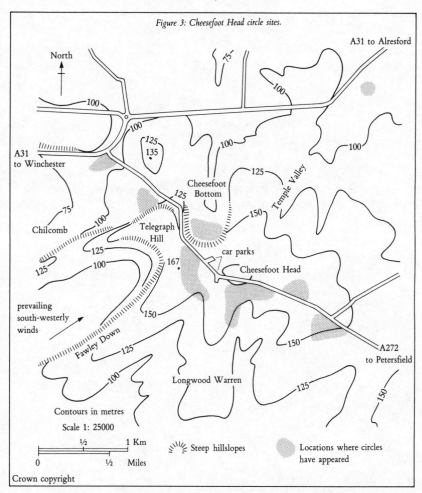

Figure 3: Cheesefoot Head circle sites.

The Westbury White Horse, near Bratton, Wiltshire

This is the location where the first modern circles appeared, in August 1980, beneath a giant White Horse carved into the chalk of Westbury Hill to commemorate King Alfred's victory over the Danes at the Battle of Ethandun in AD 878. Every summer at least a dozen circles appear along the base of this pronounced hill-slope bordering the north-facing escarpment of Salisbury Plain (a restricted area used by the military for major training exercises) (see Figure 4).

Both Cheesefoot and Westbury are sites with long-established

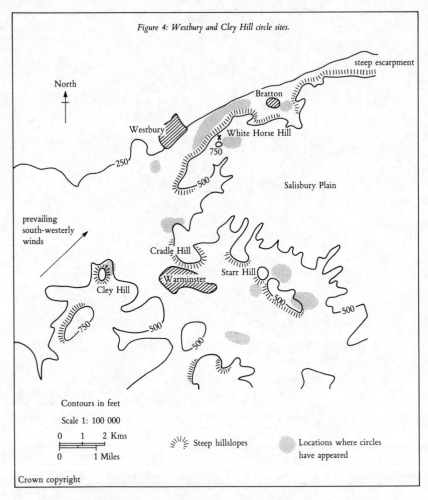

Figure 4: *Westbury and Cley Hill circle sites.*

traditions. Both sites have ancient 'devil' names, which folklorists believe may suggest that unusual occurrences have been associated with the region since ancient times.

Cley Hill, near Warminster, Wiltshire
This conspicuous hill juts up from a generally flat plain to the west of the small town of Warminster. Famous in the 1960s as a sky-watching place for UFO-spotters, Cley Hill is also accessible to walkers. Its summit is a National Trust property frequented by visitors.

Although our knowledge of the numbers of circles that appear depends very much on the amount of publicity surrounding the phenomenon, these three sites are very important, because each summer circles tend to cluster about them. Figures 3 and 4 illustrate the locations of circles discovered at each of these sites for all years since 1980. This marked association between hillslopes and circles strongly suggests that there must be some kind of causal relationship between terrain and the circles.

INTERNATIONAL DISTRIBUTION
Accounts of similar (but not necessarily identical) circles originate from many countries all over the world, including the United States of America, Canada, Brazil, Argentina, New Zealand, Australia (including Tasmania), Japan, Italy, Switzerland, Austria and France. In researching this book we nearly doubled the known number of countries reporting 'circles' – adding, for example, Norway, Sweden and Uruguay to the list. Some of these accounts can be found in Chapter 9.

TIME OF DISCOVERY
Although it is difficult to pin down an exact time at which many circles appear, most seem to form during the night or in daylight hours around dawn. We base this conclusion on the fact that most formations are discovered early in the morning by local landowners and farmers, when no circle was believed to be present at that location late on the previous evening. This characteristic was demonstrated by an all-night vigil at Cheesefoot Head undertaken by the redoubtable Pat Delgado and Don Tuersly during the summer of 1986, which proved that the ringed formation first seen at dawn on 6 July must have formed between 10 p.m. on the 5th and 3.30 a.m. (during which period it was too dark to view the field).

The nocturnal appearance of the majority of circles *might* suggest that hoaxing could be a plausible explanation for the phenomenon, because hoaxers would be expected to carry out their dubious activities under cover of darkness to escape detection and prosecution. However, several circles are known to have appeared during daylight, and because of numerous other reasons discussed in Chapter 5, hoaxing seems only remotely possible as the principal cause of the entire phenomenon.

Summary

Whatever causes these circles, they are clearly a beautiful and appealing anomaly. They come in many shapes and sizes, have been appearing all over the world and have been doing so for a very long time (see Appendix 2). It seems even more remarkable that their existence has until only very recently escaped major public notice.

What causes the patterns? Are alien intelligences really responsible? Or can there be a more earthly answer to the mystery? These are some of the questions we examine in the next part of this book. We believe you will be more than a little surprised by our quite conclusive findings.

4 The Contenders

Many theories have been suggested to account for the phenomenon of the circles. These range from the cynical to the bizarre, from the rational to the downright absurd. All have one thing in common: they represent man's love of the Unexplained, and his desire to explain it. Since we first looked up to the sky and began to wonder, strange experiences and other oddities have caused rational people to try to understand this mysterious universe around us. The crop circles have been no exception, and their promotion by the media has triggered all manner of ideas from people who, by and large, have never even visited a circle.

Here are just a few theories and our reasons for rejecting them.

HOAXING

With such a visually attractive phenomenon, none of us would be too surprised to consider the possibility that some (or even all) of the circles represent an audacious hoax. We have seen how a large proportion of the population already have a subconscious model or what UFOs look like and what they represent. This is a cultural stereotype that has been conditioned into their minds by 1,001 science fiction films and books. Because the circles closely resemble our preconceptions about UFOs, no one should be in the least bit surprised if hoaxing forms an important element within the phenomenon. Hoaxing is sufficiently important to warrant extensive consideration: see Chapter 5.

UNIDENTIFIED FLYING OBJECTS

We have drawn attention to the widespread belief that 'UFOs' (alien devices) create the circles. If UFOs really *are* creating circles, man would be on the threshold of one of the most exciting discoveries in history, but refuting the UFO proposition is, of course, the central theme of this book.

The image that UFOs must represent intelligently controlled devices is just another extension of existing folklore. In other times unusual lights seen in the sky were perceived as 'miracles' (in the Middle Ages), inventors' airships (1897), unidentified aeroplanes (1920–30s) and secret Nazi V-rockets (Scandinavia, 1946–7). The fact that these anomalies were reported in terms resembling the technology of the day strongly suggests that the reporting of UFOs is culturally dependent and that UFOs cannot represent a developing 'alien' technology that by some staggering coincidence just happens to reflect our own technological advances with each passing era. For the aliens to send us giant airships with cogs and propellers (1897), then V-shaped rockets (1947) and now shiny metallic spaceships, keeping step with our own progress, would be wildly improbable.

These comments place the UFO phenomenon in its proper context. People have seen strange things in the sky (and on the ground) for many centuries, so something seems to be there. But the concept that UFOs reflect 'alien intelligences' is just the latest extension in a continually changing belief system. Those who insist that UFOs *must* be 'intelligently controlled' have simply not opened their minds to consider less exotic solutions.

HELICOPTERS

This suggestion is frequently made in the press by people who have never studied circle sites and who are unfamiliar with helicopter flight principles. It has been established beyond all reasonable doubt that helicopters cannot be creating cornfield circles, because rotor-caused downwash spreads out radially in all directions and does not end abruptly. This fact was proved in 1985 by Lieut.-Colonel Edgecombe of the Aviation Standards Branch of the Army Air Corps (based at Middle Wallop, Hampshire), whose professional duties involved the assessment of helicopter damage to farmland for Army insurance claims.

Following BUFORA's suggestion, two BBC Television documentaries (*Running Rings Around Arthur*, 1988, and *Secret Circles*, 1989) independently attempted to re-create cropfield circles by flying different types of helicopter just above ground-level and filming the results. In each case the crop simply swirled about in a random manner without being laid flat in a distinctive spiral pattern.

Even if helicopters *could* create roughly circular patches of damage by some novel means, forming circles at night in isolated rural locations would clearly be a high-risk operation for the pilots and the public alike. Furthermore, several accounts of circles are now known to exist which predate the invention of helicopters and similar man-made devices. We will consider this impressive evidence later. These factors seem to rule out helicopter and modern aircraft activity without need to discuss the matter further.

ANCIENT FIELD MARKINGS
Another common suggestion to account for the circles arises from an understandable confusion between our novel crop-field formations and ancient field markings left because of the presence of subterranean archaeological remains such as early farms, stones, Roman roads, pits and other buried remnants. This subject was first studied during the 1920s when such pioneers as O.G.S. Crawford and Major G.W.G. Allen began systemmatically photographing sites of archaeological interest from the then new vantage-point of the air. Their work paved the way forward for an extensive examination of Britain's prehistory, which is still being updated even today.

Ring ditches which date from the Bronze Age, are particularly prone to cause markings which resemble our circles from a distance. However, these never produce precisely defined swirl patterns in lodged corn, never form in complex geometrical patterns, produce no layering and banding effects and have never been identified with crop circles by archaeologists.

COPULATING CREATURES
One of the most original and amusing ideas about the cause of our circles is the suggestion that hedgehogs, rutting deer and other creatures create the circles during some obscure mating dance. Pat Lloyd, secretary of the Master Deerhounds Association, has claimed that, 'People who have spent a long time studying this say they are roe rings.'

On the other hand, Les and Sue Stocker, who run the St Tiggywinkle's Hedgehog Hospital in Aylesbury, deny the theory that 'demented hedgehogs' create circles by running round and round in large packs. 'Poor old hedgehogs, they get the blame for everything,' moaned Les. 'They are definitely not the guilty party in this case.'

A number of farmers have discovered foxes and their cubs

playing in the circles. Not surprisingly, this has led several to assume that the circles were *created* by the foxes. although why foxes should make play areas for their cubs in complex geometrical patterns must be hard to imagine.

All these wonderful ideas at least prove that Britain is a nation of animal-lovers with colourful imaginations. Unfortunately none of them manages to account for any of the complex characteristics discussed in Chapter 3. Furthermore, if animals *are* making cornfield circles, why should they suddenly start doing so now in greater abundance and why have naturalists not identified our circles as the result of such bizarre behaviour patterns before?

GIANT HAILSTONES
Another theory, steeped in the traditions of those wonderful British *Carry on* movies, claims that the circles are caused by airliners releasing the contents of their passenger toilets from a height of several miles! These deposits freeze in the super-cold conditions of the upper atmosphere, descend into cornfields and then melt after creating circles. Perhaps this accounts for why the discoverers of a luminous white jelly-like substance found in a circle at Goodworth Clatford were all supposedly struck down with 'bugs' after imprudently handling this unusual substance!

UNEXPLODED WORLD WAR II BOMBS
This theory was first proposed by Flight Lieutenant Steve Stephens, on a BBC Radio Solent show in November 1989. He suggested that during the war abortive German air raids frequently resulted in the ditching of unexploded bombs that fell harmlessly into cereal fields across southern England. Many years later the bombs exploded, leaving behind flattened corn circles in the same formation they had held when they left the bomb rack. This theory stretches credulity to the extreme. It certainly fails to account for any of the characteristics being discovered at circle sites and cannot in any way explain the circles that appeared before there were any German bombers, and those in distant countries.

TETHERED MODEL AEROPLANE
This must take some prize as the most far-fetched idea yet suggested. According to the claim, the hoaxers tether a model aircraft to a pivot and then – well, we think you can figure out the rest!

FAIRY RINGS/CROP FUNGI
It is true that these rings (sometimes outlined by mushrooms or toadstools) are vaguely circular, but they are *not* flattened circles, have none of the internal characteristics we see in this phenomenon and are easily recognized for what they are – a fungal infection. On the other hand, they have quite often been misinterpreted as UFO 'landing traces', when eager ufologists have scanned the fields above which a UFO was reported, found one of these growths and added two and two together to make a spaceship.

'LEY LINES'
This idea is commonly paraded by the mystic community. 'Ley lines', properly called 'leys', are another of our modern mythologies. They are supposed to be 'energy paths' that criss-cross the Earth and which were recognized by the ancient civilizations more 'in tune' with such forces. Whilst ley research is interesting and has some support from some members of the archaeological community, there does not seem any logical reason to connect this with crop circles. Paul Devereux, author of various books on the subject, editor of *The Ley Hunter* and widely considered the world's leading authority, told us flatly he sees no apparent connection. For us, that is that.

THE HOLE IN THE OZONE LAYER
'Scientists believe they may have solved the riddle of the cornfield circles ... They believe unprecedented atmospheric conditions caused by the ozone crisis are behind the baffling phenomenon. Scientists have detected violent disturbances in the "electromagnetic field" in areas where the circles have appeared. Research co-ordinator Colin Andrews said "We now believe the shifts in the Earth's electromagnetic conditions caused by the ozone layer hole may be responsible"'. *Sunday Express*, 19 March 1989.

This article sparked an unexpected retraction by Andrews in *Flying Saucer Review* (June 1989): 'I categorically refute the statement attributed to me in the *Sunday Express* article of March 19th 1989, and suggesting that I had indicated a link between mystery cornfield rings and the ozone layer (sic).' Editor Gordon Creighton commented: 'It would be interesting, wouldn't it, to know what lay behind the publication of such an article, and who precisely was responsible for so remarkable an assertion.' So far as we can establish, it seems to have been a team of Japanese researchers who were supposedly liaising with Colin Andrews' CPR (Circles Phenomena Research) team on the crop-circle problem.

Yet the Wiltshire based *Gazette and Herald* (13 July 1989) and the *Kennet Star* (27 July 1989) later carried articles promoting this concept, and Colin Andrews developed similar ideas on the *Secret Circles* documentary for the BBC in Bristol (recorded later in 1989), when he claimed that, 'I think the magnetic field of the planet may well be ... being manipulated in an intelligent fashion ...'

Whilst we do accept that there could be a slight possibility of a link (if atmospheric ionization is somehow involved), we are puzzled as to why 'ozone-produced' circles should be concentrated in southern England, as alleged, when the reputed 'hole in the ozone layer' is positioned above the Arctic.

HERCULES TRANSPORT PLANE

This ingenious theory was first raised by C.P. Dennison of Leamington Spa. According to Dennison, the circles are created by 'wingtip vortices shed by a Hercules aircraft'. This massive transporter frequently flies from RAF Lyneham in Wiltshire and causes a 'rotating cylinder of air with a horizontal axis'. This cylinder breaks into smaller sections which fall gently to earth in a 'vortex bomb'! According to Dennison, this effect can be observed on frosty mornings if you happen to be in the right place to see a low-flying Hercules pass by.

Whilst it is true that some aircraft are known occasionally to create explosive wing-tip vortices that have from time to time rapidly descended to earth causing damage, this theory fails for three reasons: at least one account of a circle exists which predates the invention of aircraft; if this theory was true, the fields round RAF Lyneham would be peppered with circles (they are not), and the theory is completely inconsistent with many alleged eyewitness accounts of circles actually forming (see Chapter 7).

PLANETARY POLTERGEISTS

Dr Bernard Finch has suggested that the circles were created by a 'planetary poltergeist', although the details are left hanging. This seems to be another way of describing an anomalous energy or force (such as is reputed to cause 'poltergeist' effects in ghost lore). On 22 August 1986 the *Hampshire Chronicle* quoted Pat Delgado as suggesting what he calls an 'IUFF' (Invisible Unknown Force Field) 'in the form of a vertical rotating force field, from either below the ground or above it, [and] which creates unexplained activity similar to that caused by poltergeists'.

These ideas remain tantalizingly unproven and do not seem to us to have 'the right stuff' which a successful explanation requires. We are quite sure that other interesting speculations may be made, since the crop circles offer a delightful intellectual challenge for all crossword-puzzle fans out there.

Perhaps you have a better theory than any of these!

5   The Hoax Theory

Throughout BUFORA's decade of circles research we have uncovered clear and irrefutable proof that *some* circles are being created by hoaxers. This chapter examines both proven and suspected hoaxes. We also take a good hard look at some of the circle-making demonstrations that have tried to prove this solution, and from them we can draw important conclusions about the phenomenon as a whole.

For those of us researching anomalies, hoaxing and fraudulent claims have always posed considerable difficulties, for fairly obvious reasons. Many amateur sleuths – and a number of eminent scientists – have left themselves open to ridicule by accepting claims that more critical inquiry has subsequently exposed. Prime examples of man's fallibility include Arthur Conan Doyle's acceptance of the now admittedly fake photographs of the Cottingley fairies, and the Piltdown Man fiasco (in which a new species of 'ape-man' baffled science, following discovery of fossil bones, before being shown to be a 'mix-and-match' fabrication).

It would be foolish for any circles-researcher to claim that hoaxing cannot be a realistic answer for at least *some* of the circles that are appearing. If just *one* apparently 'genuine' formation should eventually turn out to be a hoax, the implication that *all* the circles are potential hoaxes would become viable.

Any cautious student of anomalies knows that the human need for excitement and mystery frequently breaches all bounds of normal social behaviour. Take a quick glance through the UFO literature and you will find that the myth is crammed full of entertaining, bizarre and often outrageous hoaxes, perpetrated by people whose motivations were commonly neither pathological nor financial. Instead, these people simply felt the need to fool others and achieve a brief moment of fame.

'Classic' examples of UFO hoaxes include the Ripperston Farm

(Dyfed) entity, which featured in several books and made TV headlines in 1977: a member of the local Rotarians later claimed to have dressed up in an asbestos suit and intimidated the witnesses (whose story had provoked a national 'flap' and triggered a best-selling non-fiction book). William Loosely's 'manuscript', allegedly discovered in a drawer and dating from the nineteenth century, appears to describe the very first ever alien contact, on 4 October 1871. It even had a 'crop circle' of flattened weeds left by the 'space craft'. This was published in a 'true story' book by British science-fiction author David Langford, conceived in 1978. Whilst sensible ufologists saw gaping holes in the story right away (as book reviews clearly demonstrate), others accepted it. Langford later confessed this hoax in an article for *New Scientist*, suggesting he had wanted to see how many gullible ufologists would be taken in by it. In fact, just before we went to press, David Langford reported to us his great delight that his hoax had finally found its own niche within the crop circles mystery. The *Western Evening Herald* of 30 January 1990 had carried a letter from Marilyn Preston of Saltash in which she discussed the William Loosely 'novel', apparently unaware that it was a fabrication. She commented: 'Was this UFO which came to earth 120 years ago the first to make one of the mysterious crop circles ...?'

These brief examples serve to show that 'alien' and UFO hoaxes can be very elaborate and remain unexposed for years. Clearly this has important implications for our understanding of the circles, because alien UFO-related mysteries are vulnerable to manipulation by groups wishing to promote beliefs and theories. For the ufologist, the hoax can satisfy a need to believe in something incredible, regardless of the 'clues' that should suggest that things are not all they seem to be. What is frustrating for the serious researcher is the existence of cases in which apparently 'genuine' anomalous experiences subsequently provoke hoaxing by witnesses who found themselves in the emotive position of needing to satisfy two sets of pressure groups, the 'believers' and the media. All this inevitably creates a dilemma for the crop-circle researcher.

The Proven Hoaxes

Westbury, Wiltshire, 1983
During August 1983 the *Wiltshire Times* carried an exposé of a failed hoax by two local farmers, Alan and Francis Sheppard, who

confessed to having created a fake quintuplet formation on their land at Westbury (where apparently 'genuine' circles had been appearing for some years). The Sheppards' hoaxed circle was created by using a pole-and-chain method and was filmed for posterity.

This 'experiment' was perpetrated on behalf of the *Daily Mirror*, a national tabloid newspaper, which compensated the Sheppards for the damage caused to their crop. The *Daily Mirror* hoped that a rival national newspaper, the *Daily Express*, would report the circle as the landing-marks of a giant UFO, because the *Express* was actively promoting the circles as a subject of some concern. Had the *Express* fallen for this trick, the *Mirror* could have stepped in, revealed the hoax and continued the media furore surrounding the subject whilst mildly discrediting its rivals at the *Express*. Unfortunately for the *Mirror*, the circles were a short-lived wonder in 1983, and the *Express* lost interest.

The circle (which significantly was one of the more complex formation types) remained a part of the 'genuine phenomenon' according to many people interested in the subject. Fortunately BUFORA investigator Ian Mrzyglod did quickly procure evidence which immediately suggested that a hoax had occurred, but others were happy to accept this as one more example of the alien powers surrounding the phenomenon.

On 18 August 1986 BUFORA investigator Philip Taylor took part in the *Nightline* programme on LBC radio with DJ Pete Murray. During the show, which discussed UFOs, former *Mirror* reporter Chris Hutchins phoned in and confessed to his involvement in the Westbury hoax. He said that the newspaper had manufactured the circle as 'just a joke'.

Cheesefoot Head, Hampshire, 1986

During July 1987 four farmhands from Cornwall claimed in the Southampton-based *Southern Evening Echo* that they had hoaxed the second 1986 formation at Cheesefoot Head 'by shuffling along on our knees to push down the wheat, then rolling around our bodies in a complete circle'. Two of the hoaxers, Ian Mepham and David Forster, explained that they had been in the area collecting horse-feed for their employers. 'we heard about the rings and the stories behind them from some of the local farmworkers, so we went out to have a look at the existing ones. We had no intention of making a ring, but when we got there we decided to give it a go.'

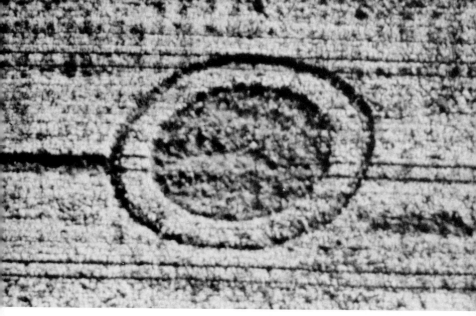

What the mystery is all about. One of the strangest types of crop mark: a ringed circle with a linear spur following a tramline. Pepperbox Hill, Whiteparish, Wilts., 1987

The circle that started the modern myth – one of those found below the Westbury White Horse in Wiltshire during summer 1980 and rapidly investigated by the PROBE group

The circles made famous by Denis Healey when he found and photographed them near Alfriston, Sussex, in August 1984. This is a classic quintuplet of one large central circle and four small satellites. Taken some weeks after discovery the formation shows severe damage from sightseers but was devoid of any tracks when first seen

Layering and banding effects within a circle at Chilcomb near Winchester, Hants., 1987. Such fine detail is hard to explain by hoaxing

Typical spiral centre of a small crop circle, showing
how stems are twisted round a fixed point

Two circles near Westbury White Horse, summer 1988. These are
between tramlines and show no trace of how any hoaxer might have got
to them without damaging the surrounding crop

Westbury again, showing that little has changed, except this 1987 circle was very large. The White Horse Hill site is 'haunted' by similar circles almost every year

Physicist and meteorologist Dr Terence Meaden takes readings at a crop circle site

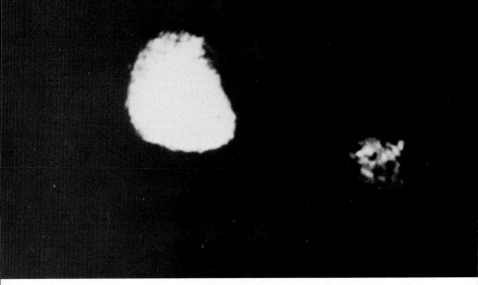

Luminous glow photographed by one of the many scientific expeditions to the UFO 'window' at Hessdalen in Norway. We believe this to be a novel atmospheric plasma

Circles researcher and author Colin Andrews at a circle site under investigation with Paul Fuller

This photograph shows a wide range of circle formations in one location: near Bratton, Wilts., in 1987

Close-up of the small circle in oats found near Mansfield in July 1989. We believe this to be a hoax. Can you tell the difference from the 'real' thing?

A precisely defined grass circle discovered in Pucklechurch, Avon, in 1989, twenty-four hours after a whirlwind was observed in the same field

THE MOWING-DEVIL:
OR, STRANGE NEWS OUT OF
HARTFORD-SHIRE.

Being a True Relation of a Farmer, who Bargaining with a Poor Mower, about the Cutting down Three Half Acres of Oats: upon the Mower's asking too much, the Farmer swore *That the Devil should Mow it rather than He.* And so it fell out, that very Night, the Crop of Oat shew'd as if it had been all of a Flame: but next Morning appear'd so neatly mow'd by the Devil or some Infernal Spirit, that no Mortal Man was able to do the like.

Also, How the said Oats ly now in the Field, and the Owner has not Power to fetch them away.

Is this an ionized vortex photographed over Trindade Island in the Atlantic, January 1958? The grainy close-up shows the internal structure. Can you 'perceive' aliens standing on the rim inside the 'spaceship'?

Cover of the *Journal of Meteorology* giving news of the mowing-devil discovery in late 1989, one of the major breakthroughs in crop circle research (see Appendix 2)

These hoaxers dismissed claims that the circles were created by UFOs as 'utter rubbish' and went on to state that, 'To get the outer ring one of us simply held the other's hand' (!) 'The stupid thing was that this was a Sunday afternoon with traffic passing us all the time.'

BUFORA already had suspicions about this circle-and-ring formation after it was discovered that a passing motorist from Horndean in Hampshire had stopped to observe the first formation between 6.30 and 6.45 p.m. on 6 July 1986. This witness had noticed a red Vauxhall Victor car parked close to the edge of the field in the 'punchbowl' itself. There is no direct road to the field, and the ground there would have been very rough. We know for certain that the second Cheesefoot Head formation appeared between 6.56 p.m., when the field was last seen by a researcher, and 7.45 p.m., when David Thurlow of the Solent Press Agency discovered the new set, so the report of a car parked unusually close to the 'punchbowl' was rather suspect and may support the Cornishmen's claims.

Taken at face value, this story would not be proof that a hoax had been perpetrated. BUFORA's attempts to contact the hoaxers for a demonstration of their circle-making abilities failed. However, BUFORA's Mike Wootten obtained a copy of the *Daily Telegraph*'s aerial photograph of this formation (taken the morning after the circle appeared) which Terence Meaden subsequently enlarged. This photograph shows that the outer ring displayed an unexpected and noticeable kink – as if hoaxers had temporarily lost their bearings and then tried to correct the outer ring by starting over. Re-examination of Delgado's plan of this circle suggests that no true spiral pattern was present across the entire zone. Indeed, this formation had a number of curious features that have not occurred in other circles and which also imply a hoax.

We believe that the Cornishmen's claim may well be true. If it is, they hoaxed a convincing circle-and-ring formation in less than twenty minutes, right next to a major road, on a pleasant summer Sunday evening and without being caught in the act! Their hoax was sufficiently convincing that it passed as the real thing from a distance. In fact, at least one leading researcher was quoted as suggesting that these circles were seemingly 'perfect' and so could not be a part of some hoax.

If they were a hoax by somebody – and we believe the evidence here strongly hints at that, it has significant implications for the entire phenomenon.

Cheesefoot Head, Hampshire, 1986
In September 1986 the message 'WEARENOTALONE' appeared near existing circles along the south-western perimeter of the Cheesefoot Head punchbowl, with letters twelve metres high and sixty-one metres in length. The N in 'ALONE' was reversed. We do not believe in extraterrestrial stand-up comedians, and clearly the only acceptable solution for such an incident is that this was a hoaxer at work. 'We are not alone' was a byline from a famous science fiction UFO movie!

A few of even the more cautious researchers did not reject this out of hand, as it surely deserved, or learned the lessons that it seems to teach.

Suspected but not Proven Hoaxes

Alfriston, Sussex, 1984
Politicians are well known for their need for constant media attention, so perhaps we shouldn't be too surprised to learn that, when a quintuplet circle formation appeared near the pretty little village of Alfriston in the heart of Conservative rural Sussex, well-known Labour politician Dennis Healey was soon involved. He innocently alerted the *Daily Mail* newspaper to the formation, which had appeared very near his summer retreat.

The *Daily Mail* was pleased to promote the Alfriston circle, and on 4 July it carried Dennis Healey's own excellent photographs of the formation along with comments about 'Healey's Comet' and 'a giant spacecraft' being responsible. In February 1990 Mr Healey even appeared on BBC television to show his photographs. He suggested, quite sincerely, that there was no obvious solution as yet. He added one interesting new fact: that his wife had reported a strange glow in the sky the night before the circles were found. He thought it may have been streetlamps reflecting off low cloud, but it may be a clue about atmospheric processes.

BUFORA investigator Philip Taylor quickly pointed out in the *Brighton Argus* that the Alfriston circle was located at a place called 'Cradle Hill' and that this was some coincidence, given the existence of an identically named location famous to all UFO sky-watchers as a key vantage-point at Warminster in Wiltshire (where other circles appear nearly every summer).

Of course, this in itself is not enough to prove that some unidentified hoaxer fooled Mr Healey, and Terence Meaden is convinced from his examination of photographs that the Alfriston quintuplet was genuine (see Plate 3). Perhaps it was, but nobody, to our knowledge, examined the circle for layering effects and damage, and no one has subsequently come forward to claim that they did fabricate the Alfriston circle. As in many anomalies, the evidence is rather suspiciously suggestive of 'game-playing', yet debatable. We simply feel it deserves caution.

Essex, 1989

During the intensely active season of 1989 two separate sets of circles attracted a certain degree of suspicion. We think it unlikely that they are the only suspect formations to have arrived during the great media hype, but many of them were not studied in depth because there was such a huge number and so little time in which to review them before sightseeing and harvesting contaminated or destroyed all sign of the traces.

The first case involved the discovery of a single, perfectly round circle in a field of ripe wheat only two metres from a footpath near Shenfield on 18 July. This clockwise circle was the first to be reported to BUFORA from Essex and had been discovered by Stephen Hall, a quality assurance engineer from Brentwood, whilst walking his dog. He had just reported a UFO to Jenny Randles and claimed that on discovery of the marks he had not heard of the circles effect, despite the extensive national media publicity that had recently accompanied the Andrews and Delgado book. We have no reason to disbelieve Mr Hall concerning this.

BUFORA's Mike Wootten visited the location on 3 August. Measuring almost nine metres in diameter, the circle was joined by a smaller clockwise formation some five metres in diameter and which arrived ten days later. Wootten noted that the second circle was situated only 1.5 metres away from the first, and he quickly showed that the spiral centre was positioned at the precise focus of both the circles and that many of the crop stems were snapped and broken at the base. These factors are rather suspicious and may indicate a hoax.

On 11 August the Chelmsford-based *Essex Chronicle* reported that a 'mysterious circle' had appeared near the village of Littley Green, causing a certain degree of consternation amongst the local community: 'Theories range from a visitation from Outer Space to a jollification by young farmers, with a range of options such as a magnetic field, a whirlwind or badger activity in between ...' The newspaper reported that the nine metre diameter circle displayed concentric rings which alternated in direction. This factor led farm bailiff John Webb to comment: 'That would not have happened if it had been a whirlwind. The wheat would have been flattened all one way.' Once again, nothing unusual was seen or heard on the night the circle appeared, and no tracks led from a nearby lane. However, Mr Jim Padfield, vice-president of the Essex Young Farmers Union, claimed that, 'It's more likely to be the green welly brigade than little green men.' The report added that after closing time at the local pub there may have been means and opportunity!

These two cases seem like prime candidates for hoaxing. They were both positioned close to public footpaths, both displayed suspicious features (broken corn at Shenfield, concentric rings at Littley Green) and both appeared during the media furore surrounding the publication of *Circular Evidence*.

One has to wonder at yet another remarkable 'name' coincidence. Finding a circle near 'Littley Green', amidst media speculation as to whether 'little green men' create these marks, begs the question as to whether someone somewhere was anticipating comment about the intervention of 'Littley Green Men'!

Media Demonstrations of Hoaxing

Several demonstrations have been carried out by various media sources attempting to show how easy it is to make a circle. These demonstrations serve to emphasize how one can create something that *looks* impressive from a distance but how difficult it is to manufacture an example that is *exactly* the same when the fine details can be rapidly investigated.

Froxfield, Hampshire, 1986

During August 1986 a freelance journalist contacted Paul Fuller and Pat Delgado, claiming to be a reporter for the *Mail on Sunday* newspaper writing a serious article about the circles. Because BUFORA had already circulated free copies of our 1986 report *Mystery of the Circles* to all the national newspapers in Fleet Street, Fuller sent him one.

Later that same week, somebody approached the *Petersfield*

Post claiming to have photographic proof that they had hoaxed all the circle formations that had appeared to date, and offering to demonstrate their circle-making abilities with local press and TV in attendance. A demonstration was arranged at Venthams Farm near Froxfield a week or so later, and BBC TV's *South Today* team, BBC Radio Solent and a number of bystanders turned up to record the results.

It was the freelancer, who arrived with two 'farmhands'. Armed with a pole and chain, the 'demonstration' got underway. As it happens, *Mystery of the Circles* described several simple methods of creating circles, including this one.

This 'journalist's' companions proceeded to trample down a large circle, using the pole as a central pivot and the chain to help force the crop down into a near-perfect circle. Over an hour later the would-be hoaxers inspected their perfectly circular hoax, commenting that they always carried a trowel to fill in the (very obvious) hole at the centre and boasting that they had been responsible for other manifestations that had appeared during that summer.

As BUFORA's report predicted, the hoaxers produced a perfectly circular zone of crushed and broken wheat with no true swirl pattern, no layering and no banding. Despite claims that they had made other circles, no photograph was supplied which showed a half-completed circle, only photographs of undamaged fields and circle formations supposedly in those fields.

Despite this lack of support, the journalist later commented: 'I'm amazed that no one has actually tried to copy the rings before. It seems to me that everyone was overlooking the possibility that these are a hoax, and that somewhere someone is sitting back killing himself laughing at all the publicity.' In fact, BUFORA's *Mystery of the Circles* had already described the Westbury 1983 hoax in some detail. The Froxfield demonstration only serves to emphasize how some sections of the media have taken advantage of the phenomenon in order to play games with the public, and again emphasizes our need for caution when thinking about the possibilities of a successful large-scale hoax.

Country File, 1988
During 1988 the BBC Pebble Mill Countryside Unit produced a documentary *Running Rings Round Arthur** about the circles

---

* In fact, the documentary was incorrectly titled, as the statue shown was of King Alfred, not King Arthur!

screened on 9 October. Six Young Farmers were invited to create a circle at Red Rice Farm near Andover in Hampshire. Their method was to walk into the field along a tractor-created tramline, advance into the untouched crop and use one person as a pivot. A second man then began trampling down the corn whilst attached to the 'ringleader' by a short length of rope. This ensured that the trampled zone would be perfectly circular, and it allowed the hoaxer's accomplices to join in the fun by trampling down the corn and then touching up the result to 'create the scorch marks'. The team's leader implied that they had been hoaxing circles for some time, but in great humour the 'Rent a Circle' team declined to elaborate further on their activities. Despite the apparent difference between the Young Farmers' hoax and 'genuine' circles, BBC TV interviewer Ann Brown seemed to dismiss the entire phenomenon with the comment, 'Thoughts of little green men were suddenly replaced with thoughts of ruddy great men ...'

Secret Circles, 1989
On the *Secret Circles* documentary from BBC Bristol (1989), two teams from the Army Cadet Corps at the local university were invited to make a circle by whatever method they chose. A team of four women created a circle by linking hands and simply marching. No circles-researchers were invited to examine these hoaxes, but it seems clear from the TV transmission that this attempt produced a perfect circle consisting of broken corn with no layering or banding effects and a poorly defined swirl pattern.

Two male cadets used the 'latest technology' available by driving a stake into the ground and attaching a rope, which they managed to rotate about the pivot with some difficulty. Their hoax was also perfectly circular and displayed broken corn with no banding or layering effects, and there was a suspicious hole at the centre of the formation.

Commentary

The evidence in this chapter proves conclusively that at least *some* circles *are* the result of hoaxing. This must imply that other circles may also be hoaxes. There is a distinct possibility that a sophisticated technique is being used in some circumstances and as part of a co-ordinated effort to promote a mystery. If so, then some of the comments below may need to be mitigated.

The existence of the proven hoaxes raises two important questions for our understanding of the phenomenon: who is doing the hoaxing, and are these hoaxed circles *identical* to those circles that are not being identified as hoaxes?

From the examples given above, we suggest that at least four groups of people may well from time to time get involved in hoaxing circles: the media, publicity-seekers, Young Farmers groups and UFO-spotters.

Clearly the dubious events at Westbury (1983) and Froxfield (1986) demonstrate that certain sections of the media have powerful vested interests in the promotion of the phenomenon. This need serves two commercial purposes: to attract the public's attention (i.e. sell more copy) and to promote the Anomaly Myth – that the circles must have a sensational explanation.

From the available evidence it seems that other hoaxes involve people whose motives are not purely commercial. We strongly suspect that the '*WEARENOTALONE*' hoax was perpetrated by someone on the fringe of the UFO movement who was aware of the increasing interest being shown in the alien explanation. By providing hints about a UFO link, the myth is reinforced and UFO-related activities (for example, sky-watching, UFO meetings, books and journals) all attract more interest.

Many observers without a deep understanding of the problem argue that *all* the circles must be caused by hoaxing. A typical example was published in *Country Life* (9 March 1989), when Robert Rosenthaal of Santa Monica, California, commented: 'If this were to happen in the United States we would immediately look for six college students with high powered weed cutters, especially as all of the circles appear to have track marks leading into them ...'

This argument is inappropriate, because circles *do* occur in the United States (see, for example, p. 159) and because many photographs now exist which were taken immediately on discovery and show no track marks leading from tramlines to these isolated circles. Historical circles frequently predate the use of tramlines, yet footprints and suspicious marks were allegedly missing from them.

These factors rule out hoaxing for the majority of cases, although at least a handful of circles seem to be the result of tricksters at work. Indeed, we suspect that the final influence of hoaxing may well be considerably greater than is presently believed, especially in recent years, when publicity has been so substantial and there is plenty of evidence of what look like 'name-games' being played. For example, there are the two different 'Cradle Hills' that sprouted circles after the fame of that name was established within ufology, or the allegation early in circles lore that those sites then visited which began with the letter *W* (i.e. Wantage, Warminster and Westbury) could all form a triangle of circles.

Table A: Are Hoaxed Circles Identical to Those Not Being Identified as Hoaxes?

BUFORA's decade of research suggests that there are important differences between hoaxed circles and 'genuine' circles. These differences are tabulated below.

Differences between hoaxed circles and the 'real' circles.

	'Genuine' Circles	*Hoaxed Circles*
Swirl pattern	Always present in one form or another	Not present or only partially covers affected area
Layering effects	Usually present	Never present
Banding effects	Always present	Present but not very uniform
Condition of crop	Usually undamaged	Stems usually broken; heads damaged
Shape	Usually elliptical	Either perfectly circular or clearly misshapen (e.g. kink in outer ring)
Position of spiral	Usually offset from the geometrical centre, but can be dead-centred	Usually dead-centred
Type of formation	All Types	Some evidence of restricted range
Damage to ground?	No	Sometimes hole is apparent at centre
Condition of surrounding crop	Undamaged	Track marks and footprints evident
Dowsing effect?	Yes	No
Degree of publicity	Only 10 per cent are reported	Most receive widespread publicity
Time of discovery	Usually overnight or around dawn	Usually during the day

Sorting out hoaxed circles from genuine circles, and false claims of hoaxing from the true ones, is problematic, but it seems clear that we can rule out hoaxing as the primary source of the basic circles, for the following four reasons:

1. the difficulty we face in replicating the very complex features being discovered in genuine circles (particularly the layering effect);
2. the very high numbers of circles being discovered every summer;
3. the long-established international distribution traced for this book and reported in Chapter 9 (dating back many years in Britain, and possibly elsewhere); and
4. the fact that we have a more reasonable hypothesis to account for many of the reported features being discovered.

It seems significant that many hoaxes are reasonably complex (that is, quintuplets and ringed circles). This suggests that tricksters choose their designs from a range of formations to match people's concept of UFO marks.

In March 1970 a significant experiment was carried out at Warminster. A group of ufologists on Cradle Hill, below which we now find many circles, observed a strange object. One man claimed to have successfully photographed it and the case was given much coverage by *FSR*, in which experts and scientists debated its unexplained status. Some years later a group known as SIUFOP (Society for the Investigation of UFO Phenomena) admitted that they had hoaxed the 'UFO' by putting a filtered spotlight on a car and parking this on a nearby slope. The photographer was a member of this team of technicians and had employed various detectable trick methods. The intention was to test how far belief would prevent critical evaluation of the evidence. As Simpson said, '[The ufologists'] statements and actions were often not those of people trying to understand a strange event, but those of people prepared to ignore relevant criticisms in order to support a cause.' [1,2,3]

We believe that this case shows how large-scale hoaxing *can* operate – and why. In our view, there is growing evidence that *some* aspects of the circles mystery are the product of such a controlled hoax.

This book outlines reasons why this cannot account for the entire phenomenon (which we believe has something else at its heart), but we have become increasingly suspicious of the rapidly rising numbers and complexity of the circles since about 1983 – which just happens to coincide with the point at which the mystery escalated from a local to a national level. This may well be connected with a long-term project to test how people respond to such a dramatic phenomenon.

To pin the blame on one specific group, such as SIUFOP, would be a mistake. There is a growing number of scientific bodies who do not approve of what they perceive as the sweeping tide of supernaturalism and who doubtless would be prepared to launch and operate a complicated experiment that could bring considerable disrepute to believers in the paranormal. Such a group might be one that has seized upon small degrees of publicity attached to an interesting natural phenomenon that was already achieving UFO-related attention in one part of Britain; or perhaps a sociological group are the hosts – seeking to study human trends of thought.

Here are just a few points to bear in mind when contemplating this idea. We think it has been given far too little credence as yet, thanks to the widespread conviction that the circles cannot be man-made.

1. The location of the SIUFOP hoax was carefully chosen. The Warminster connection was used because it was socially important. Any new hoax may well have similar motives, and the creation of a mythical 'Wessex Triangle' could be an important attribute of a long-term and well-designed stratagem.
2. SIUFOP state that they left ground traces at the point where they placed the vehicle and spotlight, although in 1970 nobody actually found them. Ground traces are seen to be an obvious candidate for any attempt at hoaxing because an uncorroborated story remains unbelievable to most outsiders, whereas traces are bound to attract the media and are visible even to non-believers.
3. As you saw, hoaxing of circles *is* possible, *has* provably happened and *was not* always detected right away, even by some of those who believe that it is quite impossible to hoax circles effectively.

For us, this indicates that some of the superficial evidence for an 'intelligence' at work might be due to human factors. Think about the imputed 'messages', escalating circle types and rising numbers of markings – plus the games that often seem to be played with researchers, such as manifesting a circle right underneath their noses the moment their backs are turned, which has now occurred on at least two occasions.

We understand that SIUFOP claim to have conducted other hoaxes, some of which have not yet been exposed. The fact that they claim to have successfully operated more long-term hoaxes shows the feasibility of someone doing this in Wessex with the circles.

We think that the possibility that some of the circles are the result of a co-ordinated effort involving experimental hoaxers, either carrying out some fact-finding mission or seeking to discredit the UFO movement (or more correctly allowing the UFO movement to discredit itself!), has to be given the strongest possible consideration.

The fact that we cannot currently replicate what is occurring in the 'genuine' circles should not be interpreted as proof that nobody has mastered a particularly clever circle-making technique, and that this method has yet to be duplicated by circles-watchers. We confidently predict that in the future there will be more provocative hoaxes and that more exotic patterns will appear in the cereal fields of Wessex.

We would urge everyone to bear these things in mind and 'watch this space' for the daring and perhaps amusing new circle patterns that some clever trickster may think of inventing. But we would also ask these suspects to remember that they are harming food crops in which farmers have invested time and money. Such lighthearted games are damaging people's livelihoods.

In our view, the joke has been a good one but has gone on for long enough.

6 'Unknown Forces'

In *Circular Evidence*, from Colin Andrews (see Plate 10) and Pat Delgado, we see the most detailed presentation of an 'exotic' solution. Some unknown force field, quite possibly guided by an unknown form of intelligence, appears to be considered by the authors to be the most likely instigator of the circles.

The book was billed as 'a detailed investigation of the flattened swirled crops phenomenon', and it was added that the purpose was 'to present the facts ... facts that you can verify by walking into a circle and checking for yourself'.[1] This was a very laudable aim and, indeed, the book does have some excellent features (notably its photographic record of the mystery). However, we must examine some of the claims made in this bestselling title and, more importantly, establish that significant evidence appears to have been omitted. This we find rather puzzling.

The Eyewitness Accounts

The omission of what is (in our view) crucial eyewitness testimony surprises us the most. These are the growing number of accounts of circles actually being seen to form in daylight by reputable people. Their absence from the book raises a number of questions. Several eyewitness accounts had appeared in the meteorological literature prior to 1989 when the text for *Circular Evidence* was finalized. If this book truly does deal with *all* the evidence surrounding the circles phenomenon, why do these authors seem to consider the eyewitness accounts unworthy of inclusion?

As well-informed circles researchers the authors would surely have known of the stories by Bell, Lewis and Shuttlewood prior to completing the text of *Circular Evidence*. These witnesses all report having seen circles formed in daylight (see Chapter 7).

We also wonder why Andrews and Delgado could be seemingly

unaware of at least some of those accounts described on pp. 102–13 of this present book. Paul Fuller sent Colin Andrews a letter in February 1988 pointing out that such eyewitness reports did now exist and that we and other researchers valued them highly. Andrews responded to Fuller's letter but has seemingly ignored the eyewitness aspects.

He also later appeared on the BBC TV documentary *Running Rings Around Arthur*, which included an on-site interview with Melvyn Bell and discussed his experience in some depth. This programme has been broadcast by BBC TV several times in just over twelve months. Andrews was presumably interested in the results of this when they were first broadcast in October 1988.

It seems that Colin Andrews knew of the Melvyn Bell observations, because he apparently reported this to George Wingfield, another of *Flying Saucer Review*'s myriad consultants. Wingfield comments in Timothy Good's *The UFO Report 1990* that, 'The witness is an associate of Dr Meaden's, so it was perhaps inevitable that this event was described by Mr Bell as a "stationary whirlwind". Despite subsequent reference to "dust, dirt and light debris spiralling into the air", which was not mentioned to Colin Andrews when he was first told the story, it does not seem that one can draw much conclusion as to what caused this Circle.'[2]

Perhaps we have misunderstood this comment, but it seems to imply that the Melvyn Bell reference to 'dust, dirt and other light debris' was an embellishment of some kind to support a natural explanation. In a lecture to BUFORA in March 1990 Wingfield emphasized this view by disputing the importance of the sighting.

Of course by commenting in this manner Wingfield infers that Andrews actually asked Melvyn Bell whether he saw any debris spiralling upwards, and, when we understand Andrews did not, in any event Bell certainly described the mechanism he observed as 'like a whirlwind' on the *Country File* TV documentary.

We have further been advised that Terence Meaden sent Andrews and Delgado copies of his papers on the phenomenon between 1985 and mid 1989 and that Meaden also discussed this work with Colin Andrews in the field.

Yet the authors term the weather concept 'an insult to one's intelligence' and 'a joke'[3] without any indication to their readers that evidence exists which strongly supports the natural solution.

Delgado went on to claim in the *Hampshire Chronicle* (July 1989) that 'They [i.e. we, the present authors] are taking a nonsensical path towards the problem. They are quoting whirlwinds – and they never come at night – despite what they say ...' This rejection of the 'whirlwind' theory continues: 'They are following a truly bad trail of investigation. Whirlwinds, or vortices [sic], are caused by pockets of hot air rising, and rotating, as it goes. There is no way it can press downwards. That is a scientific fact.'

We fully agree with Delgado. His dismissal of the 'whirlwind' theory is perfectly correct. Most *ordinary* 'whirlwinds' rely upon insolation (the sun's heat) and cannot therefore be responsible for the predominantly nocturnal appearance of circles. Unfortunately Delgado seems to conclude from this that because an *ordinary* 'whirlwind' cannot be the cause, any 'natural' atmospheric vortex must be similarly dismissed. This reasoning is flawed because Terence Meaden is not proposing a traditional 'whirlwind' as the cause of the crop circles: he is suggesting a previously unrecognized *descending* vortex which can occur by night or day. Meaden has made this very clear for several years in his many published papers.

We believe that it is unreasonable to reject a natural atmospheric solution for the data by suggesting 'whirlwinds' to be an impossible cause. They argue that meteorologists are not convinced, but Appendix 1 of this book seems to indicate that there *is* a growing body of support from this profession, now that Meaden's theories are being published in the subject's literature.

As for 'whirlwinds' not occurring at night, it is a contentious claim that, 'After extensive enquiry and prolonged personal observation, we have no evidence that these circles are created except at night.'[4] In our opinion this is not a defensible statement, and we have presented these researchers with evidence to contradict it. However, they repeat the view that, 'The evidence is over-whelming that circle creations only occur at night.'[5] Whilst it is true that most circles probably *do* form at night (or in pre-dawn hours at least), there are now extensive grounds for believing that a far from insignificant proportion appear during daylight.

Andrews' and Delgado's dismissal of a natural atmospheric solution is highlighted by an interview given on the *Gloria Hunniford Show* (broadcast on BBC Radio 2 on 3 August 1989) in which Colin Andrews dealt with the Melvyn Bell case in the following manner. Jenny Randles participated by phone from her Cheshire home.

Jenny Randles: ... [one of the] real reasons why we believe that [circles are being formed by natural forces is] because there are EYE WITNESS ACCOUNTS – which [Andrews and Delgado] studiously avoid mentioning in their book – of people who have actually *seen* circles being formed in daylight by wind vortexes [*sic*].

Gloria Hunniford: Let me stop you there, Jenny. Now what about this point, Colin?

Colin Andrews: There are so many, aren't there? I mean the lady just doesn't ...

Gloria Hunniford (interrupting): Well, let's take that eyewitness report and the weather aspect.

Colin Andrews: Yes, indeed, there's *one* eyewitness report.

Jenny Randles (interrupting): There's more than one, *many* more than one.

At this point Colin Andrews appeared to become flustered and wrongly suggested that Jenny was used to sitting behind a desk in London and not investigating circles first-hand. In response to that question about the fast-accumulating eyewitness testimony he said that they knew of one alleged account and '... I must say, Gloria, this is very important, the only one ... isn't it a strange coincidence? ... [was] an employee of Dr Meaden's. We're not prepared to accept one eyewitness account.'

Gloria Hunniford was forced to terminate the discussion at this point.

As we show in the next chapter, a number of eyewitness accounts have already been well publicized in various media sources, but Andrews' imputation (presumably accidental) terming the connection between Melvyn Bell and Terence Meaden as 'a strange coincidence' had serious repercussions. Meaden was very unhappy and ceased exchanging information and reports with Andrews' research team. In fact, Meaden asked Andrews to justify this statement, to which Andrews replied that under pressure he had mismanaged his answer. We sympathize with this but cannot apologize for the pressure. These eyewitness accounts are surely crucial to our understanding of crop-circle formation.

Meaden has since provided BUFORA with a statement that makes it abundantly clear that Melvyn Bell independently volunteered his eyewitness account without any encouragement of skulduggery from himself. Besides which, there are many other eyewitness accounts of circles being created by atmospheric forces (which have no conceivable link with Terence Meaden). Indeed, we are publishing many new examples in this book after having found them in the historical records (without enormous effort).

We must ask whether all this evidence can possibly be dismissed? In our view, these accounts do not appear to support Andrews' and Delgado's argument that the circles are being caused by 'an unknown force field manipulated by an unknown intelligence'[6] but instead favour a natural solution. Nevertheless, these accounts must be evidence of *something* and cannot simply be ignored or wished away as 'coincidence'.

Repeatedly throughout 1989 these researchers made the claim that they were working with meteorological bureaux all around Europe and that they had found 'no correlation' between the circles and meteorology. If this is so, they must have evidence which demonstrates that circles are not appearing when frontal systems and sea-breeze fronts are passing over circle locations – which Terence Meaden, as a meteorologist, insists to be the case. Unfortunately this counter-evidence has not been published anywhere (as far as we know), whereas Meaden's research and findings have appeared in reputable meteorological sources.

The Omission of Other Vital Evidence

Circular Evidence has a second puzzling omission. Despite the claim that, 'Unfortunately for [the "whirlwind" theory], many of our circles have been in locations remote from any hills';[7] the well-established association between circles and hill slopes (currently standing at fifty per cent of cases within one kilometre of such a slope) is not discussed. We have seen no media statements by Andrews and Delgado which point out that circles cluster around geographical locations such as Cheesefoot, Westbury and Cley Hill. Nor have we seen any media comments as to how the sudden fall in temperature reported during the site-monitor experiment 'Operation Whitecrow' was entirely consistent with the passage of a weak cold front known to have passed over southern Britain on the night in question, 17–18 June 1989.

We have several other examples of circles appearing when frontal systems pass over the location, and this book later offers ample evidence of such a link. These facts do not support the widespread claims that there *is* no evidence of any description for a meteorological link with the circles.

The UFO Photo

This *Circular Evidence* photograph shows 'a white disc-shaped object' hovering above the spiral centre of an unnamed circle.[8] Commenting on this oddity, Colin Andrews claims that neither he, Delgado nor Taylor saw anything when the picture was taken and that, 'We have had the negative analysed professionally, but no logical explanation has been found. It is another facet of the subject which we are unable to account for'.[9] No full account of this analysis appears.

Of course, the discovery of an image that looks like a UFO on one of the authors' photographs should be studied critically. For instance, might not some mischievous outsider have tried to fool Andrews and Delgado with evidence that boosts a UFO evaluation, awaiting an opportunity to expose the truth? It happened when the *Mirror* sought to hoax the *Express* and circles researchers may not be immune.

We suggest that Andrews and Delgado submit this photograph for computer enhancement in an effort to reveal whether or not the image is solid and three-dimensional.

The researchers have also produced photographs taken at the Chilcomb (1987) ringed circle, although again not seen at the time. Writing in *Flying Saucer Review*, 'Busty' Taylor claimed that some of his negatives of circles had been copied and tampered with without his permission. He confirmed this to the authors personally. If true, this may support our warning that the CPR group are open to a hoax by outsiders with a wish to discredit the field of circles research.

If this is so, we deplore it. We may disagree profoundly with some of the conclusions arrived at by Andrews, Delgado and CPR and dispute much of their methodology, but we respect them as responsible individuals and would not condone deliberate trickery which involved dubious or illegal activities. We raise these questions purely out of a genuine concern that this photographic evidence be either properly analysed and strengthened or withdrawn from the circles debate.

The Crash of the Harrier[10]

A bizarre claim first made (in some detail) by Colin Andrews in *Flying Saucer Review* in 1988[11] is that a plane crash was possibly linked with circles. This is referenced briefly in *Circular Evidence*.

The facts are that on 22 October 1987 a British Harrier jump jet took off from Dunsfold in Surrey on a test flight for British Aerospace. Passing over north Hampshire and Wiltshire at a height of at least six kilometres, the pilot passed a routine radio message to RAF Boscombe Down, and then all radio contact with the aircraft was lost. Boscombe Down immediately put out a general alert to all other air traffic in the area, and some time later an American military plane flying over the Atlantic just south-west of Ireland intercepted the Harrier in unusual circumstances.

Tragically the aircraft was minus both its cockpit canopy and its pilot, a scene which the astonished Americans filmed from their own aircraft and which was subsequently given national TV exposure. The Harrier flew on for nearly 700 kilometres on 'automatic pilot' before crashing into the unsalvageable depths of the cold Atlantic. The pilot's body was discovered by a gamekeeper the following evening, close to Winterbourne Stoke in Wiltshire. His main parachute was recovered several miles away but his secondary chute and the aircraft's dinghy were discovered in the same area.

Speculation immediately abounded over this strange incident. What could have caused this experienced pilot unexpectedly to bale out whilst leaving his plane to fly on with no apparent technical problems? Why had both his chutes failed to operate? Why was his ejector seat never found?

According to Colin Andrews, as soon as he heard of the incident he had 'a strong inner feeling' that there was some connection with the circles. Rushing to the site where the pilot's body had been found, he was not surprised to discover a full military operation taking place. This 'strong inner feeling' occurred even before he knew where the body lay, so naturally Colin Andrews reported what he knew about the circles to the investigating military authorities, who were apparently 'very interested' in what he said. 'We will be in touch with you again soon', they commented. Unfortunately no such contact seems to have occurred, but Andrews noted: 'My discussions with these officials have left me with the very clear impression that there is far, far more in all this than meets the eye ... and that there is profound uneasiness about the UFOs and about the circles.'[12]

Why should someone believe that this terrible accident was

related in some way to the circles? Certainly at the time of the incident all the cornfields would have been harvested at least two months beforehand. According to the map published in *FSR*, the pilot's body was in fact over one kilometre away from the location at which the 1987 Winterbourne Stoke circles had last been seen some two months previously, and despite Andrews' claim that the aircraft had made a slight course-change over this very field where the circles appeared, no proof of that has yet emerged.

No explanation was immediately forthcoming for the Harrier incident, but at the subsequent inquiry it emerged that the most likely explanation was relatively mundane, albeit tragic. In a normal emergency an ejector seat fires the pilot through the canopy, then a manual separation device allows the pilot to break free of the seat, and it falls to earth by parachute. In this case the ejector seat had not fired but seemingly the separation device had accidentally triggered, throwing the unlucky pilot through the canopy, causing his death. This unexpected ejection would account for why the ejector seat has not been found (because it was still in the plane at the bottom of the Atlantic). The pilot may have been badly hurt before leaving the cockpit. This seems to fit the facts perfectly adequately.

As far as we can ascertain, the Ministry of Defence has not responded to the CPR team's offer in the *Southern Evening Echo* on 12 July 1989 (and in other places) to 'get together' to try to solve the mystery of the circles' alleged connection with the Harrier incident.

The Billy Meier Saga[13]

Pat Delgado discusses a 'fascinating' book, *Light Years*, by journalist Gary Kinder, in which the rural Swiss Eduard 'Billy' Meier discovers a number of swirled circles in grass near his home. These marks were created by UFOs (according to Meier) which he has met frequently.

Perhaps Delgado was unaware that the Billy Meier case is widely viewed in the UFO community as one of great controversy. Between 1975 and 1978 Meier claimed to have held more than 130 meetings with denizens from the Pleiades, a cluster of stars more than 400 million light years from Earth. Meier's astonishing claims were supported by a series of superb close-up photographs of the Pleiadeans' 'beam ships', disc-shaped craft which he discovered were driven by a 'hyper-space drive system'. The pictures rapidly became a sensation, and several books have explained in graphic detail how the craft were built, who manned them and why the Pleiadeans were visiting Earth.

However, many serious ufologists have major reservations about this extraordinary saga. Surely scientists are duty-bound to treat extreme claims with at least as much caution as ufologists have, because by the very nature of what is being reported no team endeavouring to set up a scientific data base for circles research should introduce a hotly debated case into this unless it is absolutely necessary. The circles do look like the same phenomenon under discussion, from viewing photographs in Kinder's book. But how much strength should be placed upon them alongside Meier's more bizarre claims?

Critics point out that many of the UFO photographs are taken pointing straight at the sun or against a clear light sky – conditions which would suit trick photography. A great deal of other evidence emerged from the exhaustive research into Meier's case conducted by Kal Korff (summarized by Peter Brookesmith[14]). This includes the discovery of models of the Pleiadeans' spaceships in Meier's home – which the witness insists were made by his children based on the photographs he had already taken of real spaceships. The witness may be sincere, but it seems prudent to reserve judgement on the value of his evidence.

The Martian Mars Bar

One of 1989's most endearing media stories concerned 'Busty' Taylor's discovery of a 'luminous white, jelly-like substance' at the Goodworth Clatford quintuplet back in 1985.[15] This story subsequently formed the central theme in many media articles (some implying that it was a 1989 discovery). It seems to be the basis for that claim in *Fate* about *several* sites generating unknown material (see page 16).

The 'Mars Bar' was subjected to independent analyses at the University of Surrey and the National Testing Laboratory at Wisley. The result of the University of Surrey's analysis is published in *Circular Evidence*, and the conclusions it reached seem to us to be quite clear. The analyst said that the substance was 'some kind of confectionery that had gone off' – it even smelt of honey. The analysis at Wisley was not particularly contradictory and added that, 'No distinctive or unusual features were observed.'

Unfortunately it seems that many are reluctant to accept an ordinary explanation for this substance. The case for this reluctance stems only from the statement in the University of Surrey's analysis which reported that Fehling's test failed to indicate the presence of glucose syrup (which is present in most, but not all, types of commercial confectionery).

Yet surely any confectionery left out in the open must deteriorate and react with its surroundings? We have no idea how long the 'white goo' was in the field before it was discovered. This is presumably why the Wisley analysis reported that the so-called 'Mars Bar' contained 'normal soil flora' (picked up as it broke down and interacted with the ground) and why Fehling's test failed to prove conclusively that glucose was present.

Had either test reported anything 'unearthly' about the sample, we agree that there might be an argument for some interest. But that is not the case. Yet this is the sample from which the notorious tabloid, the *Sport*, discussed careless alien travellers dropping extraterrestrial chocolates and making circles-researchers go down with out-of-this-world bugs!

Indeed, a massive media myth developed around the discovery of the Martian 'blob'. We see no reason why the 'alien choc' was not simply discarded by a careless and thoughtless litter-bugging visitor or (just conceivably) someone with a mischievous sense of humour who decided to leave the 'evidence' for circles-researchers to discover and use in their promotion of the phenomenon.

Inconsistencies in *Circular Evidence*

Although *Circular Evidence* carries many spectacular photographs of circles and is undoubtedly a valuable record for future researchers of the subject, we have been confused by a number of claims which these authors have made which seem to conflict with the text of the book.

THE CLAIM THAT *CIRCULAR EVIDENCE* REACHES NO CONCLUSIONS
On the dust cover of *Circular Evidence* the authors state that their book does not set out to prove any particular theory or explanation about the circles. This statement was repeated in many media quotes. For example:

' "I just don't know what causes them," said Mr Delgado ... "We have just laid down the facts for people to see. There is a serious scientific investigation going on now and the Government has asked for reports. But no one knows the answer".' (*Winchester Gazette & Extra*, 29 June 1989)

' "It's a mystery", said Andrews, "a complete mystery. And for the time being that's really all one can say".' (*London Evening Standard*, 3 July 1989)

Whilst we accept that no definitive comprehensive solution is offered by the CPR group, and this is fair enough, it seems evident to us that the authors lean towards a UFO-related explanation. This UFO connection is clear when we examine some of the topics discussed throughout the book:

1. When discussing the 1987 ringed circle at Chilcomb, pp. 97–8, they raise the question of the Joyce Bowles encounter with a landed UFO and a 'humanoid', which was reported to have occurred about 1.5 kilometres from this site in 1976 (i.e. eleven years previously);

2. On p. 35 the authors attempt to link the sighting of a giant circular UFO resembling a 'funfair wheel' reported by pensioners Pat and Jack Collins with the discovery of the Goodworth Clatford quintuplet the following morning (although BUFORA investigation strongly suggests this UFO was a bright astronomical body);

3. In Chapter 6 Andrews and Delgado describe more than twenty UFO reports at length which they attempt to link to crop circles. On p. 179 they report a sighting of a UFO as 'a large circular craft'.

Along with their statements about 'unknown forces' and 'unknown intelligences' in their own written material, this seems to support our assumption that Andrews and Delgado consider UFOs to be controlled by an 'unknown intelligence'. Despite their having worked with Dr Terence Meaden for many years, there is not one reference to Meaden's published work or the results of BUFORA's decade of research anywhere in their text, which has almost only UFO material listed as references.

THE CLAIM THAT THE CIRCLES HAVE 'NOTHING TO DO WITH LITTLE GREEN MEN'

Throughout 1989 Andrews and Delgado were repeatedly quoted

as claiming that the circles had 'nothing to do with little green men'. For example:

' "Some people are even claiming they are left there by space ships. But I think the little green men from outer space theory is rather silly".' (Pat Delgado, *Wales on Sunday*, 2 July 1989)

'One question that is guaranteed to make [Delgado] wince is: are they the marks of an alien's spaceship? "We've had a gutfull of UFOs and little green men. We've gone through it and come out the other side".' (*Southern Evening Echo*, 26 June 1989)

' "This is definitely NOT Little Green Men from Mars".' (Colin Andrews, *Secret Circles*, BBC TV documentary)

Unfortunately in their own book Andrews and Delgado repeatedly proffer the idea that the circles are created by some kind of 'intelligence',[16] whilst on one occasion they strongly imply that the source of that 'intelligence' may be 'extra-terrestrial'.[17] Perhaps we have misunderstood their expressed viewpoints, but they seem to introduce devices in the mechanical sense, claiming that, 'UFOs are capable of producing the most extraordinary behaviour and phenomena. Their control of force fields unknown to us may well result in rings and circles. It may well be within the capability of a UFO to manipulate a rotary force-field.'[18]

We are genuinely confused. How do we understand these comments in any way other than a belief that UFOs (i.e. some sort of device) are controlled by some kind of 'intelligence' and may lie behind the circles? Is that not what Andrews and Delgado are alleging? If it is not, we feel that it is time they expressed themselves more clearly and set out who or what these 'forces' and 'intelligences' are inferred to be. We fully understand why many people may equate 'intelligence' with 'little green men', although we accept that even intelligently controlled UFOs need not come from outer space, as popularly believed. If they mean something different, we urge them to explain what that is. At present we are forced to guess what these 'unknown intelligences' are reputed to be, and that is leading to misunderstanding and provoking disputes.

The first part of this chapter set out to demonstrate that, whilst *Circular Evidence* is clearly an honest attempt to produce an interesting book, written in a thought-provoking fashion by two dedicated and hard-working researchers, nevertheless some of the evidence presented in its pages is misleading and on occasion, we feel, fundamentally flawed.

The Media Myths of 1989

1989 was the year in which the myth of the alien cornfield circles 'took off' with a series of sensational and bizarre news stories. For many believers, the ultimate truth was finally revealed beyond all doubt.

This section examines the social machine that swung into action with the release of *Circular Evidence*, and we investigate the way in which a myth was created and portrayed to the public by various media sources. The sight of so many 'ufologists' desperately yearning for an exotic solution to the phenomenon reminded us of the scene in the Monty Python movie *The Life of Brian* in which a man is mistaken for Jesus: when he loses a shoe, he is suddenly surrounded by believers eagerly proclaiming this to be a 'sign' of some higher intelligence.

Overview

So in 1989 the cornfield circles came of age. The media pot that had been quietly simmering for nearly a decade finally bubbled over with a series of odd claims that alternately bemused and amused. We have selected some of the stories that appeared in the press which we believe require closer examination. We cast unfortunately necessary critical comment on some of those claims:

1. The discovery of a strange 'luminous white jelly-like substance' in the Goodworth Clatford (1985) quintuplet, which apparently caused 'severe breathing problems' to anyone who came into contact with it, and resulted in a dog becoming violently ill and lying 'listlessly on its back' with 'respiratory problems' for several hours. (*Kennet Star*, 27 July 1989)
2. The claim that the circles were 'not appearing in random fashion' but were intelligently 'referencing themselves to man-made features such as lanes, telegraph poles and roads'. (*Wiltshire Gazette & Herald*, 6 July 1989)
3. The story that the pilot of a lost Harrier jump jet had been forced to bale out because he accidentally crossed a high-energy beam being controlled by an 'unknown intelligence' that was creating the circles. (*Southern Evening Echo*, 12 July 1989 etc.)

4. The report that cereal crops were 'contaminated' and that they should be 'kept out of the food chain' (*The People*, 9 July 1989 and many other media sources)

5. The recording of a strange, high-pitched 'warbling sound' emanating from circles during the filming of the BBC TV documentary *Daytime Live*, 30 October 1989 (billed as 'UFO blasts TV crew from circle of corn' in *Today*, 31 October 1989)

6. The claim that the governments of Canada, Australia, France and Japan were showing great interest in the British circles but that the British Government was uninterested and trying to explain the circles away 'to take the pot off the boil through fear of the unknown'. (*Wiltshire Gazette*, 17 August 1989)

7. The revelation that the Queen had 'sharply questioned' Mrs Thatcher about the cause of the circles in 'secret talks' at Buckingham Palace (*Wall Street Journal*, 28 August 1989) and that the royal family had 'chosen *Circular Evidence*' as 'one of only 32 books published this year to grace the [royal] bookcases'. (*Southern Evening Echo*, 3 August 1989). Readers may be astonished to learn from this that the royal family are restricted to reading only thirty-two carefully chosen books a year!

8. The claim that a dead fly discovered clinging to a stem at the centre of a circle had been 'zapped dead' by some kind of 'mysterious force'. (*Sunday Times*, 9 July 1989)

9. The idea that the 'mysterious force' that creates the circles can respond to the subconscious thoughts of the 'scientists' researching the phenomenon. (*Sunday Times*, 9 July 1989)

10. The uncovering of a 'staggering' ninety-eight circles on a mountainside in the Black Mountains that 'eliminate the hoax theory once and for all'. (*Sunday Express*, 30 July 1989 and others)

11. That researchers visiting circles sites have 'felt their own blood crystallise on certain occasions' (*Telegraph Weekend Magazine*, 8 July 1989) and that the circles could be a message from some 'form of intelligence' telling us that, 'If you destroy this food, your planet is finished.' (*Wall Street Journal*, 28 August 1989)

12. The report that army helicopters from Middle Wallop and Hampshire & Wiltshire Police are photographing circles from

the air and exchanging details of sightings with civilian operators. (*London Evening Standard*, 3 July 1989; *Sunday Times*, 9 July 1989)

13. The account that the Royal Commission for Historical Sites had 'put planes' at ufologists' 'disposal' to search for circles. (*Hampshire Chronicle*, 3 August 1989)

14. Indeed, the media stories continue. In 1990 Terence Meaden has already been called upon to respond to one report that mysterious energy forces were causing mass-murderers to go on the rampage!

ANALYSIS

Readers may find themselves utterly confused by this collection of allegations. How can they fit something as mundane as we are contending? At times we found ourselves wondering if we have been investigating another phenomenon altogether!

We must attempt to place these tales in their proper context. We stress that by doing this we are not pointing the finger of suspicion at anyone in particular and that (with some exceptions) we are not automatically precluding that the claims have substance. Our aim is simply to demonstrate how the media failed in their responsibility to the public, which, in our view, was to research and then objectively present the facts about strange reports and not help stimulate a myth.

In the text that follows, (???) indicates a point at which sceptical questions should have been asked.

The Myth of the 'Contaminated' Crops

THE CLAIMS

The circles started appearing in 1946 [???] but since 1975 it has gone beserk (???) 'Tory MP Teddy Taylor said "People are becoming alarmed. [???] Something strange is going on." The affected areas of Hampshire, Wiltshire and Dorset are criss-crossed by ancient ley lines associated with energy forces dating back to the Druids. [???]' (*The People*, 9 July 1989)

'The latest twist, claim the researchers, is a molecular change in affected crops which is passing into the food chain [???] ... Of the 95 circles reported in Wiltshire until last week, one third were developing the same molecular damage [???].' (*Sunday Times*, 9 July 1989)

'Scientists investigating mysterious circles that have appeared in cereal fields throughout southern England say crops involved should be banned from the breakfast table. They warn that the cereals undergo a change in molecular structure and shape and have urged the Government to take action [???]. "We have written to the Ministry of Agriculture, Food & Fisheries", said Colin Andrews, a spokesman for the scientists, 'It is possible that a molecular contamination is taking place", added Mr Andrews.' (*Sunday Express*, 9 July 1989)

ANALYSIS

1989 was a year of 'food scares', but the claim that the circles were 'contaminating the food chain' could be interpreted as one of the least responsible. This myth of contaminated crops is a fine example of the promotion of a claim without adopting rigorous investigative standards. BUFORA and TORRO have been investigating these circles for a decade, yet in that time we have not discovered one example of this change taking place in the affected crops, despite PROBE having samples analysed by Bristol University as long ago as 1980.

In *Today* (10 July) we are informed that '60 of the country's leading authorities in areas as diverse as plant chemistry and astronomy' were involved in the search for an answer, but once again no names were cited, no credentials listed and no questions asked. Certainly for such a serious claim – one which could conceivably bring the British cereal industry to the brink of financial disaster – media sources should at least have checked with these scientists, even if the evidence might have been too technical for their audience to comprehend.

The Ministry of Agriculture, Food & Fisheries specifically denied to us that they were aware of any such evidence that the affected crops were 'contaminated' or 'unfit for consumption'. This was during a telephone conversation with Paul Fuller in December 1989. In January 1990 the Ministry wrote to confirm that they denied any receipt of any information that crop circles were contaminated. They further denied having 'advised farmers to change their normal cropping pattern'. This seems to confirm our fears about this food scare. If a 'molecular change' does occur, we would be the first to suggest caution and warn of dangers regarding these crops. Certainly the *possibility* that affected crops might be 'contaminated' was raised by Pat Delgado in 1986 at an open meeting held at Alresford. However, as far as we know, there is no data available in print to prove such a suggestion.

Not surprisingly, some involved observers were less than happy with these claims. Farmer Charles Hall, chairman of the Hampshire Branch of the National Farmers Union, slammed the stories and suggested to us they were irresponsible.

The Involvement of Mrs Thatcher, the Queen and the Ministry of Defence

THE CLAIMS

'Mrs Thatcher ... [says] she had read [Andrews'] recent book on the subject and was passing a funding report to the Ministry of Defence [???].' (*Sunday Express*, 9 July 1989)

'British agriculture and defence officials want to know more. So does Queen Elizabeth, who is said to have sharply questioned Prime Minister Margaret Thatcher about the circles recently. While those talks are kept secret, a Buckingham Palace spokesman says the Queen took a hurriedly published book about the circles to her summer palace in Scotland this month; as Britain's biggest landowner, she has every reason not to be amused.' (*The Wall Street Journal*, 28 August 1989)

ANALYSIS

Crop circles are not a new phenomenon and have been appearing for many years across the British countryside. We also have the response by Richard Ryder (Deputy Minister for Agriculture Food & Fisheries), given to a question by MP Michael Colvin on 29 July 1989. Ryder says that the government's official view is that circles are, '... most likely to result from a combination of wind and local soil fertility conditions in cereals which are prone to lodging'.

It seems strange that despite this apparent belief in a mundane explanation, Mrs Thatcher was still 'passing a funding report' to 'worried' officials at the Ministry of Defence. Why should Mrs Thatcher need to 'step in to help find an explanation' (*Southern Evening Echo*, 12 July 1989) if one of her major government departments was already aware that the circles have an ordinary explanation and if the deputy head of that department was publicly to support this explanation in the House of Commons?

Next we turn to the interest being shown by nameless

high-ranking 'defence officials' at the MoD. Why are they so reluctant to come out of their Whitehall shells to discuss their 'concern' about the appearance of these 'mysterious circles', especially given the military facilities in Wessex?

The *Southern Evening Echo* makes great play of the claim that 'defence officials' are 'worried by the appearance of circles within highly sensitive military areas of Salisbury Plain'. Had the ministry fallen for the Wessex triangle myth or do they know that circles appear all over Britain?

Despite the official view that circles have a logical solution, the *Southern Evening Echo* goes on to state that 'as Mr Andrews revealed, no farmer' accepts a weather-based solution to the mystery. In fact, BUFORA had sent them a press release days before which could have put them into contact (just for starters!) with the nineteen cereal farmers who responded to our survey indicating that they *were* happy to entertain a weather-based solution. Colin Andrews presumably knew this, because he conducted a post-survey follow-up on our behalf and spoke to some of the farmers concerned (something he was quick to point out on p. 29 of *Circular Evidence*, even though he later said on Radio Solent that he had never exchanged any information with us).

Regretfully our research suggests that the media claim about Margaret Thatcher's 'personal interest' and the involvement of the Ministry of Defence is rather unlikely, but again no media source appears to have bothered to check the facts with No. 10 or the Ministry. Only the Plymouth-based *Western Independent* seems to have tackled them on these issues, and their story was most interesting: 'The Ministry of Defence says it is not concerned about the corn circles and says it knows nothing about reports that the Prime Minister has passed a circles research funding report to the MoD ... "We have no interest in these circles whatsoever" said a spokesman who admitted the ministry knew nothing about worries threats [sic] they could be a danger to aircraft. "It's all a load of old rubbish".'

On 10 July 1989 we wrote to the Prime Minister questioning her reputed interest in the circles. Our letter was answered by a Whitehall officer, Clive Neville, at department Air Staff 2a: '[I] would first of all like to assure you that ... the Ministry of Defence does not intend to investigate the cause behind the corn circles. As you rightly say, these rings have been occurring throughout the

United Kingdom for a number of years and we do not believe they represent a threat to the security of the defence of the country.'

The Prime Minister's officer also responded personally to us on 8 August with a polite note expressing not the slightest hint of interest or concern at this top level of government. Similarily the MP who first raised the issue in the Commons, Teddy Taylor (Conservative), wrote to Jenny Randles (using official House of Commons notepaper) on 13 July, saying: 'I can assure you that I have had no direct contact with those directly involved [in circles research] ... the answers I have now had from Ministers simply say that the flattening of circular areas in cereal fields is a phenomenon known to occur from time to time.' Finally in February 1990, Labour MP and circles witness Denis Healey declined on BBC television to call for a government inquiry, suggesting this was unnecessary for a 'natural phenomenon'.

In fact, we understand that Mrs Thatcher and the Queen have both been 'presented' with copies of *Circular Evidence*, so their interest was presumably passive (possibly little more than a polite acknowledgement?) rather than their taking some kind of active role. Where the comment about 'sharply' questioning Margaret Thatcher at the Palace comes from, we have yet to discover.

Army Helicopters and Police Spotter Planes Searching for Circles

THE CLAIM

'Police air support units have been busy photographing them, along with Army helicopters from Middle Wallop. Scientists have been descending to take measurements while farmers complain about damage to their crops.' (*London Evening Standard*, 3 July 1989)

ANALYSIS

We already know that the 'official' Whitehall view is that the circles are 'most likely to result from a combination of wind and local soil fertility conditions'. Why then should the media claim that the Army and the police are assisting civilian researchers by 'photographing' circles and 'exchanging details of new circle formations'? We therefore prompted two MPs to raise these issues in the Commons, and the replies they received suggest that this claim also has problems.

For 11 July 1989, Hansard, which transcribes parliamentary activity, notes:

> Mr Teddy Taylor: To ask the Secretary of State for Defence what progress has been made in the enquiries initiated by Army helicopters based in the south-west in investigating the origin of flattened circular areas of wheat; and if he will make a statement.
>
> Mr Neubert: The Ministry of Defence is not conducting any inquiries into the origins of flattened circular areas of crops. However, we are satisfied that they are not caused by service helicopter activity.

And on 18 July 1989:

> Mr Michael Colvin: To ask the Secretary of State for the Home Department if he will call for a report from the chief constables of Hampshire and Wiltshire on their investigations into the cornfield circles in Hampshire and Wiltshire; what is the estimated cost of these investigations; and if he will make a statement.
>
> Mr Douglas Hurd: I understand from the chief constables of Hampshire and Wiltshire that there have been no investigations into the cornfield circles by their officers.

Once again the public are left confused and bewildered. Who are we to believe, Hansard or the newspapers? Despite this contradiction, what *is* clear is that Army helicopters *do* occasionally hover over circles and even take photographs of them. *Circular Evidence* carries two photographs of military helicopters in this role and even carries a photograph taken from one of these helicopters.[19]

Colin Andrews claims that, 'I later made enquiries through an Army contact, who confirmed [the helicopter's] presence and even sent me the report and photographs submitted by the pilot.' We know that in 1985 Lieut.-Colonel Edgecombe of the Army Air Corps sent the Ministry of Defence a report which he kindly allowed us to reproduce in BUFORA's 1986 summary *Mystery of the Circles*. This suggests that military personnel *occasionally* photograph circles and submit reports to the Ministry of Defence. Why not? These pilots are human beings, and they are bound to fly near circles on the many missions undertaken in Wessex every day. Is it surprising they may sometimes detour to take an aerial peep at these wonders of nature? But we have found no evidence that there is official study of these reports or that Whitehall is 'concerned' about the phenomenon.

'Planes at Their Disposal'

THE CLAIM
'The Royal Commission for Historical Sites is interested in [CPR's] findings, and have put planes at [their] disposal. They are also providing 3½ million aerial photographs, going back forty years.' (*Hampshire Chronicle*, 3 August 1989)

ANALYSIS
BUFORA checked this claim with Professor Charles Thomas, acting chairman of the Royal Commission on the Historical Monuments of England. Again, our investigations seem to cast a very different light on this story. According to Thomas, no planes had been put at CPR's 'disposal', and no formal agreement had been made about the use of the commission's 3½ million aerial photographs (which are in any case freely available to the public).

Circles Are Intelligently Locating Themselves

THE CLAIM
'... but what we can't account for is the referencing of them to man-made features such as lanes, telegraph poles and roads. They are not appearing in a random fashion ...' (Colin Andrews, *Wiltshire Gazette & Herald*, 6 July 1989)

'Sites tend to be clustered around military installations – that might be significant in itself – and ancient archaeological sites – ditto.' (*Sunday Observer*, 14 August 1988)

ANALYSIS
The claim that the circles were 'intelligently locating' themselves was a major reason why CPR rejected Meaden's meteorological explanation. This reasoning seems to assume that wind vortices have a uniform geographical distribution and that circles should appear at random across southern England. This is not accurate, for the following reasons:

1. Meaden's theory depends heavily on the generation of circle-forming vortices in the proximity of steep hill slopes.

This immediately suggests that circles should cluster about certain locations. The discovery of the Aylesbury quintuplet (see p. 124) seems to prove that slopes can generate trailing vortex systems up to seven kilometres from the hill concerned. This implies that it may not always be clear which slopes are associated with circle formations.

2. Southern England is literally saturated with 'archaeological sites, reservoirs and military establishments' – sites that some suggest might be of interest to some kind of 'unknown intelligence'. Chance correlations are bound to appear if these are located at places where natural factors enhance the probability of a Meaden Vortex, such as Silbury Hill.

3. No statistical analysis has (to our knowledge) been presented which demonstrates that circles are clustering around such 'interesting' locations with a greater-than-chance probability. Until such an analysis has been produced, the claim must remain unsubstantiated. Even if it were established, hoaxing would have to be given consideration as an explanation.

The Discovery of the 98 'Circles' in the Welsh Black Mountains

THE CLAIM

'A team of top scientists is travelling to Wales to investigate a massive outbreak of mystery circles. A staggering 98 were found on two hill tops near Llanthony in the Black Mountains ... Colin Andrews, spokesman for the scientists, said the new find could prove vital in solving the riddle. "The new circles have appeared on the tops of hills in less than one week. We believe we have something of major proportions ... Because of the scale of the formations, we are sure there is no human involvement. We can eliminate the hoax theory once and for all." ' (*Sunday Express*, 30 July 1989)

'Red-faced scientists who investigated the 98 mystery circles in the Black Mountains of Wales have discovered they were made by a local farmer – to encourage grouse to settle ... But yesterday, Mr Colin Andrews, spokesman for the scientists, said "These circles are nothing to do with the investigation. They were cut by the local landowner ..." ' (*Wolverhampton Express & Star*, date unknown)

ANALYSIS

The Black Mountains 'circles' probably received a more balanced press coverage than many of the other anecdotes discussed in this book. To the media's credit, the discovery of this 'massive outbreak' of circles was tracked down and exposed within a day by a reporter from BBC Wales, who took the simple step of speaking to the landowner concerned and discovering that there was a mundane explanation which had nothing to do with UFOs or atmospheric vortices – or crop circles, for that matter.

This episode serves to highlight how careful anomaly researchers must be if they hope to avoid looking foolish in the press. Innocent this mistake doubtless was, but it could have damaged circle-research credibility. Certainly the discovery of so many 'circles', clustered together and consisting of a 'new' type of formation ('tadpole' shaped) should have provoked suspicions, not instant publicity.

The Japanese Connection

THE CLAIM

'In September Mr Andrews is travelling to a scientific conference in Tokyo to present a paper on the cornfield rings. "We have been working with the Japanese who are looking into the possible connection – and that is all it is – between the markings and the ozone layer problem".' (*Wiltshire Gazette & Herald*, 25 March 1989)

'Mr Andrews, an electrical expert with the Test Valley Borough Council, says he has been working in close contact with a professor at Nihoy University, Tokyo. "He is a plasma fusion expert who is studying the electric field distribution around the planet, and it is probably changing because of the ozone problem, the greenhouse effect," he said.' (*Wiltshire Gazette & Herald*, 6 July 1989)

ANALYSIS

Throughout the circles controversy, the involvement of 'Japanese scientists' has been a recurring theme. We have been in contact with some of these scientists and from their remarks in Appendix 1 there is no evidence that these particular ones (at least) consider the ozone layer to be involved. This seems to be no more than a topical idea that stimulates 'news'.

The Japanese conference referred to was the URSI Symposium

(URSI being the Union Radio-Scientifique Internationale – International Union of Radio Science) on the subject of Environmental and Space Electromagnetics, held at Tokyo University on 4–6 September 1989. Although Colin Andrews was certainly invited to speak at this conference, he apparently did not attend. It should be added that Dr Meaden did attend. His paper was extremely well received, and his novel interpretation of the mysterious crop circles achieved considerable sober media attention in Japan as a result.

Conclusions

This chapter demonstrates how the media can sometimes jump to conclusions and misinform the public when debating anomalies. Even the reputedly 'better-quality' press are just as vulnerable to the belief that the supernatural is unimportant, so that mistakes do not matter. But they *do* matter, and the crop circles are *not* a supernatural phenomenon in the first place.

We accept that this occupational hazard is partly down to the fact that reporters tend to be in a hurry for stories. We would again stress that we believe that Pat Delgado and Colin Andrews are sincere and honest researchers who are not setting out to deceive people with any of their claims. They hold these opinions, are entitled to express them and may well have suffered media misrepresentation from time to time. Our criticism merely aims to give you the facts, an exercise which we believe is important to allow correct evaluation of the problem.

7   The Plasma–Vortex Theory

From the very start of this inquiry, a group of professional meteorologists working principally (but not exclusively) in the West Country has put forward proposals for a scientific solution to the circles. This soon won the support of Ian Mrzyglod and PROBE, then BUFORA and ourselves. The circles mystery is over.

Most fundamental news of all is that a number of people have *seen* crop circles as they were being formed in broad daylight by what these eyewitnesses usually described, somewhat inaccurately, as 'whirlwinds'. However, this was merely part of the evidence which convinced those scientists (and us). In fact, as the theory has become more refined it has accommodated all the major features displayed by these crop circles. It is now possible to predict new discoveries, and we may be led unexpectedly into discovering links with 'fringe' phenomena, such as UFOs.

We certainly need to take a long, hard look at this ubiquitous concept.

The Meaden Theory

Dr Terence Meaden heads the Tornado & Storm Research Organization, an independent group of scientists based in Bradford-on-Avon, Wiltshire. (See Plate 8). Meaden is editor of the prestigious *Journal of Meteorology* and is widely regarded as a leading authority on atmospheric vortices (tornadoes, whirlwinds and waterspouts). His active interest in the circles predates that of *all* other media-touted experts researching the phenomenon, and does so by some years. The theory he is proposing has now attracted interest and guarded support from leading atmospheric physicists and meteorologists all over the world (see Appendix 1).

Meaden suggests that the cornfield circles are being created by a rotating ball of electrically charged air. This ball is known as a 'plasma vortex' because it consists of tiny molecules of air that have lost negatively charged electrons, thus resulting in a positively charged cloud of ionized gas.

This spinning ball of air can become highly charged and may glow in a variety of colours. The plasma vortex has properties similar to another enigmatic atmospheric phenomenon, known as 'ball lightning', often described as a luminous sphere of light, though it forms in all shapes and sizes. This frequently seems to adopt inquisitive or 'intelligent' behaviour, although that is because of its tendency to follow lines of least electrical resistance.

Like ball lightning, this 'Meaden Vortex' forms in the atmosphere and hovers for many tens of minutes before descending onto crops to produce crop circles and other unusual ground traces. The vortex is generated by the flow of air over and around steep hill slopes (such as those at Cheesefoot and Westbury), and it tends to be surrounded by a strong electro-magnetic field that induces electrical effects beyond the vortex itself, whilst causing unusual effects on mechanical and electrical apparatus (which, in this strict definition, can and does include people, since we all have electro-chemical properties!).

Because ordinary 'whirlwinds' normally ascend, the plasma vortex is a newly recognized phenomenon that has yet to be fully accepted by science. However, we have begun canvassing support for Meaden's theory from the meteorological community (see Appendix 1), and this was not difficult to obtain. It is very significant that ball lightning specialists seem quite willing to accept Meaden's theory, at least in its basic form. Indeed, his idea is generating both excitement and responsible debate within the meteorological and atmospheric physics communities, although some researchers find it difficult to accept that the more complex circle formations can be accounted for by reference to an atmospheric process. We deal more fully with this problem in the next chapter.

For the ufologists, Meaden's plasma vortex offers perhaps the first detailed and testable model that has been proposed by a scientist who, by and large, is unfamiliar with the quagmire of cases we know as 'the UFO phenomenon'. His theory is flexible enough to account for a possibly substantial proportion of reported 'UFO experiences' and is already generating keen interest amongst those ufologists who are prepared to debate the matter. The implications of Dr Meaden's theory seem to be revolutionary. Literally thousands of UFO reports, on the face of it, may be a product of the mechanism the physicist has discovered.

However, it is important to remember that at this stage Meaden's theory is only just being disseminated to the meteorological community. For that reason it would be wrong to suggest that his ideas are fully formulated and that everything being suggested in this book is a hundred per cent correct. Researchers may not yet be able to withdraw to the safety of their beds and catch a well-earned rest. Certainly a number of outstanding questions remain to be answered, and more work is needed before the 'circles effect' can be tied up in a neat bundle that positively explains everything that is occurring.

Nevertheless, we, the authors, would like to make it clear that, even though we have problems with certain aspects of this theory, we are totally satisfied that it works as a basic explanation for the 'mysterious' crop circles and that it utterly dispenses with the need to suggest exotic forces or 'intelligences'.

The evidence for the plasma-vortex theory is summarized in the following pages.

Eyewitness Accounts of Vortices Creating Circles

Meaden's theory is supported by several good 'eyewitness accounts' of unusual atmospheric vortices creating circles in daylight.

Littleton Down, Wiltshire, 1983

In the *Journal of Meteorology*[1] and on the BBC TV documentary *Country File*, Melvyn Bell, of Keevil, Wiltshire, described his observation of a 'whirlwind' which he watched flattening wheat into a circle. This was towards dusk in late July or early August 1983, and the place was a dry valley running from west to east on Littleton Down, at OS reference ST 9752, which is below Great Cheverill Hill. Mr Bell was horse-riding at the time and stopped when he became aware of a whirlwind starting up below him, in a field adjacent to the bridlepath. Fifty to sixty metres away he could see dust, dirt and other light debris spiralling into the air, and in a matter of only a few seconds a ten- to twelve-metre diameter circle was flattened out in the wheat as he watched. At that distance he was not aware of any accompanying noise. On the BBC TV documentary, Melvyn Bell described the mechanism he observed as 'like a whirlwind'.

This eyewitness account is important because Melvyn Bell reported a very short-lived event which occurred near a hill and which involved a mechanism that was clearly rotating (because 'light debris' was observed spiralling up into the air).

Such a description is, of course, exactly what we would expect from someone observing a small thermally induced whirlwind, which is a relatively common occurrence in British summers at that time of day. The very short duration of this event suggests that chance observations of circle-forming would be quite rare in rural locations. We see no evidence from this account that Melvyn Bell observed an 'intelligently controlled' force. The question as to whether he truly observed the creation of a genuine crop circle is dealt with below.

Warminster, Wiltshire, 1980
In an article published in the short-lived news magazine *Now*, well-known UFO author and local journalist Arthur Shuttlewood described his observation of a circle forming before a large group of startled UFO-watchers close to Warminster.[2]

'One evening there were about 50 of us sky-watching along the Salisbury Road. Suddenly, the grass began to sway before our eyes and laid itself flat in a clockwise spiral, just like the opening of a lady's fan. A perfect circle was completed in less than half a minute, all the time accompanied by a high-pitched humming sound. It was still there the next day.'

Here we have another report of a short-lived event which also occurred near a hill and which was accompanied by unusual acoustics (a 'high-pitched humming'). Ordinary dust whirlwinds frequently produce humming sounds because these indicate the presence of ionized and electrical discharges. (You can find many references to this within the literature of atmospheric physics concerned with such matters. The books of researcher William Corliss, who popularizes scientific titbits from the professional literature, are recommended to anybody who wishes to pursue this angle with a wealth of such data.)

The humming (or buzzing, whirring, swishing) noise will recur many times throughout the rest of this book and is a highly significant clue to the fact that Meaden's Vortex must be electrically charged, not just spinning air.

Westbury, Wiltshire, 1982

In the scientific formulation of his theory Meaden includes the following account sent to him by Ray Barnes of an experience which probably took place on Saturday 3 July 1982.[3]

> ... I was fortunate enough to see one of these [circles] form in a field at Westbury. It happened ... just before six in the evening after a thunderstorm earlier that afternoon; in fact it was still raining slightly. My attention was first drawn to a 'wave' coming through the heads of the cereal crop in a straight line at steady speed; I have since worked this out to be about fifty miles an hour. The agency, though invisible, behaved like a solid object throughout and did not show any fluid tendencies, ie no variation in speed, line or strength. There was no visual aberration either in front, above or below the advancing line. After crossing the field in a shallow arc the 'line' dropped to a position about 1 o'clock and radially described a circle 75 feet radius in about four seconds. The agency then disappeared.

Whatever Ray Barnes saw, it seemed to brush the top of the corn before coming to rest and then carving out a circle in the field. Ray Barnes described this mechanism as like a 'wave coming through the heads of the corn'. This description suggests that the causal mechanism was air pressure, sweeping across the field like the crest of a wave. A mechanism which lightly brushes the top of the crop easily accounts for circles in which the affected crop is only slightly depressed (for example, at Bratton, August 1987, and Charity Down, June 1988).

Terence Meaden interviewed Ray Barnes the day after receiving his letter and learnt that, as the crop was being flattened, the witness heard a 'hiss and a rustle'. The 'rustle' can be explained as the sound of the falling of stalks, and the hissing sound probably emanated from the agency responsible for the creation of the circle.

Once again a prominent hill slope was within a short distance (the Westbury escarpment).

Dundee, 1989

This eyewitness account of a circle forming during the early hours of the morning first came to light via the BBC TV programme *Daytime Live* (where the account was inexplicably portrayed as the *first* known eyewitness account – in fact, it was by no means the first). The programme went out on 3 November 1989 when half-a-dozen such incidents were already known.

The witness, Sandy Reid, is a naturalist who often trails and studies foxes near his Tayside home, not far from Dundee. One morning in late August, at approximately 4.25–4.30 a.m., Reid was walking along a slightly raised embankment dividing two fields of spring barley. Suddenly he became aware of a violent rustling of the corn only a few metres from where he was standing. Thinking that he had disturbed a deer, Reid immediately froze and then slowly crouched down to avoid detection. However, instead of being confronted by an animal, he was astounded to observe a small portion of the barley being severely buffeted by a highly localized movement of air. Despite being only fifteen metres or so away from the disturbance, Reid reported feeling no wind where he was crouching. He watched the disturbance continue for at least thirty seconds. It came to an end when the crop suddenly lay down flat in a circular area some fifteen to eighteen metres across.

Reid walked into the circle and immediately felt 'an unusual condition of the atmosphere', a peculiar sensation that he found difficult to put into precise words but which might suggest either a change in air pressure or the presence of ionization at the site. Significantly, Reid reported that when he first entered the circle not only had the wind stopped buffeting the corn but all the birds had ceased singing.

Sandy Reid had not heard of crop circles prior to his observation of this event, so perhaps it is understandable that his description of what he found in the circle seems unusual. Neither a swirl pattern nor a radial burst was discovered, but as he walked across the circle he saw that the corn pointed first one way and then the other. Later that morning he returned to the same field with a friend, discovering a second, newly formed circle only fifty metres from the first.[4]

Thanet, East Kent, 1989
At approximately 12.30 a.m. on 10 August Wilfred Gomez and a friend were driving along an unclassified road near Lydden on the Island of Thanet when they observed a 'solid hurricane of light' with a fuzzy, indistinct top but a more clearly defined lower base, hovering over an adjacent cornfield. The column of light was white with a bluish tinge and seemed to be rotating. Mr Gomez wound down his side window and heard a low, even 'humming' sound

emanating from the object. The witnesses observed the column of light for approximately four seconds as they drove past. The column then 'blinked out to one side', and the humming stopped.

The two witnesses drove a short distance up the road before stopping and walking into the field in which the light had been. Because there was a half moon, they soon discovered a small circle approximately five metres in diameter and about ten metres from the path. Five metres further into the field they discovered a huge twenty-metre-diameter circle with undamaged corn swirled in an anti-clockwise direction. As with the previous Silbury (1988) circles, power lines crossed the field *directly* above the site, making the approach of any hypothetical 'spaceship' completely impossible.

Although this account did not involve a pronounced hill-slope location, there was a small incline some fifteen metres in height sloping down towards the position of the circles. At the time of formation weather records show there was a 5 knot wind flowing *down* the slope from just east of south.

The farm-owner subsequently confirmed that he had not been aware of these circles prior to 19 August, when the local press visited the area. The farmer had not seen circles on his land before 1989, and he was sceptical that they could be the result of something extraordinary, preferring instead to blame 'whirlwinds', which he had seen lifting corn 'hundreds of feet into the air' from his fields on several previous occasions. The meteorological office at RAF Manston (situated only four kilometres away) confirmed that this location was particularly prone to 'dust devils' (more standardized atmospheric vortices), particularly during the late summer.

A sensational account of these events appeared in the Canterbury-based *Adscene* on 25 August 1989 (with the headline 'ALIENS!'). Several national newspapers requested interviews. Fortunately an accurate case study was compiled by Paul Harris, who made this available to TORRO and BUFORA.

Observations of Vortices at Locations at which Circles were Subsequently Discovered Within a Very Short Interval of Time

Avebury, Wiltshire, 1988
At 7.15 a.m. on 16 June Roy Lucas was enclosed in a tractor cab cutting grass verges on a track three kilometres to the west of the

village of Avebury. Following a misty night, the air was very humid and the sky overcast. Terence Meaden describes what took place next:[5]

> Looking across the field of winter wheat to the east ... [Roy Lucas] suddenly noticed at a distance of eighty metres what he took to be a large puff of white 'bonfire smoke' rising to 15 feet (5m) maximum height. The outer part of this 'smoke' was scarcely rotating but the middle part, which was too thick to see through, was spinning rapidly. In a couple of seconds the effect had ended; the spinning central column had gone and the residual 'smoke' or cloud of fog drifted gently in the prevailing light north-east wind towards the south-west and dissolved after going several yards. He used the word smoke out of convenience but said that the effect was more likely caused by water vapour, cloud droplets or fog. He further emphasised the swiftness of the appearance and disappearance of the phenomenon. It had arrived suddenly like 'smoke from a distant cannon' or just as if 'a smoke-filled or fog-filled balloon had suddenly burst' ... He made the further point that the spinning column might have been very much longer than he could judge, for he realised that the only part he could see was the part rendered visible by the smoke or fog. The diameter of the cloud was about the same as its height, viz four or five metres.
>
> [Meaden continues:] A similar occurrence a few seconds later in practically the same place, and five minutes later there was a repeat performance, but this time beyond the field boundary ... From the elevation of his tractor Mr Lucas looked for signs of marks in the crop, but he could not see any. Nevertheless, regarding the sighting he added 'After seeing what I saw I am quite convinced that this is what caused the circles.'

A few hours later the farm manager discovered these – i.e. two single circles (diameters eight and nine metres) in a barley field only 350 metres west. Overall, ten circles appeared at this location during the period preceding 29 June 1988. All of them lay in a zone to the south and south-west of Windmill Hill, a thirty-metre-high obstacle which, Meaden said, was '... sufficient ... to provoke turbulence with vorticity in its lee as the wind flowed south-westwards above it'.

Meaden suggests that Roy Lucas observed the lower end of a tall, spinning column of air which became visible only because its lower end penetrated a layer of very humid air trapped just above

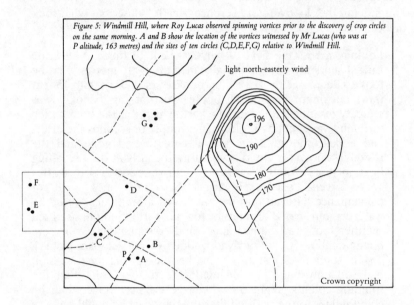

Figure 5: Windmill Hill, where Roy Lucas observed spinning vortices prior to the discovery of crop circles on the same morning. A and B show the location of the vortices witnessed by Mr Lucas (who was at P altitude, 163 metres) and the sites of ten circles (C,D,E,F,G) relative to Windmill Hill.

the ground by a small temperature inversion. Rapidly spinning air tends to result in the reduction of air pressure within the vortex, and as this happens, small droplets of water in the saturated zone begin to condense to form a 'fog' or 'smoke'. In this case, the spinning columns formed only one kilometre to the south-west of a prominent hill jutting up from a generally flat landscape. Figure 5 shows how on the morning of 16 June there was a light north-easterly wind which would have flowed over Windmill Hill right towards the location where the circles appeared.

We are convinced that Dr Meaden is correct and that this is the same type of process that occurs in many other situations to produce crop circles.

Pucklechurch, Avon, 1989

Some observers have repeatedly claimed that the cornfield circles cannot be caused by a natural atmospheric phenomenon because, 'All rotational winds, such as whirlwinds and tornadoes, move across the countryside leaving a swathe of destruction and, usually, anything but neat markings.'[6] This is simply not the case, as can be easily demonstrated with well-investigated accounts such as Jacqui Griffiths', describing her experiences on 5 August 1989:

> While driving south-west out of Pucklechurch on the B4465 towards Mangotsfield, I was passing the Remand Centre entrance and approaching Dennisworth Farm on my right, when I noticed what appeared to be a whirlwind in the field on my right.
>
> I pulled over to stop and watch. The whirlwind was in the field and appeared to be as tall as the trees which bordered the farm grounds; these trees were rushing to and fro as if in a gale. I could see tufts of grass, twigs and bits of straw whirling round (this is what first attracted my attention).
>
> The whirlwind appeared to move towards and then over the hedge, where it appeared to 'lose' its bottom part, came over the road and then died. It was a very hot and windless day.[7]

The next day a local researcher, Peter Rendall, went to the location of the incident with the witness and discovered several swirled patches of flattened grass and straw close to where the 'whirlwind' was seen. Rendall's photographs of these swirled patches clearly show one roughly elliptical area of swirled, flattened grass with two spiral centres. From Rendall's photos it seems clear to us that the *central* zone of the circle had been subjected to a *descending* force, whilst the *outer* part of the circle had been subjected to an *ascending* force. This combination of rising and falling air currents is exactly what occurs inside an ordinary heat-produced 'whirlwind'. Readers will appreciate immediately that had a mature arable crop been present (instead of just grass and straw), typical crop circles would undoubtedly have been formed by this natural atmospheric force (see Plate 13).

Marple, Cheshire, 1988
This important event came to BUFORA's notice a year after it took place (on 15 June 1988). The initial report was a news cutting from the *Manchester Evening News* for 17 June 1988 (sent to us by Michael Thomas), headed 'The day it rained hay'. It read as follows: 'Residents of Marple are used to it raining cats and dogs. But they'll never forget the day when, suddenly out of a clear blue sky, it began raining hay. The deluge lasted several minutes and appeared to come from at least 200 feet (sixty metres) up.' Apparently neighbours and workmen also saw it and just stood and stared.

Graeme Brock, headmaster of Marple All Saints Primary

School, read the item in the *Evening News* and decided to report the strange events that had manifested on 15 June next to his playground. The first incident occurred at approximately 11 a.m. when he glanced out of a window and saw pieces of hay rising into the air in a random fashion beside the fence. Thinking the children were responsible, he went outside, but by the time he reached the group of youngsters, the hay had stopped rising and he was forced to accept their claim that the hay had moved on its own.

At 12.45 p.m. Graeme Brock was supervising a lunch-time game of rounders in the school playing field when suddenly hay began rising from a point some thirty metres into the field adjoining the playground. The children's sport was rapidly forgotten! As the group watched, more and more hay lifted off the ground and swirled upwards in an anti-clockwise direction before forming into a dense oval-shaped mass some thirty to fifty metres above the ground. For a second or two this oval mass simply hovered above the astounded onlookers. Then it proceeded to move away in a straight line, passing directly over the heads of the children before eventually disappearing in a south-westerly direction.

Questioned a year later, Graeme Brock described how he and the children had noticed a strange sensation as the object floated above them. He described feeling a kind of 'soft pressure' pushing down on his head and shoulders; several of the children confirmed that they had felt 'funny' as the object passed overhead. These accounts suggest that ordinary downwards air pressure was involved in the incident, but unlike some of the other eyewitness accounts no light phenomena or acoustics were reported.

Within moments of these events, the residents of one residential road observed the hay cloud drifting towards them, depositing its load and then moving overhead. Although most witnesses were too surprised to record details, a Mrs Cobain telephoned the *Manchester Evening News* as the event unfolded, returning to watch as the cloud drifted away into the distance.

It seems clear that the cloud had expanded to some fifty metres in diameter and consisted of one central clump surrounded by several smaller clumps. The description is not unlike the quintuplet patterns being discovered in cereal fields. This may be only coincidence – or perhaps an important clue.

By this point the cloud of floating hay had flattened out into a thinner discus shape (not unlike a 'flying saucer'!) and began to disintegrate into small clumps which fell gently to earth. Some of these clumps resembled small birds' nests, and the hay within them was intertwined into portions about thirty to forty centimetres across. Although a great deal of hay fell on this road, the cloud itself carried on drifting slowly to the south-west, down the hill slope in the direction of southern Stockport, until it presumably totally disintegrated over a golf course half a kilometre away.

Following this amazing sequence of events, one of the children allegedly saw a small circle some five metres in diameter in the long grass at the precise spot at which the hay was sucked up. Unfortunately it was not possible to establish conclusively whether a circle had been discovered, because the only adult who examined it in 1988 turned out to be a 'UFO-investigator' who (according to bemused local residents) had suggested that the hay had been 'sucked up by a UFO' and that there was a 'massive government conspiracy to conceal the truth'. Jenny Randles and co-investigator Roy Sandbach made sure they told nobody that they too were ufologists when they visited the scene a year later. Otherwise this present report might have been rather short!

The Marple hay fall is crucial evidence for Meaden's theory, because it suggests that ordinary ascending vortices may be involved, somehow, in the processes that leave circular ground traces in long grass or, had it been present, in a mature arable crop. This case also shows that

1. atmospheric vortices *can* remain stationary for an appreciable length of time;
2. atmospheric vortices *can* form at least quasi-geometrical patterns in the atmosphere;
3. acoustic and electrical effects are *not* always apparent during these events;
4. air pressure was clearly involved; and
5. the event took place on the lee slope of a prominent hill.

In this example, it is important to bear in mind that the circle may have been formed before the ascending column of hay was noticed. This possibility suggests that a *descending* column of air might create the circle before turning itself into an *ascending* column and producing the hay cloud. Witnesses also reported having felt what seems like *descending* pressure after the hay rise occurred. Whether the circle was formed during the ascending or descending stage of this vortex event remains unclear, but even if the circle was formed when the hay was sucked up, this indicates that unrecognized natural vortices might still do things that recognized (ascending) vortices are able to do.

Ross-on-Wye, Herefordshire, 1981

This event was reported in a letter to a magazine chronicling odd phenomena.[8] John Lewis, who noted that he lived on a ridge that sloped steeply down on the north side, described how he heard 'a very loud roaring sound, not unlike an express train'. This noise increased to 'something like the sound of a falling bomb' (i.e. a screaming, whining yell). The following morning Lewis discovered two newly formed circles about twenty-five feet in diameter in a nearby barley field. After Lewis tried to ascertain the source of the incident, it was learnt that an adjacent farmer had experienced 'a quite fearsome whirlwind ... that had run along the side of the ridge and through the farm, scattering hay and straw bales like feathers. It then moved on towards the field where I had found the circles.'

This had apparently occurred at about the same time as Lewis had heard the noises (around noon on a late summer day). Some golfers also reported watching the whirlwind (i.e. a rotating air funnel) begin above the surface of the M50 motorway! The witness concluded with the following comment: 'There is little doubt in my mind that the flattened circles, the so called UFO nests, are caused by whirlwinds: it is too much of a coincidence to be otherwise.'

As with the Pucklechurch case, a seemingly ordinary 'whirlwind' creating ordinary damage was associated with the arrival of 'two circles' in an adjacent field. Whilst this event was not directly observed, all the components were – the vortex, the reported acoustics ('a very loud roaring' and 'something like ... a falling bomb') and the sudden appearance of the circles. You can see examples of similar features (for example, the sounds) in association with other vortex effects.[9]

Bolnhurst, Bedfordshire, c. 1968

Following an appeal in the *Daily Express*, the following account was sent to Dr Meaden:

> Some twenty years ago my wife and myself were staying with friends at a fairly remote fourteenth century farmhouse in Bedfordshire. During the night we experienced acute

headaches which were totally alien to our usual health condition. Accompanying the headaches were a very unpleasant buzzing and pressure in the head. Eventually we went off to sleep again. After breakfast we took a walk ... to examine the tall beans in the field adjacent to the house. Usually our host's dogs would race into those beans and one would see the beans moving and the clicking sound as the dogs raced about in this growth. On the particular morning in question however the dogs looked petrified and just would not go into the beans. We decided to investigate and walking through them for about twenty yards we found a precise circle, with a burning appearance and a distinct smell of Kerosene. Diameter of circle about thirty feet ...[10]

Meaden's correspondent later clarified his account with the following: 'At the time I "thought" that something was making that circle, there was a pressure in the air in the way of a type of humming. It was this that brought about the abominable headache. I assumed that the circle was made at 02.00 hrs because I distinctly recall looking at my watch at the time and I was fully awake ... The headache came at 02.00 hrs and went when the pressure humming noise ceased.'[11]

This account seems significant, because the circle clearly formed during very humid conditions, and acoustics may have again been related. However, it is wise to stress here that no proof exists that the circle formed at the precise moment claimed by the witness (2 a.m.), and that the oppressive atmospheric conditions may conceivably not be related.

Norton Bavant, Wiltshire, 1988
Mr Sharp of Norton Bavant, Wiltshire, described how he heard a sudden noise that he compared to a 'whirlwind' striking his garage not long after dawn one morning in July 1988. Less than 200 metres away, two newly formed circles were discovered later that same morning.[12]

Similarities between Characteristics of Corn Circles and Characteristics of Recognized Atmospheric Vortices

THE 'COINCIDENCE' OF THE SPIRAL PATTERNS
'Dust-devils, or rotating columns of sand travelling rapidly across open spaces, are not uncommon objects to desert travellers. Their

height and breadth is often very considerable and the evidence of the eddies causing them very great. The smallest of this type I have seen was only five feet (1.5 metres) high, that is, the visible column of sand, and less than a foot (30 cm) in diameter. It passed so close to me that it was easy to see its narrow cycloidal path marked on the sand, which was deposited and lifted as the eddy travelled on at not less than 15 mph (i.e. 25 kmph), although the wind was actually very light.'[13]

This account from William Corliss demonstrates a fact well known to meteorologists who study 'whirlwinds' – that atmospheric vortices appearing over water surfaces or dusty deserts frequently produce intricate spiral patterns due to the need for a constant supply of air at their base. This is because air flows in from all directions before spiralling upwards inside the vortex. These spiral ground traces clearly mimic the patterns found inside corn circles. We cannot believe that this is merely coincidence.

THE ABILITY OF SOME VORTICES TO REMAIN STATIONARY

One of the main reasons why some observers rule out a natural atmospheric solution for the circles is the widespread belief that all atmospheric vortices constantly move about and that no account exists of vortices that remain stationary. The Marple hay fall proves this preconception is quite false. Several good accounts exist which suggest that vortices can remain stationary, although the conditions under which this can occur may not be clear at present. Here are some examples of stationary vortices.

A vortex was observed remaining in the same North Dakota field for three-quarters of an hour.[14]

A standing eddy vortex was observed in the lee of a hill at Carron Reservoir, Scotland, in May 1983.[15] The vortex extended from the forest canopy to the base of low overlying clouds and was rendered visible only because (like Roy Lucas's vortices) a layer of saturated air lay close to the surface of the lake.

Perhaps the most interesting account of a stationary vortex was reported by Capes whilst walking in the Egyptian desert: 'Hearing a swishing sound behind me, I turned and observed a large revolving ring of sand less than a foot (30 cm) high approaching me slowly. It stopped a few feet away and the ring, containing sand and small pieces of vegetable debris in a sheet less than one inch (two cm) thick, revolved rapidly around a circle of about twelve foot (three metres) diameter while the axis remained stationary. It then moved slowly around me after remaining in one spot for at least thirty seconds, and slowly died down.'[16]

THE EXISTENCE OF A PRECISELY DEFINED VORTEX FUNNEL

Anyone who has seen the Disney film *The Wizard of Oz* may remember the foreboding tornado that whisked Dorothy away to a magic land. Perhaps this is the most famous cinema vortex of all time.

Many people insist that atmospheric vortices are always surrounded by a zone of severe atmospheric turbulence and that therefore no 'whirlwind' could ever be sufficiently delineated to create our precisely defined cornfield circles, especially if adjacent witnesses feel no wind. With little effort we have discovered several accounts (and photographs) of vortices displaying what seems to be a precisely defined funnel at the centre of the vortex.

This ties in closely with what Roy Lucas observed – a vortex with a slowly rotating, poorly defined outer zone (the sheath) but with a rapidly rotating, well-defined inner zone (the funnel). For many vortex events, the inner funnel seems to be entirely masked by the outer zone of turbulence. If this is so, ground traces created by the (precisely defined) funnel will normally be obliterated by the less well-defined outer sheath. However, Corliss records good eyewitness accounts to suggest that under particularly stable atmospheric conditions some vortices may be capable of creating precisely defined circles should they come into contact with pliable arable crops at ground-level.

This possibility is enhanced by many eyewitness accounts of vortex events that seem to affect very small geographical areas. Note, for example, this account: 'Suddenly a dull sound was heard, rather like the rumble of a carriage drawn by a horse at full gallop, then a whirlwind of irresistible force was formed, which suddenly and instantaneously carried off the roof of the house, and dispersed it in all directions. This whirlwind was neither preceded nor followed by any rain. It is also extraordinary that this house alone was affected and at ten metres distance no disturbance of any kind was experienced.'[17]

Meaden suggests that the reason why the plasma vortex is precisely defined is that there is surface tension between volumes of ionized and normal air.

Clearly those who claim that 'whirlwinds' cannot be precisely defined have simply not consulted the established meteorological literature. It seems logical to assume that, if photographs and eye-witness accounts suggest that vortices do at times have a precisely defined funnel, the very sharp cut-off zones for the majority of cornfield circles cannot be a reason to exclude such a natural agency for their creation.

THE COINCIDENCE OF THE SHEATH EFFECTS

Waterspouts (which are minor vortices forming over water surfaces) occasionally exhibit (up to three) very thin outer sheaths which are concentric with the central funnel. These sheaths can ascend and descend at will during the vortex event, and their existence was verified by laser probes of waterspouts off the coast of Florida during 1976. Significantly sheaths always rotate in sequence (for example, clockwise, then anti-clockwise, then clockwise) to maintain their conservation of momentum, and they are normally positioned very close to the parent funnel.

Many accounts of sheaths appear throughout the meteorological literature. This is typical:

> So far I have described nothing unusual, but the following was quite new to me and seemed of great interest. Surrounding the central core, but separated from it by a clear narrow space, was a sheath, the lower end of which faded away some distance above the water. The profile of this sheath was undulating, it being thicker in some places than in others. A curious point is that this sheath seemed to pulsate rhythmically, but I could not say whether the appearance of the pulsation might not have been an illusion caused by waves travelling up its outer surface. The pulsation gave an uncanny suggestion of a live thing ...[18]

Meaden suggests that an electrically charged vortex creates these outer rings by electrical induction. This means that, if we could watch a vortex creating a circle at night, we might notice several rings rotating about the central vortex, each rotating sequentially in different directions. A number of good accounts exist of nocturnal waterspouts and tornadoes which display bright luminous bands or rings.[19] These accounts include British examples of glowing nocturnal 'whirlwinds'.

THE ABILITY OF VORTICES TO FORM IN MULTIPLES

Opponents of Meaden's theory tend to state that vortices cannot form in multiples because they are too unpredictable and violent.

This is contradicted by such accounts as the following:

> What was unusual were the numerous distinct fingers of columns of vapour swirling out of the steam fog layer directly into the over-lying cumulus clouds. It is estimated that they were 50–200 metres in diameter, travelled more or less with the wind, and showed a slow but distinct rotation (mostly cyclonic) of up to several rotations per minute. The steam devils tended to be rather short-lived, the longest surviving perhaps for 3 or 4 minutes. An even more interesting view ... was taken from a commercial airliner on January 30th 1971 ... visible are small cumulus ... plus the steam devils and a highly patterned effect on the surface steam fog. It definitely appears that there were quasi-hexagonal cells elongated along the surface wind direction, the largest steam devils being present at the vortexes of the hexagons.[20]

Such accounts clearly suggest that under certain, perhaps limited, conditions groups of ascending vortices can form and operate in unison. The Marple hay fall surely must have involved natural atmospheric forces, and these were reported to have formed quasi-geometric clusters of hay in the sky.

Overview

We have presented a number of witness accounts of vortex mechanisms creating circles, and further accounts of circles appearing at locations where rotating vortex mechanisms were well observed at more or less the same time and place. Several involve observations of luminous phenomena that may be explicable by proposing a glowing ionized plasma as the creative force. These accounts are just a part of the growing body of evidence which offers strong support for Meaden's theory.

So far as we know, there is no equivalent evidence for the concept that the circles are in any sense 'alien' or 'exotic' or that their explanation requires anything other than conventional atmospheric forces, which may possibly be operating in a relatively novel fashion.

Terence Meaden has so far offered the only scientifically testable hypothesis to explain the crop circles. Perhaps the forces can be demonstrated in a wind-tunnel. It stands or falls on one issue, and one issue alone. Can atmospheric vortices do all the things they need to do in order to be capable of forming such intricate geometrical patterns in cereal crops?

So far Meaden's theory of the ionized vortex has been able to account for all data laid before it and has adequate support from a study of the conventional meteorological literature. Later in the book you will see that its support from the more unconventional literature of ufology is even more dramatic.

At the very least, the proposal that crop circles are the product of this ionized vortex has to be worthy of more detailed exploration and makes debate about 'unknown intelligences' seem utterly pointless, if not downright old-fashioned and misleading.

8 Assessing the Vortex Theory

It is now necessary to give a critical examination of Meaden's theory and attempt to assess its strengths and weaknesses. We believe there are major reasons why he seems to be on the right lines. Indeed, if his theory is to be shown erroneous, critics must refute the following arguments.

In Favour of Meaden's Theory

THE EYEWITNESS ACCOUNTS OF VORTICES CREATING CIRCLES
We find it very difficult to dismiss the 'eyewitness accounts' and the accounts of vortices seen at locations where circles were subsequently discovered, given in the previous chapter. Faced with such powerful evidence for a 'natural' atmospheric solution, we wonder why anyone should need to view the phenomenon as being the product of an intelligence or unknown force.

These accounts all describe basically the same type of event, and the witnesses themselves usually considered them to be meteorological. Indeed, despite our decade of research into the phenomenon, we know of no reputable cases in which the witnesses felt the need to resort to exotic explanations when describing observations of circles they saw being formed, except those reported in a clear UFO context – that is, *not* as crop-circle events at all; and these tend to be manipulated by public opinion. Unless there is some massive conspiracy deliberately to mislead the meteorological community, these witnesses to crop-circle formation are observing events that resemble atmospheric vortices and creating ground traces that strongly resemble crop circles.

This leaves us with perhaps the two most crucial questions in this book: are witnesses observing the creation of our specific kind of crop circle, and are they observing atmospheric vortices?

At this stage we must admit that, with the exception of the

Pucklechurch case, we cannot prove beyond doubt that these witnesses observed the formation of precisely defined layered circles with undamaged corn and well-developed swirl patterns. Unfortunately no other witnesses examined the circles they claim to have observed under formation, and none of them immediately photographed the effects or took measurements. This apparent failing has been seized upon by critics who suggest that these observers merely saw the creation of poorly defined areas of roughly uniform corn. This seems a desperate attempt to dismiss powerful evidence.

This argument must assume that two types of circles and two independent mechanisms are creating different, but near identical, circles. Both the meteorologically produced circles and the 'intelligently controlled' circles had never been reported before modern times, but they appeared as if by magic at about the same moment.

Frankly, we consider this to be nonsense. It would be a coincidence of unimaginable proportions for an 'intelligent' phenomenon to produce geometrically defined crop circles whilst a meteorological phenomenon was creating similar damage. If there are two kinds of 'circle', where are the eyewitness accounts of the 'intelligent' circles under formation?

Regretfully, in the real world, chance observers of unusual events frequently do not know where to report them. Now that the circles phenomenon has become established in the public consciousness, we predict that it will not be long before someone *does* succeed where these witnesses allegedly 'failed' and gets this requested evidence.

Unless Meaden's critics can demonstrate the misleading nature of these eyewitness accounts, we accept them as genuine observations of the mechanism that creates the circles. In any event, critics of Meaden's theory must explain why the Pucklechurch whirlwind appeared at a location where precisely defined swirled circles were photographed within a day of the event. For a naturally occurring vortex to appear by coincidence where an 'intelligently controlled' force left a circle within hours is, for us, too hard to accept.

By proposing intelligently controlled UFOs capable of manipulating earth forces, no natural phenomenon would *ever* account for the circles, because by applying that dubious logic any naturally occurring phenomenon seen in association with the circles could be the result of an intelligently guided UFO.

Given our acceptance that these witnesses are reporting bona fide observations of the circle-forming agency, why should we accept that they are observations of atmospheric vortices rather than observations of some other (more exotic) mechanism? We believe there are eight good reasons for assuming that these witnesses observed some kind of 'natural' atmospheric vortex:

1. All the witnesses reported that the agent rotated, as do atmospheric vortices.
2. Several witnesses described acoustics that are consistent with natural atmospheric vortices – humming (Arthur Shuttlewood) and a 'very loud roaring sound' (John Lewis).
3. Several of these eyewitness accounts were described by the witnesses themselves as resembling 'whirlwinds' (for example, Melvyn Bell and Jacqui Griffiths).
4. Two specific kinds of weather conditions were reported for all these events: very hot days with little or no wind (Pucklechurch, Marple) and stormy conditions associated with ordinary violent vortices (Ray Barnes).
5. We have discovered many similar accounts from the UFO literature which bear distinct similarities to these accounts (see Chapters 9, 10 and 11).
6. All these accounts describe basically the same kind of event, often with other evidence of atmospheric forces (such as wind or pressures).
7. All these accounts seem to describe a mechanism that would be consistent in an atmospheric sense with what is required to create circles.
8. All these accounts are consistent with accepted accounts of atmospheric vortices in the established meteorological literature. There is therefore no need to suggest hypothetical new forces to explain them.

In the light of these findings, it seems difficult to dismiss the suggestion that atmospheric vortices are creating circles. Why force a paranormal solution onto the data?

THE COINCIDENCE OF THE SHEATH EFFECTS
One of the most important clues that atmospheric vortices are creating circles is the remarkable similarity between characteristics of ringed circles and characteristics of waterspout sheaths.

Corliss has an illustration of a double-walled waterspout seen over Lake Victoria, Uganda, in 1922. This waterspout consisted of a broad vortex funnel separated by a short distance from a thin outer sheath. Some circles are surrounded by a thin outer ring which is positioned only a short distance from the parent circle. This coincidence strongly hints that some kind of natural atmospheric vortex created the circle. We can imagine that this circle was created by the vortex as it came into contact with the standing crop. When the vortex found that its descent was impeded by the ground, it started to expand to cover a larger area. Then, when it was reaching its maximum diameter, a sheath descended about the outer circumference of the vortex to create the ring.

CONTRA-ROTATIONAL EFFECTS

Despite claims that the existence of close-proximity contra-rotations 'seems unnatural and, on the face of it, a deliberate attempt to display intelligent manipulation',[1] the natural vortex theory clearly explains why some circles display contra-rotations in the outer rings and within the circles themselves.

Let us imagine a single-vortex funnel descending onto a mature arable crop and spinning in a clockwise manner. As the vortex meets the crop, its diameter begins to expand and a progressively larger crop circle is formed with a well-defined clockwise swirl pattern. Next a small sheath descends slowly around the funnel, rotating in an anti-clockwise direction as it approaches the crop. Finally, as the vortex begins to wane, the outer sheath reaches ground-level, displacing the outer zone of the affected area in an anti-clockwise manner, creating a typical contra-rotation effect. This model may account for why some circles have outer rings, because if the sheath descends to ground-level when the funnel has expanded to its maximum width, the sheath will create a ring that is separate from the circle itself.

During 1989 three ringed circles were discovered that failed to display contra-rotations in the outer rings. Critics of Meaden's theory leapt upon this as 'proof' that his theory must be wrong (whilst conveniently forgetting the existence of the eyewitness accounts). One responsible critic, Ralph Noyes, commented in a review for the *Ley Hunter* magazine that, 'Within days of the publication of Terence Meaden's book a circle event occurred which impertinently contradicted one of his generalizations. On page 96 Meaden tells us that "single rings around single circles always rotate in a sense opposite to that of the interior." Well, they have always done so before ... But from 18 June 1989 we'd better not say so again. And there have been similar jokes before ...'[2]

Noyes and others considered the discovery of non-contra-rotating ringed circles 'a joke', because they felt that the phenomenon 'plays games' with its researchers. If so, this might once again imply that human tricksters were at work, perhaps people who had access to Meaden's findings and wanted to discredit a 'natural' atmospheric solution. In any event, the rule seemed such a consistent finding that Andrews, Delgado and ourselves also published it. We were all wrong!

Meaden suggests that for those circles which display *non*-contra-rotating circles, there are *invisible* rings between the circle and the first ring. This invisible ring would contra-rotate with the observable ones, and faint effects might be visible through the heads of the corn where the unseen ring should be.

This might sound like a 'cop-out' from an embarrassing situation. However, it should be emphasized that the increasing use of aerial photography has revolutionized the study of this phenomenon. Researchers now have the ability to search photographs for these almost undetectable effects that are often not apparent on the ground and which might have been missed before. For instance, some formations displayed additional outer satellites that were not visible from the ground.

It is also important to stress that only a small number of circles in Meaden's archive display outer rings. So far, most *do* contra-rotate.

Meaden's suggestion is that the strong electro-magnetic charges present in the parent vortex induce outer rings. This is consistent with what we know about the electro-magnetic properties of existing atmospheric vortices. His theory generally explains why only the larger circles produce outer rings, because the charges present within smaller vortices are not strong enough to induce ionized 'race tracks' beyond the funnel. The only known exception to this was the Kelston, Avon case (August 1989), which measured only a few metres across.

All these similarities between ringed circles and vortex sheaths seem far too strong to be mere coincidence. Both the positioning and the dimensions of the outer rings match those found in vortex sheaths.

THE CLUSTERING EFFECT

In Chapter 3 we saw how circles seem to cluster about locations with steep hill slopes. Three types of location have been identified: escarpments (e.g. Westbury) and ridges (e.g. Salcombe), *punchbowls* (e.g. Cheesefoot Head) and lone hills that jut up from otherwise flat landscapes (e.g. Cley Hill).

Despite these similarities, we accept that a small proportion of circles do appear at locations distant from steep hill slopes. A good example of this is the Aylesbury quintuplet, which appeared over the weekend of 20–22 July 1989 on flat terrain on the eastern outskirts of the town. A regularly occurring Cheshire site is also some kilometres from any notable high ground.

Figure 6 illustrates the relationship between the Aylesbury formation and the nearest steep hill slope – the 125-metre-high north-west-facing Chiltern escarpment some six or seven kilometres to the south-east. Meaden has demonstrated that this formation appeared at a time when the prevailing wind was from the south-east. This suggests to him that the Aylesbury quintuplet still appeared at a lee-slope location, but that lee-slope effects here extended for up to seven kilometres from the feature responsible.

That steep hill slopes can trigger vortex formation has been well established in the standard meteorological literature for some years. In one well-known study,[3] three independent analyses (examination of aircraft-incident records, wind-tunnel experiments and an examination of structural damage during major storms) all proved that for wind speeds above a certain critical level and from certain directions a huge elongated rolling-vortex some five kilometres in length forms to the east of the Gibraltar Rock. Aircraft flying through this vortex whilst trying to land at the airport frequently experience severe atmospheric turbulence.

A similar 'trailing' vortex was discovered in the lee of Ailsa Craig, an elliptically shaped 330-metre-high island in the Scottish Isles.[4] These 'trailing' vortices seem causally related to the circles effect, as a number of other circle formations are known to have appeared on lee slopes when date and time, and therefore wind direction, are known accurately for circle formation.

THE LACK OF DAMAGE TO THE CROP

One of the main problems we encountered with the hoax theory was the way in which all currently known methods of hoaxing damage the affected crop. The advantage of a 'natural'

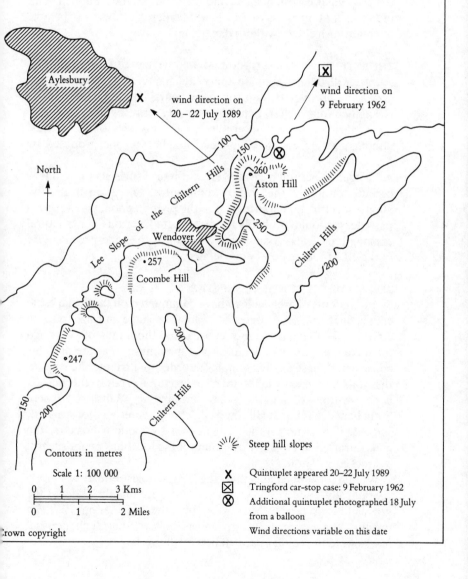

Figure 6: The Aylesbury 'hot spot'. The quintuplet of 20 – 22 July was formed almost seven kilometres from the crest of Aston Hill during light south-easterly winds. That circles form in the lee of steep hillslopes is a consistent characteristic and a major assumption underlying Dr Meaden's theory. Can it be a mere coincidence that one of Britain's best-known car-stop cases occurred only a few kilometres to the north-east and that this also happened in a lee slope location?

atmospheric solution is that air pressure seems to be an ideal force which would leave affected corn intact.

This assertion is proved by examining ordinary wind damage to cereal crops. In such cases the crop is smashed down in all directions, with none of the sculpturing and layering effects seen in crop circles. However, even when we examine simple lodged corn, the crop itself is largely intact and the stems are not snapped. This indicates that air pressure inside a 'Meaden Vortex' must be able to create corn circles without damaging the crop.

THE EXTENSIVE GEOGRAPHICAL DISTRIBUTION OF CIRCLES

As we will demonstrate in the next chapter, circles have been appearing all over Britain for many years. These factors greatly strengthen our belief that a previously unrecognized 'natural' mechanism must be responsible for the mystery of the circles, although we accept that this need not be the one proposed by Meaden.

Meaden's natural plasma-vortex theory suggests that under certain conditions the vortex would glow, taking on a ghostly, almost spectral appearance, and so the phenomenon, when seen in past ages, would probably have attracted various supernatural explanations. This is one of the reasons why the widespread nature of the effect is only now being defined.

THE ARCHAEOLOGICAL CONNECTION

Some students of archaeology have commented on the remarkable coincidence that crop circles are similar in shape and size to stone circles and other mystic sites constructed thousands of years ago for unknown purposes. Could it be, they muse, that the ancients constructed these sites as temples in order to attribute the rings to the gods and memorialize them in stone? Certainly the highest concentration of circles seems to be in Wiltshire, where Stonehenge, Silbury Hill and Avebury were all constructed. Indeed, if it is not a trick engineered by modern hoaxers, the concentration of crop circles around these locations might suggest a direct correlation.

We might anticipate that the crop-circles effect was only sporadically visible in times when crops were mainly wild and the grassland was largely overgrown by other vegetation. We can imagine that ancient Britons might believe that such unusual marks were the result of a visitation by the gods.

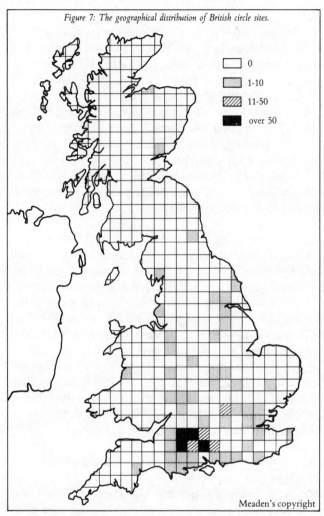

Figure 7: The geographical distribution of British circle sites.

Meaden's copyright

Indeed, the circles even occur in the Stonehenge area around mid-summer, which is an important date for what many suggest is a great astronomical calendar constructed by a long-gone race. This connection remains largely hypothetical, and we mention it only because so many have noted the apparent connection. But if it is true, such a long-term history for the circles strongly supports a natural, rather than supernatural, explanation. We propose a coordinated study of the geographical and meteorological status of stone circle sites.

ASSOCIATED UFO REPORTS

Perhaps the most exciting and surprising consequence of Meaden's theory is the brave new world that the plasma-vortex theory introduces for our interpretation of the UFO phenomenon. Despite our concern that media-inspired UFO reporting gives a false impression about 'aliens' and 'spaceships', it seems clear that a small proportion of the circles are being accompanied by anomalous light phenomena of one kind or another. This suggests that electrically charged atmospheric vortices may account for a number of related UFO reports. If this aspect of Meaden's theory has any basis at all, ufology will quite simply undergo a major paradigm revolution during the next few years. This revolution is discussed in more depth in Chapter 10.

THE PRESENCE OF SOME KIND OF RESIDUAL FIELD EFFECT

Some kind of 'field' is being left by Meaden's Vortex, which is presumably electro-magnetic in origin. It seems to be responsible for the more unusual anecdotes being reported. In particular we believe this can account for: the so-called dowsing effect; the strange high-pitched 'warbling' (termed 'sparrow-like') recorded by BBC *Daytime Live* and also during 'Operation Whitecrow'; the apparent spinning of compass needles at spiral centres;[5] the mechanical problems that have arisen with cameras at circle sites.[6]

We accept that such an effect cannot as yet be fully explained by a recognized 'natural' force, but it is surely natural in essence (rather than 'alien'), and we see no reason to dredge up some kind of 'unknown intelligence' to account for it.

THE GROWING SUPPORT FOR MEADEN'S THEORY AMONGST METEOROLOGISTS

Meaden is a respected physics doctorate, research scientist, specialist meteorological consultant and journal editor. He has more than adequate qualifications to discuss the likely relationship between crop circles and vortices. Indeed, he is best known for his work collating records and offering technical support on atmospheric vortex mechanisms.

One of the most difficult problems BUFORA has faced during the past decade has been the marked reluctance of professional meteorologists to examine Meaden's developing theory. However, we believe that this reluctance is a perfectly natural reaction, because any scientist who speaks out on a subject that has been associated with UFOs must have some concern about his professional reputation. We suspect that part of this problem has also been the unconscious assumption by the UFO community that all meteorologists are equally qualified to judge Meaden's theory and are fully familiar with what he proposes. Both these assumptions are wrong.

Meaden's theory was not introduced to the main channel of the international meteorological audience until January 1989.[7] Only a small proportion of meteorologists specialize in vortex-generation and the electromagnetic properties of small-scale atmospheric phenomena and so are able to comment.

Nevertheless, there *is* support, and it *is* growing (see Appendix 1).

A METEOROLOGICAL EXPLANATION IS ACCEPTABLE TO THE FARMING COMMUNITY

During 1987 BUFORA decided to carry out a survey of cereal farmers in Hampshire on behalf of TORRO to establish (amongst other things) whether or not the farmers knew what was responsible for the circles. As Table B demonstrates, most of the farmers held no strong opinions about the cause of the circles, but of those who did hold a strong opinion 'hoaxing' and 'the weather' clearly gained far greater support than 'intelligently controlled UFOs' or other ideas, such as animal tracks. This finding flatly

Table B: Numbers of Cereal Farmers Responding to Suggested Causes for the Circles (1987)

	Hoaxers	The Weather	UFOs
Numbers Agreeing	29	19	3
Numbers Disagreeing	8	9	15
No Response/Don't Knows	53	62	72
	Proportions (Including Non-Respondents)		
Numbers Agreeing	32	21	3
Numbers Disagreeing	9	10	17
No Response/Don't Knows	59	69	80
	Proportions (Excluding Non-Respondents)		
Numbers Agreeing	78	68	17
Numbers Disagreeing	22	32	83

contradicts the statements made in various media sources that all farmers reject the 'whirlwind' theory and that the circles cannot be the result of hoaxing. Throughout this book we carry numerous comments by farmers who seem happy to accept both 'whirlwinds' and 'hoaxers' as the principal cause of the circles.

Disadvantages of Meaden's Theory

Critics of Meaden's theory normally raise one or more of the following arguments. Many of these make false assumptions about natural atmospheric vortices. Several are based on an unfamiliarity with the emerging evidence. Some come from pure wishful thinking. We shall attempt to answer these points.

THE CIRCLES 'INTELLIGENTLY' LOCATE THEMSELVES AT MYSTICAL SITES

We believe we have successfully dealt with this argument (p. 96). No analysis has yet shown that circles are clustering about 'mystical' sites with greater-than-chance probability. However, even if such a relationship *were* to appear, the most realistic solution would surely be that some kind of human intelligence was responsible. Only recently has such information even been considered as evidence for the presence of some kind of 'alien intelligence'.

Although we reject the claim that the circles 'intelligently locate' themselves, certain 'mystical' sites (for example, Avebury and Silbury) have produced large numbers of circles during modern times. This may be because some of them are prone to vortex-generation (for example, Silbury Hill is shapèd like a miniature Ailsa Craig). Are long-term Meaden Vortex effects the reason why they are considered 'mystical'? Or it may be because hoaxers need to manufacture the myth that the circles are the product of an alien intelligence. Proven hoaxes identified in Chapter 5 largely feature the more complex patterns, as at these sites. Note also that the first visitors to the multiple formations at Silbury Hill in 1988 reportedly discovered footprints under the corn. This was considered sufficiently unusual for them to comment and seems entirely consistent with hoaxing.

THE NUMBER OF CIRCLES IS INCREASING EXPONENTIALLY
EACH YEAR

This is a false argument, because the number of reported crop circles depends entirely on how many researchers search for them. This in turn feeds off the degree of publicity surrounding the phenomenon and that has varied widely from summer to summer.

Prior to 1989 fewer than ten people were known to be actively searching for circles, and all these researchers lived in the South of England. Apart from sporadic national attention, most of the publicity came from the media in Wessex. Then suddenly the phenomenon became a topic of international recognition, with people searching for circles everywhere (and *finding* them!). We also know that many discoverers of older circles tended to dismiss them as the products of animals or the weather before they knew there *was* a 'crop circle mystery' of epic proportions; so it is very probable that many unreported circle events occurred in the past. The BUFORA-TORRO survey proved this. Furthermore, by 1989 the social climate surrounding the phenomenon had changed, and the public's perception of what was occurring was now of something far more dramatic (and newsworthy). All these things combined to escalate the reported numbers of circles at a seemingly prodigious rate.

However, even if these factors did not apply, there are good grounds for believing that trends in British agriculture may influence the increasing number of circles now being reported. These may also account for part of the concentration within Hampshire and Wiltshire (where cereal farming is dominant) and the apparently excessive number of reports in Britain as opposed to other nations. If Britain has recently introduced or operates unusual agricultural practices, that might trigger circle formation.

We need to study the types of crops being grown, the lengthening period in which those crops are reaching maturity, the increased use of pesticides and other chemicals (some of which are known to cause lodging in cereals if applied excessively) and the ability of those crops to withstand a sudden down-current of air. This latter factor depends on such things as the density of crop stems (which tend to lean against each other, thus building up strength) and the introduction of crops with longer heads and fatter stems. It is likely that these may help to make long-existent natural forces suddenly visible as crop circles.

If the circles are created by a Meaden Vortex (or indeed by any 'natural' mechanism), changes in the surface area devoted to cereal crops must also affect the number of reported formations. Agricultural statistics show that since 1950 the area devoted to cereal crops in the UK has increased by twenty per cent, and within that increased acreage the area devoted to winter crops has increased substantially. We know that during the 1950s cereal crops were sown largely in the spring and reached maturity in late summer. By the 1980s, the introduction of winter-sown crops (which reach maturity from late May onwards) doubled the time period in which cereal crops are of sufficient pliability and can permanently deform. For this reason, even if the number of circle-forming events remained constant, the opportunity for cereals to record that mechanism would predictably have undergone a substantial increase.

One of the main prerequisites for Meaden's Vortex seems to be the need for a very stable layer of air lying close to the ground. This situation occurs most frequently at night or in the very early hours of the morning (when the majority of circles seem to form). A plasma vortex will not form in highly turbulent atmospheric conditions, and if there is a greater incidence of such large areas of well-stratified air, that would be crucial. Perhaps the introduction of farm mechanization and the widescale removal of hedgerows have altered field size enough for more of these highly stratified areas to form and then hover in the lower atmosphere, increasing the chances for a Meaden Vortex to appear.

NO 'NATURAL' PHENOMENON COULD CREATE SUCH PRECISE PATTERNS
This is possibly one of the most common objections made by critics of Meaden's theory. In many ways this is a perfectly understandable reaction, and both authors of this book sympathize. It *is* very difficult to contemplate a 'natural' solution for such apparently artificial creations. However, the Marple hay fall, the Pucklechurch tornado and the mass of UFO events to be described later all involved the creation of precisely defined circles by an obviously natural mechanism. Meaden's suggestion that ionized air becomes self-contained (forming a geometric shape by surface tension) seems to be reasonable, although it would be nice to see firm evidence that this can occur.

Earlier we reminded you that a number of 'natural' phenomena exhibit very precise definition – for example, the Giant's Causeway in Antrim, snowflakes and even some electron microscope images depicting the molecular construction of matter itself. These are beautiful to look at but are produced by 'forces of nature'. This demonstrates that it is mere human arrogance, masquerading as prejudice, which assumes all natural phenomena to be imprecise and causes us to introduce the pleasing but needless speculation about order and pattern going hand in hand with some sort of guiding (alien) intelligence.

WHERE ARE THE ACCOUNTS OF 'NATURAL' CIRCLES BEFORE THE 1980s?

FSR consultant George Wingfield has publicly dismissed Meaden's theory for several reasons, but this is perhaps his least well-argued objection: 'Why did these "stationary whirlwinds" seemingly reappear around 1980, and occur in increasing numbers throughout this decade? This is hardly indicative of a meteorological effect.'[8]

We completely agree with Wingfield. No meteorological phenomenon should suddenly appear without precedent, although we acknowledge that in the so-far-unproven event of a large-scale climatic change (for example, the onset of a glacial period or the 'greenhouse' effect caused by the ozone-layer hole) the atmospheric boundary layer's capacity to generate plasma vortices might be significantly altered. Also we seem to be dealing with a meteorological process recorded on the ground thanks to geographical factors, and if these have altered, they may suddenly have triggered the appearance of circles in modern times, even if the weather phenomenon has always occurred. Even so, there should be occasional evidence of circles dating back some years from around the globe.

Also social and agricultural factors seem to have affected reporting mechanisms, so that it *appears* that the phenomenon suddenly arrived during the 1980s. But it has been known for some years that circles had been discovered dating back as far as 1918.[9] Now we have discovered for this book *many* other incidents, and these factors disprove absolutely the allegation that cornfield circles have appeared only during the 1980s. (Refer also to Appendix 2.)

METEOROLOGISTS REJECT MEADEN'S THEORY

This is probably the most serious argument. But many great scientific discoveries were laughed out of court when they were first proposed. Wegginer's theory of plate tectonics (otherwise known as 'continental drift') had existed for more than forty years before it was even considered by many geographers. Darwin's theory of evolution was ruthlessly discredited by its opponents before it began to gain acceptance. Einstein's theory of relativity was understood by only about a dozen physicists when it was first published. However, as we have already shown, rejection of a Meaden Vortex is fast disappearing, as the idea is understood. To date meteorologists have generally assumed the validity of vague media reports which imply that Meaden believes circles to be the product of whirlwinds. This is quite implausible and they have understandably rejected the idea. However, it is not what Meaden actually does propose.

HOW CAN MEADEN'S VORTEX PRODUCE THE LINEAR SPURS?

The existence of the linear spurs (see pp. 49–50) has provoked much debate. Perhaps it is important to stress that only three of the known 800 or so circles have displayed appreciable spurs, so the importance of this issue should be viewed in proportion. Nevertheless, we believe there is an acceptable solution.

Meaden tentatively suggests that the linear spurs are created at the very end of the circle-making process, as 'parcels' of charged particles cluster together in the outer rings. When the vortex mechanism breaks down, physical processes blow these particles away from the newly formed circle into the adjacent crop. In the Whiteparish formation this happened to be along the lines of greatest weakness induced by the presence of tramlines, whilst in the Childrey circle the general wind direction was probably orientated in a different direction to the tramlines, which is why the spur takes another path. In both cases Meaden claims that the general wind direction at the time of formation would be consistent with this interpretation.

We are not fully convinced by Meaden's explanation of the linear spurs. There is good evidence that these features were added onto genuine circles by hoaxers in two of the three known formations with long spurs.

At Childrey (July 1986) a small hole (approximately 30 cm across and 23 cm deep) was discovered in the crop beyond the spur where some soil had been removed. The spur itself was shaped like an arrowhead, causing some commentators to suggest that the whole formation resembled the scientific symbol for man (and used in astrology for the planet Mars!). This is found on the plaque for the Mariner 4 space mission. In our view this implies that the spur was a subsequent addition to a (possibly) genuine circle, to enhance the 'mystery'.

At Whiteparish (July 1987) the irate farmer made it very clear to us that circles had been appearing on his land every summer for at least twenty-eight years. Despite the comments in *Circular Evidence* that the farmer had claimed to have seen 'perfectly formed pod marks' in his fields (quintuplets ?)[10] the book omits to mention that the farmer also claimed to have chased hoaxers off his land when he caught some people trespassing with an incriminating length of rope.

This strongly suggests that in Wessex a small group of people are 'touching up' genuine circles to create evidence that supports the alien myth. The annual invasion of Wessex by 'travellers' and hippies during the summer solstice period may be relevant. Both groups are heavily into astrology and therefore likely to be well aware of the meaning attributed to the dramatic manifestation of the 'Mars' symbol at a circle site. Clearly, unless a novel meteorological explanation can be found for these features, it seems reasonable to interpret the linear spurs as further clues that there is more mischievous hoaxing at work than some researchers seem prepared to accept.

THE CIRCLES BECOME MORE AND MORE ELABORATE WITH EACH PASSING YEAR

This, in our view, may be the single biggest stumbling-block to a general acceptance of Meaden's theory. In many ways we accept that, *if* it can be shown that the circles *are* evolving into ever more complex patterns, this would *not* be consistent with a 'natural' meteorological explanation.

That the concept of 'evolving formations' is an illusion was first proposed by Paul Fuller.[11] He drew attention to the fact that each summer the reported formation types seem to change. When his article was written (late 1986), the known formation types had apparently 'evolved' from reports of singles (1981) and linear triplets (1983), (see Plate 11). Fuller's article also drew attention to the lack of 'mixing' in reported formation types. In other words, all the known 1985 circles consisted of quintuplets, and more than half the 1986 circles apparently displayed (previously unseen) outer rings.

However, examine the temporal distribution of the quintuplet formations.

During 1985 six apparently unprecedented quintuplet patterns were discovered which seemed (for some) to represent an 'intelligent' progression in the phenomenon. Then Colin Andrews uncovered a quintuplet event that had occurred at Headbourne Worthy near Winchester in 1978, and study of aerial photographs of the 1980 circle at Westbury indicated the existence of faint satellites visible only from the air which made that into what would probably have been a quintuplet.

The apparent 'evolution' was due simply to our lack of knowledge about historical circles rather than being a real characteristic of the phenomenon itself. By implication we believe that the same argument can be applied to other 'new' formation types. For example, triplets were originally supposed to have appeared 'suddenly' during 1981 – we now know of several pre-1981 triplet formations, including that at Earl Shilton, during 1940–41; ringed circles were supposed to have appeared 'suddenly' during 1986 – we now know of ringed circles at Twywell in Northamptonshire in 1977 and at Evenlode in Gloucestershire in 1960. These examples strongly suggest that, if ufologists were to wait for a few more years, each proven formation type would have a documented historical precedent. The apparent lack of them at present is due only to poor historical recording.

Why do certain formation types appear to dominate each year's circles? No full analysis has been carried out on the vast Terence Meaden archives to substantiate the claim, but we suspect it is an artefact of the reporting method – that is, only the more exciting 'new' types receive publicity. Certainly there is good evidence that single circles tend to be ignored by the media, whilst circles with outer rings or satellites are promoted. Of course, this creates an impression that the more complex formations replace less complex ones. Copycat hoaxing of the type of circles heavily publicized that year may be another factor.

Table C: An Evaluation of Three Major Theories to Account for the Circles Effect

Characteristic	Status	Intelligent UFO
Precise definition	Displayed by almost all circles	Reports of precisely defined UFOs do exist in the UFO literature. However, these may all be reports of Meaden Vortices and/or of non-intelligent but unrecognized natural phenomena.
Corn undamaged	True for at least 95 per cent of the affected areas	Physically real 'spaceships' would damage the corn. However, spaceships creating wind effects might be possible if alien spaceships exist at all.
Swirl pattern	Displayed by all genuine circles	Some UFOs have been reported to rotate. However, are these 'intelligent' UFOs or are they Meaden Vortices/ other rotating natural phenomena? (If intelligent, the aliens must like getting dizzy!)
Layering effects	Displayed by most circles	But why?
Banding effects	Displayed by most circles	But why?
Outer rings	Displayed by a minority of circles	But why?
Contra-rotation	Displayed by only a few circles	But why?
Complex geometrical patterns	Displayed by only about 10 per cent of circles	But why? To test *our* intelligence?
International distribution	Most circle formations now have foreign precedents	Yes, if an intelligence is visiting us, we might expect them to visit many countries
Have been appearing for more than 300 years	Only one example so far (many others pre-1980)	Yes, but this seems utterly pointless behaviour.

Dowsing effects present	Apparently universal for all genuine circles	But why?
Linear spurs	Only three examples of lengthy spurs so far discovered	But why?
Camera problems	Reported on only a few occasions	But why?
Strange patterns in regrowing crops	Reported in a regrowing crops handful of circles. No conclusive evidence has yet emerged	
Sick dogs	Reported twice?	But why?
Discovery of the 'Mars Bars'	Reported just once	But why?
Unusual luminous effects noticed at time of formation	Reported a few times	Consistent with UFOs, but are UFOs 'intelligent' or 'natural'?
Nocturnal dawn appearance	Most circles seem to appear at this time	Consistent with intelligent UFOs avoiding contact with man (but why?)
Referencing to tramlines	Alleged, no conclusive evidence has yet emerged	But why?
Association with steep hill slopes	Most circles seem to cluster near such features. The Aylesbury quintuplet may prove that *all* circles lie within 7 kms of steep hill slopes	

Characteristic	*Hoaxing*
Precise definition	Yes, by using a pole and chain, trampling or rolling around on the ground as in the Cornishmen's hoax
Corn undamaged	No, all known attempts damage the corn. Would require a novel method of hoaxing circles
Swirl pattern	Yes, by using a pivot (although this would leave evidence of a central hole)
Layering effects	No known method at present
Banding effects	Debatable
Outer rings	Yes, several methods can create rings, although these may not display some of the characteristics already described
Contra-rotation	Yes
Complex geometrical patterns	Yes, to imply that an 'intelligence' exists behind the phenomenon
International distribution	Yes, because the need to hoax circles would presumably extend to other cultures
Have been appearing for more than 300 years	Yes, but seems very unlikely for all 800 circles in Meaden's Archive – particularly for the many circles appearing before the 1980s when there was little media interest to encourage hoaxing
Dowsing effects present	No known method exists for creating this effect; seems most unlikely to be explained via hoaxing
Linear spurs	Yes, to imply that an 'intelligence' exists behind the phenomenon
Camera problems	Hoaxers would presumably have to be present when these effects occurred
Strange patterns in regrowing crops	Yes, to imply that some exotic solution exists for the circles
Sick dogs	Possibly by leaving some poisonous substance behind
Mars Bar	Yes, as a joke or a red herring to fool later investigators
Unusual luminous effects noticed at time of formation	No, unless novel method of creating UFO hoax available
Nocturnal/dawn appearance	Yes, to avoid detection whilst committing criminal damage to farmers' fields
Referencing to tramlines	Yes, to imply the presence of an 'intelligence'
Association with steep hill slopes	Debatable. If hoaxers are reading this book, please choose flat locations in future!

Characteristic	*Meaden's Unrecognized Plasma Vortex*
Precise definition	Areas of ionized and ordinary air may be precisely defined due to surface tension. Other 'natural' phenomena (e.g. snowflakes) are also precisely defined
Corn undamaged	Yes, air pressure could create circles without damaging the corn. Just look at ordinary wind damage in corn.
Swirl pattern	Yes, a natural consequence of Meaden's theory
Layering effects	Yes, by moving around whilst creating the circle
Banding effects	Yes, a by-product of rotation
Outer rings	Yes, via 'sheath' effects
Contra-rotation	Yes, via 'sheath' effects
Complex geometrical patterns	Debatable, but could be caused by multiple vortex funnels and/or complex electrical induction effects
International distribution	This would be a natural consequence of any 'natural' theory, as well as Meaden's
Have been appearing for more than 300 years	Yes, any 'natural' phenomenon should have extensive historical precedents
Dowsing effects present	Possibly, but not fully understood at present
Linear spurs	Seems unlikely under current theory. Possibly 'touching up' of 'genuine' circles by hoaxers?
Camera problems	Yes, by leaving some kind of charged ground trace. Not fully understood as yet
Strange patterns in regrowing crops	Awaiting further evidence
Sick dogs	An unrelated event
Mars Bar	An unrelated event
Unusual luminous effects noticed at time of formation	Yes, plasma vortices should glow in the night
Nocturnal/dawn appearance	Yes, because meteorological conditions (e.g. existence of stable layers of air) favour nocturnal vortex generation
Referencing to tramlines	Possibly, because a charged body of air needs to earth itself to particular structures that affect local magnetic fields
Association with steep hill slopes	Yes, because steep hill slopes generate 'trailing vortices'

Summary

We have attempted an objective look at Meaden's theory and are happy that it can accommodate almost all the serious objections being made. We note that critics assume that science progresses by instant solution to all problems. If a characteristic is discovered that apparently does not fit, this does not falsify a theory.

Table C sets out the known characteristics of the circles phenomenon, their present status and how well each theory accounts for them. We believe that at present no theory explains all the reported characteristics, but this table makes it seem very obvious that the natural atmospheric solution proposed by Meaden makes more sense and explains more of these characteristics.

It may be that there are other legitimate criticisms of the ionized vortex theory which nobody has yet formulated. We are not foolish enough to say that Dr Meaden has all the answers and that the issue is settled, but we do sincerely contend that the evidence in favour of his basic premise – that an atmospheric force creates these patterns – is overwhelmingly endorsed by the current evidence.

9   A Vortex Case Book

Visual Accounts of Vortices

The meteorological data is packed with reports of short-lived or peculiar vortices (often described in lay terms as whirlwinds or tornadoes). However, in modern days they are sometimes reported outside the meteorological community as UFO sightings. It is instructive to look at some of these cases to gain an impression of the sort of thing which is being observed, and then compare and contrast this with the meteorological accounts given earlier and with the effects of Meaden's Vortex.

Hampshire, 1967
Bertram Stride was fishing for lobsters just off the coast from Highcliffe in the early morning of 18 July 1967 when he perceived a tornado funnel sucking up water in a swirling motion. At about the same time airline pilots over the Channel area between Kent and France observed 'clusters of objects streaming trails of lights'.[1]

Just five kilometres north-west of Highcliffe is the stretch of road between Avon and Sopley on which one of Britain's strongest documented vehicle-interference cases occurred on 6 November 1967, at 1.30 a.m.

A Leyland Comet truck and a Jaguar car were approaching a crossroads when a purplish-red rugby ball shape glided to a halt above a telephone kiosk. The car's engine and lights faded and then failed; the truck's lighting also failed, but its diesel-powered engine continued to operate. The visual phenomenon made a continuous humming sound, and a pungent odour (likened to ozone) filled the air during its presence. Next day, when the truck driver was taken by police to collect his vehicle, he saw that the highway was being resurfaced with fresh bitumen at the precise location of the incident, the phone booth was newly painted, dark markings that had been seen on the grassy embankment (circles perhaps?) now had men with what looked like geiger-counters prodding about. The truck had to be tow-started by an army lorry in order for it to be driven out of the police compound at Christchurch; it had very costly damage, with all electrical circuits burnt out and requiring a new dynamo, starter motor, regulator, ammeter, batteries and bulbs.[2]

Those who decry the lack of any physical, scientific evidence in UFO cases would do well to ponder this report. Its clear link with the crop-circle vortex will become apparent later.

Berkshire, 1979

Paul Wilson, a computer scientist, was beside a cornfield near Maidenhead with his fiancée at about 2.30 p.m. on a warm, sunny day in early September. The corn was just being harvested. There was no obvious wind.

The witnesses report that, 'The corn began rising in a spiral' in a field beyond the hedgerows. These were 'lazy swirls which rose to just above tree top height and then petered out into nothing'. They noted how the phenomenon remained *totally static* for approximately sixty seconds – ceasing instantly. Some bits of harvested corn were scattered down nearby, and Mr Wilson comments that these were 'completely intact and undamaged'.

Unfortunately there was no easy access into this field and no crop-circle mythology to suggest to the couple that such a visit might be productive, so no search of the ground was undertaken by these witnesses. However, the harvested nature of the crop may have made full-blown circles improbable.[3]

Clwyd, North Wales, 1983

Witness Alan Foster was waiting for a train on Rhyl railway station at approximately 5.30 p.m. It was a warm, sunny day in late June.

A column of debris and dust was seen rising upwards in the south-west. It was inclined towards the right at a slight angle to the vertical and rose approximately twenty metres into the air. Inside the tube was seemingly transparent. The whole thing remained *totally stationary* for about fifteen seconds and then just disappeared. The strangest aspect was the way the tube cut off at the top, taking debris not into cloud but seemingly into a 'white hole' in space. Mr Foster said: 'It was as if there was a giant vacuum cleaner scooping up samples.'[4]

Here we see how vortices *can* remain quite stationary, last for very brief periods of time and rotate just like the force that produces circles.

A report from Cheddar, Somerset, on 7 July 1984 is instructive. Mrs Taylor put her washing out to dry on a rotary clothes-line. After going indoors for just sixty seconds (on a fine day), she returned to the garden to find her washing scattered all over the grass. Some silent force (according to Terence Meaden, it was a vortex) had caused this to occur. Some clothing was wrapped very tightly round the vertical pole, whilst one of the horizontal metal struts was bent downwards – indicating that at least part of the energy in this incident was akin to the effect producing crop circles.[5]

Strange Effects from Vortices

Rains of hay, as at Marple, are very common consequences of rising vortices. Hundreds of cases are on meteorological records.

One of the earliest reports of hay falls comes in J.J. Daniell's *History of Warminster*, describing how it rained clumps of wheat around this modern centre of UFO and circle lore. That happened in summer 1696!

It may even be that this vortex side-effect could be responsible for a phenomenon known in ufology as the 'angel hair' mystery.[6]

Researcher Aimé Michel found that on 17 October 1952 at Oloron in south-west France something strange happened in a clear blue sky.[7] Yves Prigent, the headmaster of a local school and a former meteorologist, saw to the north 'a fleecy cloud of curious shape' that drifted slowly along. Tilted at a 45 degree angle was 'a long narrow cylinder' which was non-luminous. 'Puffs of white smoke were escaping from its top side', and ahead of this were about thirty 'shapeless smoke balls' that appeared as rings through binoculars. They were zigzagging about and seemed tied to one another by a white trail 'like an electric arc'.

Many witnesses watched as it moved off to the south-west, drifting very slowly. For hours afterwards the local trees, rooftops and telephone wires were strewn with gelatinous white 'goo' that was thread-like and which melted rapidly on touch. Most experts dismissed it as spider's web, although possibly electrostatic forces attracted this.

A vortex may be described as like a 'flying saucer' when glowing during daylight.[8] What about at night?

On 9 December 1986 Puxton Drive in Kidderminster, Worcestershire, had a strange visitor. Derek Perks and his wife were woken at 12.50 a.m. by their windows vibrating. A high-pitched whistling noise was also threatening the peace of this quiet suburban area. Mr Perks used the analogy of a 'giant spinning top – slowly winding down' to describe the fifteen-second sound. Going outside, the Perks were joined by several neighbours and saw that a very short trail of destruction had been left in this one localized area. Thick wooden fenceposts were snapped and metal casings on street lamps were twisted through 90 degrees. Most residents correctly assumed that a vortex was to blame. The Perks' teenaged daughter, Rachael, had seen some lights drifting away immediately after the sound disappeared.

Terence Meaden, assessing the case, said it was a fine example of a very short-lived vortex and that the lights might have been tiles or posts being carried away and reflecting streetlights as they tumbled. Of note is the fact that the weather had been wet earlier in the night but a clearing frontal system immediately preceded this episode. There are many reports in the UFO literature in which a 'close encounter' took place during almost identical weather patterns, the most famous being the Alan Godfrey 'abduction' at Todmorden in November 1980, which we will look at later.[9]

Observations of Strange Clouds

Eastern Seaboard, USA, 1904

Noted paranormal writer Hilary Evans first referred to a secondary source and suggested more research. In *Fortean Times*, American analyst Michael Shoemaker responded, doing a first-rate job checking local newspapers and shipping manifests. He found the basic details to be historically accurate and provided a definitive account.

Slight confusion occurs about the date. It is taken by the context of the account to be 30 July 1904, but as the account reads 'When the British steamer *Mohican*, from Ibraila, Roumania, which reached this port on Saturday, was making for the Delaware breakwater ...' this implies it was arriving, when the records show it was actually leaving Philadelphia then. Possibly the report comes from a port it passed through on its way out, or the incident occurred on the previous Saturday (23 July) when the *Mohican* may have arrived. Arrival was not logged, an unusual event in itself. Perhaps, if something odd accompanied that arrival, the port authorities preferred to record nothing. Either way, according to the testimony of the ship's master, Captain Urquhart, when the *Mohican* was at latitude 37° 16′ and Longitude 72° 48′, the whole crew encountered something that '... was beyond me ... I never saw anything so terrifying in the years I have been at sea.'

It was just after sunset, and the sea was dead calm. Then a 'strange grey cloud' appeared in the south-east. It drifted slowly towards the ship and then enveloped it. It had 'a peculiar grey tinge ... [with] bright glowing spots in the mass'. These spots became more vivid as it approached the metal hulk. When it swallowed them up, the entire decks '... blazed forth like a ship on fire ... from stem to stern and topmast to keel everything was tinged with the strange glow'.

Hair reportedly 'stood straight on end' and '... beards stuck out like bristles on a pig'. The compass needle was 'flying around like an electric fan'. This latter effect has been reputed to be associated with crop-circle events and occurs in a number of well-attested UFO cases.

Naturally there was great panic. Some sailors even prayed. The captain tried to make them work, to distract attention, but the iron chains – indeed everything metallic – were stuck firm to the hull by an enormous magnetic force. Eventually a peculiar calmness descended, possibly suggesting that the crew entered an altered state of consciousness. Captain Urquhart says: 'My sea legs began to fail me for the first time ... there was a great silence over everything that only added to the terror.'

After an estimated thirty minutes the cloud lifted off the ship and drifted away. All returned to normal.[10]

This remarkable story suggests that the *Mohican* had chanced upon an ionized cloud very much akin to the vortex that Terence Meaden is proposing and that the temporary immersion of these witnesses resulted in the electrical and magnetic effects described – plus (possibly) an induced altered state of consciousness. Ufologists recognize this from their data, calling it the 'Oz Factor'.[11]

Suspicions about vortex activity in this Philadelphia case are enhanced by other local press stories that Shoemaker found, describing highly unusual weather phenomena at the time. These include a tornado at Doylestown (28 July) and several ball-lightning cases (1 August). A similar case to this occurred aboard a ship off the Florida coast in 1928.[12]

Tibet, Autumn 1947
Another case concerns the charming widow of a REME colonel.

Crossing the desert plateau from Nepal into Tibet with a truck convoy and Gurkha guard, she, her husband and some Plymouth Brethren stopped for supper. Sitting on the truck, they all felt a strange tingling sensation (suggesting an electrostatic charge from ionization) and then the colonel crashed to the ground like a felled tree when going to investigate. A heavy pressure in the air was now causing the trucks to vibrate, and coming toward them was 'a grey floating mass' which '... seemed to be solid in the middle but outside seemed like vapour'. They all felt a '... prickly feeling ... as though my hair was standing on end. All my exposed parts were touched by it ...'[13] Her husband regained consciousness, and they fled the area (abandoning what had been a several-day trek on an important mission). The three people who came closest to the phenomenon (her husband, herself and the Gurkha) all suffered illness and a red rash on the exposed parts of their skin, which lasted two days and may have come from exposure to a radiation field.

This vortex was probably visible through particles of dust and sand attracted into the charged field.

Antarctica, 1966
Early in the morning of 22 May 1966 two members of the British Antarctic Survey, stationed near Mount Gundrey on Adelaide Island, saw a strange dense cloud appear in the south which behaved oddly.

According to the testimony of Eric Wilkinson, senior meteorologist with the team, the cloud rose vertically, reached an altitude of between 150 and 250 metres and was about thirty metres by thirty metres in size. During the approximately forty-five minutes that it remained in view, the cloud seemed alternately to expand and contract and emitted a low buzzing noise described as similar to bees. At one stage during the observation a thick black 'ray' emerged at an approximate 45 degree angle and struck the snowfield. At the point at which it struck the ground, snow was whirled up in a rising spiral, like a dust devil. A secondary ray bounced off from the place of impact at a 75 degree angle in the opposite direction.

Weather was dull, with a five knot wind. There was no thunderstorm activity. Reports were made to the yearly meteorological record and the US Air Force, but most importantly of all Wilkinson took slides of the event, so we have a clear idea of what the vortex phenomenon looked like in this case.[14]

Shropshire, 1988

The most remarkable case has been left until last.

The principal witness was aged forty-five at the time of these events – on, we believe, 9 February 1988. He had spent twelve years in the armed forces but was at the time looking for farm work in the Oswestry area.

It was about 8 a.m. on a clear, sunny day and after an unsuccessful farm visit outside the market town he was returning home along the A4083 to the south east. He passed a grass verge by some fields and saw an elderly woman beside a car parked just off the road. Her dog (a spaniel) had been allowed off the lead and was running across the road into fields to the south, barking and yapping – 'going beserk'.

The source of this distress soon became obvious. Straddling the hedgerow and path opposite was a strange cloud. It was 'like a yellow fog' at least fifteen metres in diameter and glowed brilliantly. There was a 'power noise ... not a motor or vibration – more like the wind rushing', due to a rotational motion of the mist, and 'leaves and dust were blowing about like there was a whirlwind.' During the couple of minutes whilst this thing appeared, a sensation 'like hair standing on end' was felt, and there was a 'terrible musky smell – vile and horrible and sulphurous' and also an 'eerieness'.

The dog ran *into* the glow and completely disappeared. By this point the woman was screaming, and our witness had to calm her, even though the glow was stationary in the same position just yards away. The glow vanished instantly, 'like smoke disappearing'. They now found the dog prone on the ground with its body on the footpath and head on the kerb. Going over to it, the man picked up the animal and felt that it was both soaking wet and very warm to the touch – 'steaming like it had just come out of a bath'. Its eyes were red and bloodshot and it was panting heavily, but seemingly alive. The man carried it into the car, placed it on the passenger seat and covered it with a blanket.

In shock he watched as the woman leapt into her car and drove away. However, he was able to note her car licence plate and managed to trace her. Three days later he phoned the woman, who told him that the dog had fully recovered and was running around as fit as ever. A vet was never involved.

The dog apparently died before this story was reported (that is, within six months of the incident), but it was an elderly animal, and neither the owner nor the other witness felt this was connected with the experience. Meteorologist David Reynolds advises that the wind was blowing from the direction of the only local hill, a ridge 300 metres high to the west. There are other cases on record involving severe effects on animals, especially dogs. At Sizewell, Suffolk, on 24 February 1975, a pumpkin shape glowing like a TV screen gave off an ozone smell as it terrified both dog and owner on a beach.[15,16]

Crop Circle Reports

In the following pages are accounts of circles from all over the world. These are mostly new reports we discovered during our research for this book. They prove that this is a phenomenon not restricted to one country (Britain) or to one small part of that country (Wessex).

All the foreign circles have been well documented in reputable sources within the UFO literature, even though they seem not to represent UFO events in the traditional sense. Many were put on record *before* the start of the modern circles mystery in 1980 – further disproving the claim that there are no historical precedents.

BRITISH CASES
Earl Shilton, Leicestershire, 1940/41
Following an appeal by Dr Terence Meaden in the *Daily Express* in 1988, a triplet was reported which was followed up by BUFORA's Midlands co-ordinator Clive Potter. He soon established that the exact location of the circle was near Earl Shilton in western Leicestershire. This formation had appeared during August 1940 or 1941 and involved one large circle (about ten metres in diameter) plus two much smaller circles (each about two metres in diameter). Potter's correspondent reported that he understood such circles to have been fairly common in the Earl Shilton area during the 1940s and that local farmers believed them

to have been made by foxes making a play area for their cubs.

The lack of photographs of early circles makes it very difficult to determine whether they are identical to those currently appearing. This means that we can only make value judgements from the accounts.

Gloucestershire, 1960
This was the first complex circle type known to have been reported in the local media. It was investigated for BUFORA by John Llewellyn in 1960 but was seemingly unknown to Andrews and Delgado. They state that circles outside Wessex are recent, yet *all* the half-dozen oldest known sites are *outside* Wessex, which surely proves that the uniqueness of Hampshire and Wiltshire is an artefact of modern intensive searching and 'Wessex Triangle' hype.

The original report in the *Evesham Journal* on 10 June 1960 described how a farmer from Evenlode found 'two mysterious circles, one inside the other'. Jenny Randles spoke to him in June 1989 and found this was a double ring pattern, the inner ring having a diameter of five metres and the outer ring a diameter of seven metres. The width of each ring was about ten centimetres and the grass was depressed approximately two centimetres. Mr Edwards had found the marks early on 3 June and last crossed the field on 1 June (although he was beside it on the evening of 2 June). There were no tracks leading into the field and no access roads close by. The purpose of hoaxing a circle formation in this location is difficult to imagine.

We also have a letter from the local reporter called to the site that day, and he adds that these circles '... were perfectly formed, as if someone had been using a giant pair of compasses. They were mathematically faultless, one inside the other. I got the impression that the inner circle was imprinted slightly more strongly than the outer circle.'

North Yorkshire, 1974
We are aware of 'rumours' of circles in the Stockton and Darlington area during the summers of 1974–6 – more than 500 km from those appearing in southern England. Industrious readers might like to track them down by reading through local newspaper records for these summers. We have also been told of circles appearing near Hebden Bridge and Todmorden, eighty kilometers

further south. Todmorden has generated many classic UFO sightings, including a very significant close encounter in the town which we will discuss in Chapter 10.

Buckinghamshire, 1977

This story began the very day that a circle was also found in Morayshire, astride a railway embankment, after a humming object was seen.[17]

In a series of sightings teenage boys in Woburn Green reported 'yellow shimmering lights'. Detailed BUFORA investigation found that most of the lights had possible explanations as aircraft (and by late May the boys were skywatching and looking out for UFOs).

However, what mattered was a site investigation carried out by Barry King and Andy Collins a couple of weeks after the key event, which was on 19 May. They found '... two circular depressions in a barley field – one depression had a diameter of sixteen metres and the other nine metres: they were eleven metres away from each other, the smaller being to the south west of the larger one. Directly above the smaller – about seven metres up – was a telegraph line ... The depressions were caused by the barley being at slightly a lower angle than the rest of the field – the odd point being that each area was exactly circular.'[18] Geiger-counter and magnetic-field readings were taken and proved negative.

These interesting circles were photographed and possibly were discovered by sheer coincidence upon searching the site for clues about the fairly mundane (and quite probably explicable) lights that were reported.

The July 1977 Wave

Between 3 and 7 July 1977 northern England was hit by a veritable wave of vortex-related events. This narrow concentration in one time spell suggests that weather factors were probably important.

On 3 July a vortex was seen at Apperley Dene in Northumbria. It was 3 p.m. and Barry Hall and family were in the garden when a disturbance appeared in trees at the rear. Barry said that it was a 'black oval shape rising from behind the trees and bringing the disturbance up with it in a vortex it seemed to be creating'.

Swirling round and round was much dark material in a column sucked up beneath the oval. At the height of some pine trees (about fifteen metres) it paused and hovered. As it did so, with his parents looking on, Barry walked along the garden towards it. By now it was already drifting slowly towards the house, and Barry noted (as other witnesses have commented before) that the debris just seemed to be dissolving into nothing rather than falling down. The vortex passed directly over Barry Hall's head, and he saw 'a black hairlike substance' inside. As it moved away, it seemed to thin slightly but nothing was ever found on the ground. The Halls reported that during its passage there was a short sudden blast of wind, and neighbours recall a 'hurricane-like blast' which they heard (seeing nothing as they were indoors).[19]

Whilst no circle was left here, just eight hours later (11.15 p.m.) this did happen in the small village of Crook, Cumbria, in the foothills of the Lake District, with the country's highest peaks.

According to the investigation by Ian Cresswell, Police Constable Bill White observed two white spotlights that pulsated behind the Sun Inn. Another officer saw the lights from elsewhere in the village, although little co-operation was offered. The field above which the lights were seen is easily accessible, due to its proximity to the pub, and in daylight next day a single circle of depressed grass was discovered, approximately eighteen metres in diameter.

During this period of hot, stable July weather there were many more reports of strange lights in the Kendal–Windermere area. These were supplemented at 7.20 p.m. on 7 July by the experience of a man at Stainton who chanced to see 'a large cloud spinning in an anti-clockwise direction'. Whilst the wind was taking normal cloud on a course to the south-west, this strange mass remained stationary. It was egg-shaped with a slight bulge at the base and glowed sufficiently that it seemed to illuminate normal cloud immediately around it. Its edges were slightly fuzzy.

The man ran indoors to grab a camera but unfortunately only one frame of film was left. However, the spectacle was captured for posterity. After his taking this shot, the mass began to rotate faster, decreased in diameter and suddenly vanished. This was accompanied by a flash of white light. The whole experience took twenty-five seconds, and the witness himself contrasted what he saw with a tornado or waterspout.[20] Finally that week, at East Brierley near Bradford in West Yorkshire, Nigel Mortimer reports that witness Mrs Frater was walking through fields beside Copley Springs Wood in the lee of Hunsworth Hill on a warm, sunny day. She noticed a hat-shaped object hovering low over the grass. After a moment it started to 'wobble' and then began to rotate swiftly in a clockwise motion. Red sparks or flames came from the underside, and it shot upwards and then just vanished.

When Nigel Mortimer examined the field much later, he found something interesting at the precise spot. It was fallow grass, hardly ever used, and it contained a single ring that he says measured 16.666 feet in diameter. The ring itself was about one foot wide, was of a much lusher green than the central grass and was also growing taller than the centre.

Northamptonshire, 1977

Despite the claim made in *Circular Evidence* that no examples of ringed circles were known prior to 1986,[21] BUFORA has discovered several historical accounts of ringed circles both in Britain and elsewhere. There is reference to a phenomenon akin to this at East Brierley above, and a double-ringed single circle appeared on the night of 31 August/1 September 1977 near Twywell in Northamptonshire.

This formation was originally reported in the local *Evening Telegraph* and then 'rediscovered' and investigated by Ernie Still for BUFORA during 1988. Still's investigation established that the formation consisted of two rings plus an unusually small inner circle. The formation appeared in a grass field being used for cattle.

Cheshire, 1981 onward

We withhold details of the precise location of this series of events to protect the farmland on request. (They were never publicized in the local media.) However, it is south of the city of Chester in the flattest area known to produce circles on a regular basis. The family concerned moved here in 1978, but it was 1981 before the first circles were seen. They were totally unaware of any other events down south.

The house is surrounded by winter wheat, barley and rape fields, and circles have appeared in several of them. One of the family described them as follows: 'Their symmetry and intricate design I found fascinating. Because of the flat nature of the country almost all were invisible from roads.' There is a high vantage-point from which the family took to looking for them, and once they knew they were there and the right time of year to search they were able to go close to the fields and find them. Certain fields produce circles approximately every couple of years, others less regularly. At first the family imagined that foxes were responsible but then they 'found ones so huge it would be impossible'.

Most of these circles are anti-clockwise in rotation, and they are usually singles of varying sizes. The most spectacular was in 1981 or 1982 – a formation of four consisting of a large sixteen-metre circle and three smaller ones of about eight-metres all arranged to *one side* of the parent and equidistant from each other in a straight line. 1987 produced the largest single circle (up to thirty metres) and convinced the family that it was not a wildlife problem but likely due to the weather. The circles tend to appear in very late August and are visible for just a few days before harvesting. Unfortunately, despite high hopes and intensive checking (including microlites flying over the area checking the fields), nothing turned up in 1989.

The family knows a farmer in the Stanlow area (north of Chester) who claims that his father used to report the circles on his land and that he sees them occasionally himself. He reports: 'They are done by the wind on hot still days, and they're a bloody nuisance!'

Oadby, Leicestershire, 1988

This formation was discovered by flying-instructors in a wheat field during the third week of June 1988 and was subjected to a first-class investigation by Clive Potter and Ernie Still for BUFORA. The ringed circle probably appeared on the night of 18 June, and it quickly attracted local media interest. At present this three-satellite pattern is unique – which may be important.

Salcombe, South Devon, 1989

Circles have been appearing at an isolated location near Salcombe in South Devon for at least a decade. A former meteorologist, David Bargman, reported in *J Met* for November 1989 that, 'Walking the countryside every day with the dog, my wife and I have often seen circles in standing crops, both cereal and grass. These have been completely isolated with no evidence of human or animal intrusion. With only shallow thought I attributed their presence to some form of wind damage. We live remotely and it would be a very strange human to have manufactured them and

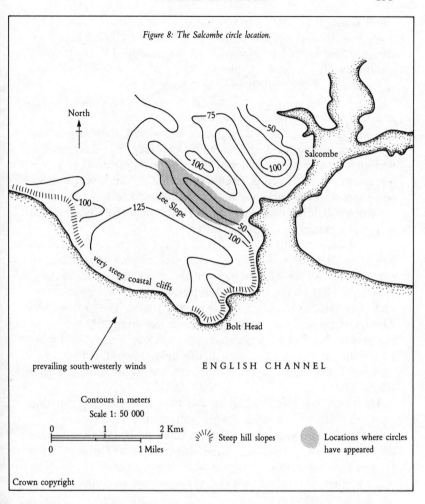

Figure 8: *The Salcombe circle location.*

concealed the evidence on the offchance a rambler would be impressed.'[22]

Just as at Cheesefoot, Westbury and Cley Hill, the Devon circles appear alongside a steep hill slope, a ridge some 120 metres high bordering steep coastal cliffs. Again the presence of steep hill slopes suggests that there might be some causal relationship that results in the formation of circles under certain conditions (see Figure 8).

A few kilometres to the north, two circles appeared in a field of spring barley on a farm at East Allington during early August

1989. Both these circles were six metres in diameter and again were linked with UFOs by the local press ('UFO Theory on Rings', *Western Independent*, 20 August 1989). TV South-West weathercaster Trevor Appleton was quick to dismiss this suggestion, offering 'whirlwinds' as the answer.

Mansfield, Nottinghamshire, 1989
This single circle (Plate 12) was first discovered on or before the evening of 16 July by a midlands UFO Society. Significantly, this was the very same afternoon that the BBC broadcast a TV documentary about crop circles to coincide with the publicity surrounding the launch of *Circular Evidence*. For this reason we were immediately suspicious that this circle might be some form of hoax perpetrated by a copycat viewer.

A full case investigation was carried out by Jenny Randles on behalf of BUFORA on 27 July. The circle appeared in a field of oats south-west of Mansfield over the weekend of 15/16 July. Again the circle was in an isolated position away from habitation and was invisible to people using nearby roads. The only nearby vantage-point was the Mansfield Incinerator some 100 metres to the north. The circle was situated at the bottom of a gently sloping incline in the south-west part of the field. Hamilton Hill, on a generally flat landscape, is about one kilometre to the south-south-west.

The circle lay about ten metres in from a high hedge running along the side of the field. By the time Jenny visited the site, a large swathe of damage had been cut through the crop by a group of 'UFO investigators' who had driven up the adjacent lane (removing barricades designed to stop vehicles) and then, according to the nearest resident, simply stomped across the field to visit the 'landing mark'.

The circle was distinctly oval-shaped with diameters varying from five to six metres as measured through the spiral centre. The affected area displayed a clockwise swirl pattern with little evidence of layering and a patch of bare earth some fifteen centimetres across where the spiral centre should have been. No sign of a hole was found at this point, ruling out pole-and-chain hoaxing. The edge of the circle was rather ragged and may have been damaged by visitors to the site. There were other suspect features.

Jenny managed to find a resident who 'knew exactly what had

caused the circle'. In 1986 a drilling rig had been placed at the exact spot where the 1989 circle appeared. This accounts for the suspicious gap in the hedgerow which is just where the circle was found, as it had been used by the oil company after their unsuccessful operation. This coincidence suggested to some that the circle might have been due to soil collapse of some kind beneath the surface following drilling, but Terence Meaden speculated that an ionized vortex might 'home in' on this point of weakness. For us it was another reason to be wary.

However, we strongly believe this is one of several media-inspired hoaxes during the 1989 circle season and this offers further proof of our suggestion that even experienced researchers *cannot* always tell the difference, despite pronouncements to the contrary. This is something which requires very serious consideration.

WORLD-WIDE CIRCLES

Just as an intensive search through past archives has uncovered many cases in Britain prior to the official start of the circles myth, so we have made similar discoveries about the rest of the world.

We have purposely avoided reports of burnt or scorched circles. Andrews and Delgado cite a number of these, but whilst they may well fit in with an ionization field, and we found dozens of them in our research, it was considered prudent to concentrate only on the same sort of circular damage that we had set out to resolve.

The following selection is just a selection. They are typical of the others and prove beyond all doubt that this is *not* a new effect that has manifested only in southern England and just since 1980.

West Palm Beach, Florida, USA, 1952

This case is impressive because of the intensive official investigation conducted by Captain Edward Ruppelt of the US Air Force.[23]

On the night of 19 August a scoutmaster (ex-Marine) was driving some boys home after a meeting. It had rained heavily in the period leading up to this night but was now fine. They went to see if a stock-racing circuit was flooded and were returning inland from the coastal highway when they saw glowing lights in the thick bushes. Fearing an air crash, the man left the boys in the car, switched on a radio and told them to wait until a fifteen-minute programme ended, then go for help if he was not back. They saw him enter the snake-infested swamp with two torches and a machete.

The scoutmaster stopped after fifty metres. He smelt 'an odd odour – sharp and pungent' (possibly ozone) and nearly lost consciousness. The air temperature also seemed to have risen. Heading east, he stopped at a clearing, where it felt 'oppressively moist, making it hard to breathe', and his skin began to prickle and tingle. Looking skywards, he saw a hugh dark mass and lit it with his torch. It was dome-shaped and slightly concave in the centre and had a circle of spokes or vanes emerging from the middle. From the base a ball of red fire or sparks descended towards him and expanded into a red cloud. He dropped all he was carrying, to protect his face, then he became unconscious.

The police found the man in a dazed state with the still lit torch discarded on the ground. The other torch and machete were never traced. An area of grass was also discovered pressed down hard and flat beneath where the mass had hovered. In the car returning to town, it was found that there were small burns on the arms and face of the scoutmaster, and tiny single holes in his peaked cap. An Air Force surgeon checked him in daylight as he awaited interrogation. This man found mild sunburn like skin effects and singed hair 'indicating a flash heat'.

Thirty-six hours after the incident the area was gone over with a geiger counter. There was also no burning evident within the flattened grass. The USAF lab analyzed soil and grass samples from the site and wanted to know how the surface blades were unscathed and not heated, but the roots were *charred*. The USAF speculated about there being pipes laid under the swamp, but this sounds like the effect of induction heating from some ionizing radiation (similar to the way in which microwaves cook food inside, leaving the outside untouched).

The witness later told ufologists that whilst he was under the mass, 'I was absolutely paralysed. I could not move a muscle ... [the thing] made a slight hissing sound similar to air escaping from a compressed area.'

As a further clue, the Center for UFO Studies catalogue of trace reports from Ted Phillips records two other interesting events within a week. At 5.35 a.m. on 25 August in the small town of Pittsburg, Kansas, a blue glow was seen to rise from a field, making a noise 'like a covey of quail'. A mass of weeds and grass displayed the effects of having been blown over as a result. And two days later, at Lumberton, North Carolina, another blue glow with coloured sparks from the underside climbed upwards at 12.50 a.m., rotating as it did so. A similar area of depressed grass was found beneath the point of departure.

Premanon, France, 1954

Four children of the Romand family were puzzled when a dog started to bark at 8.30 p.m. on 27 September. By their barn was a glowing mass; it was still. One boy threw pebbles and was suddenly knocked to the floor by an 'invisible force'. A luminous red ball was now seen moving away. Next day police found an oval of grass that was flattened in an anti-clockwise swirl and which was sharply delineated. It measured four metres in diameter and had some holes in the centre. A flagpole outside the circle was damaged, with bark torn off the wood – suggesting considerable force.[24]

Near Vaddo, Upland, Sweden, 1958

At dusk on 16 November two men in a car suddenly noticed that their engine and lights failed. A circle of blue light with a yellow rim swooped down nearby and then climbed up again and vanished. The car engine now started again, but they stopped and got out. At the spot on which the thing had 'landed', they felt the air was 'close' and 'heavy' and saw that an area of grass was 'pressed down or blown down'. A flat stone from this depression felt warm to the touch.[25]

Hubbard, Oregon, USA, 1964

At 7.30 a.m. on 18 May Michael Bizon saw a small silver object zoom up from a wheat field. It made a 'beep' noise and issued a smell like gas fumes. Inspection of the field revealed three circles of flattened wheat that were about one metre in diameter and approximately one metre apart from one another.[26]

Delroy, Ohio, USA, 1965

On 26 June elderly farmer Joseph Stavano heard a mysterious explosion whose origin he never traced. Two days later, whilst cutting hay, he found an area of wheat field oddly damaged. An eight-metre diameter circle was nearly denuded of crop, with patches where it had been pulled out by some force. The very centre had just bare earth. Stubble and wheat fragments were scattered over the surface. Outside this circle of destruction was an outer ring some four metres wide where the wheat was undamaged but flattened 'like spokes in a wheel'.[27]

Chapeau, Canada, 1969

On 11 May Leo Paul Chaput, a pulp-mill worker, saw a bright light hovering over a field. Next day four circles were found depressed into the grass (?). One of these was a half-circle, two others were ringed circles, diameters ten metres and eight metres with ring width of just under one metre. The smallest circle was three metres in diameter and was not ringed.[28]

Ibiuna, Brazil, 1969

Andrews and Delgado record the primary event but surprisingly omit the most important sequel.

Initially at 2 a.m. on 17 June a man and wife saw a bright curved oval glowing 'like mercury lamp' with vertical 'bars'. It hovered for forty-five minutes, projecting a beam of light into trees, then vanished. In daylight an eight-metre diameter circle of flattened vegetation was found swirled anti-clockwise.

Nine days later, at 2.30 p.m. the local justice of the peace in the same area heard a sound 'like the humming of a swarm of bees' and saw an object 'rocking from side to side'. This fell out of the sky into bushes and then took off as he approached. He was knocked off his feet by a terrific blast of wind at this departure, and another flattened circle and broken tree branches were discovered at the 'landing' spot.[29]

Near Garrison, Iowa, USA, 1969

This is another case referenced by Andrews and Delgado and which appears to be inaccurate. They cite their source as a book called *Life in Space* published in 1979, but we have found several much earlier and first-hand accounts. It was investigated at the time both by APRO (an erstwhile American group) and by the J. Allen Hynek Center for UFO Studies.

At 11 p.m. on 13 July two teenagers, Patti Barr and her cousin Kathy Mahr, heard a screaming, roaring noise whilst they were upstairs in their house at Van Horne. They briefly observed a dull grey, Saturn-shaped mass ringed around the middle by reddish glows which was rotating anti-clockwise. It took off at great speed, and a red glow was temporarily left on the field.

Next morning at breakfast they told Warren Barr, and he checked his soya beans. A twelve-metre diameter circle of denuded plants was found, although there was no trace of heat or flames. The leaves were 'hanging wilted and dehydrated', according to Ted Phillips from his inspection, but 'The plants surrounding the area were normal.' The damaged plants dried up and died.

Andrews and Delgado, apparently referring to the same case, give the date as the 12th, do not refer to the UFO sighting (which appears to be a classic vortex), say that heat was the suspected cause and describe the size as 120 metres, ten times the size quoted in both independent reports that we have studied.[30]

Lynchford, Tasmania, Australia, 1971

Mr C. Archer was woken up at 2 a.m. on 25 May by his dogs yelping and barking. A strange humming noise 'like a big, loud generator' was heard. He looked outside but saw nothing. Then the noise ceased.

Next day on waste ground an elliptical area of grass and blackberries, measuring some nine metres by five metres was found flattened. In the centre was a 'spiral pattern'. The land had last been seen on the 24th, when it was undamaged. On the 27th the family's healthy four-month-old kitten died. The police even performed an autopsy, as its presence outside during the events suggested a possible cause. No cause of death was found![31]

Wellington, New Zealand, 1972

The *Wellington Times* of 6 October reported how on the night of 1 October Henry Thomas and family heard a 'strange noise' and next day found a field of grass flattened into a circle of about nine metres.

Rosmead, South Africa, 1972

An impressive case, well known within the UFO archives but with a whole new interpretation thanks to Terence Meaden's theories.

At 8.25 p.m. on 12 November the headmaster of a primary school in the Karoo came home after a trip to see a light beaming onto the school's tennis courts. (Meanwhile some soldiers at a nearby camp had seen red lights rotating in a circle and debated, for fear of ridicule, whether to speak up.) The headmaster reached the court and discovered severe damage. Sergeant Goosen was called in to investigate the 'vandalism' and found no hint of this – the court was securely locked. Major inquiries achieved no success. Police chief B.I. van Heerden told investigator Cynthia Hind some years later that it remained 'the most puzzling case in his career'.

The damage comprised five holes about one metre in diameter and other smaller holes, where the tarmac had been literally torn up by a great force. Pieces of tarmac were found a long way outside the court, some imbedded firmly into a garage wall! And trees beside the court showed some sign of heat effects. Extensive police investigation at the time concluded that the destruction was due to a downward force. A scientist at Witwatersrand University said that a whirlwind might have descended onto the court. But this was late evening, the weather was warm and dry, and he could not account for the strange heating effects that singed nearby trees.

High Point, North Carolina, USA, 1974

At 10 p.m. on 23 March two men were driving down May Road toward Highway 109. They saw a triangle of pink lights that descended towards fields and became more red on doing so. Next morning they returned to the site and found a classic crop-circle triplet in the grass. The central one was the largest and most strongly depressed (diameter about three metres). The two satellites were a few metres either side and a little less notable. The grass was depressed and some blades were broken. Interestingly there was also some even less obvious damage (slight bending of grass) trailing off to either side of the smaller satellites in a straight line.

This appears to be prime evidence of how a descending vortex can produce a triplet of circles, with its energy strength decreasing the further away from the centre it gets. In grass the resistance was sufficiently low to leave this evidence visible, whereas in crops the reduced force outside the (less-marked) outer satellites was presumably not great enough to cause damage to the stronger, more resistant cereals.[32]

Langenburg, Saskatchewan, Canada, 1974

Yet another case reported by Andrews and Delgado with crucial data missing – and for which they quote no reference. We refer to a personal investigation by Ted Phillips of the Center for UFO Studies which is most interesting, to say the least.

It was 11 a.m. on 1 September, when Edwin Fuhr observed five small domes above a crop of – A & D say 'rape', Phillips 'grass'. They were causing motion in the 'grass' through 'wind'. It was a dull day with light wind, and a faint drizzle was falling. Each dome rotated very swiftly near ground-level, then ascended rapidly into cloud venting white vapour. Upon their departure a massive blast of wind from each dome flattened the crop below.

Marks were found at each of the five spots. Andrews and Delgado term these 'five circles of clockwise spiralled plants'. According to Phillips, they were much more interesting than that: 'Five *rings* were found, arranged in a semi-circle; four were three metres in diameter, one two metres. Grass was not disturbed in the centres while flattened in a clockwise pattern in the rings.'[33]

Salto, Uruguay, 1977

At 4 a.m. on 18 February rancher Angel Maria Tonna, his family and farmhands observed strange lights. They were herding cows when the generator-powered lights on the barn failed. The rancher and his three-year-old police dog, Topo, went to investigate the Saturn-like mass which glowed orange.

Cows were running wild and farm dogs barking furiously. The glow was lighting up the barn, and the thing was rocking from side to side, generating a wind that was strong enough to tear branches off neighbouring trees. Poor old Topo flew towards the hovering mass to 'attack' but froze in his tracks and began to howl when within five metres. Six beams of 'white lightning' now streaked from the underside into the ground, and Tonna – further away than his dog – was struck by a wave of heat and electrical tingles strong enough to term shocks. He was also paralysed. The glow now turned red and shot away. As it did so, the generators started but the lights still did not come on. All the wiring was burnt out. The dog stayed in all the next day and refused to eat. Tonna had a severe skin rash that persisted some days. At the site where the trees were broken there was a circle ten metres in diameter flattened and singed into the grass.

Three days later Topo was found dead at the exact spot where the thing had hovered. An autopsy by the local vet found that the animal had been 'cooked' by internal heating (microwaves? infra-red radiation?), and its blood vessels had ruptured.

10   What UFOs Really Are

Throughout this book we have said many times that ufology dwells under a delusion that aliens riding spaceships are here. This dominates the phenomenon and denies it scientific respectability. However, we have also said that there is a sensible side to UFO research. So what is it?

This chapter will examine some of the serious work that is presently in hand. There is a sort of quicksand of wild ideas, but there are also some logical and exciting theories to account for the data. In fact, Dr Meaden's concept has some important precedents which bear contemplation.

Meteorology

We were quite surprised to discover that an idea very similar to his vortex theory was published in BUFORA's own magazine some years before the crop circles first came to light. The concept featured in two articles by meteorological commentator G. Burrows.

In his first piece, published in 1974, he noted: 'The writer's experience with the characteristics of an electrical discharge in a vacuum leads him to believe that the nature and behaviour of UFOs can be explained in terms of known physical phenomena.'[1] He discussed how 'troughs of low pressure' in the atmosphere and other instances (for example eddy whirlpools) are evidence of '... vortex motion which can occur spontaneously under suitable conditions ... In certain cases a cylindrical hollow may form inside the vortex in which the value of the pressure may become very small ... [or] a partial vacuum.'

Burrows then referred back to research he had first reported in 1943 regarding the passage of electrical charge through such a vacuum. He had found that a mixture of air and water vapour at very low pressure produces ionized gases and '... can give rise to an accumulation of negative electrical charges in one part of the atmosphere and positive charges in another.' In fact, the breakdown in the atmosphere between these two can – in extreme, thunderstorm conditions – produce what we call lightning.

His speculation was that UFOs were ionized vortices which glowed different colours according to chemical composition of air but were (presumably) not at sufficient levels to generate lightning bolts. The presence of such hypothetical phenomena would, Burrows said, be demarked by floating, glowing masses that followed prevailing air currents; they would '... interfere strongly with radio receivers and motor car ignition systems, because the ionized gas would activate the emission of electromagnetic radiation covering a wide range of frequencies', thus producing electrical noises such as crackling, and would be attracted or repulsed by sources of electromagnetic and electrostatic energy in the environment (for example, radio masts, pylons and metallic bodies such as cars). He went even further, postulating that the puzzling 'angel hair' (or spiders' web as alleged) was really fine snow produced within the vortex by condensation of water vapour and that electrostatic attraction of dust and debris into the vortex might coalesce into shapes which could look like alien pilots (or, we might add from the data in this book, dark blotches mistaken for windows).

In many ways this was well ahead of its time. It gained little support. Although Scottish ufologist Steuart Campbell later conducted various personal investigations for BUFORA in such terms, he too was largely ignored.

In response to criticism, Burrows wrote what appears to have been his last word on the subject.[2] Along with this was a photograph of a tornado funnel and also one of a glow which the writer thought might be an ionized vortex over Guildford, Surrey. This picture from 1968 was taken – coincidentally, we presume – by none other than what seems to be the same David Simpson from the Surrey group soon to carry out the Warminster hoax photo experiment!

This new article refers readers to the 24 January 1975 issue of *Nature* in regard to research into 'trailing vortices' created by aircraft passage. Burrows also recognized one of Dr Meaden's most crucial points which is summarily dismissed even today by many critics of the vortex theory of circle formation. He notes:

'Vorticity is a fairly common phenomenon, which can occur anywhere both before and after sunset and during both summer and winter ... a tornado is an extreme development which occurs only rarely.'

He further rejects claims that his theory would work only under extreme thunderstorm conditions, by reporting that, 'A build up of an electrical charge in the atmosphere can occur even though the sky is almost free from cloud cover ... It is evident that ionization of air can occur anywhere at any time, and in many instances may be excited by X-rays and gamma rays from outer space, or by radioactive radiation and emanation from the earth.' As for the shape of the ionized glow, this would be less constrained in the atmosphere than it would inside a laboratory. It will '... assume a shape determined by the relative strengths of the moving electric charge and of the surrounding magnetic field ... [i.e.] cigar-shaped, cup-shaped, or saucer-shaped'.

Terence Meaden considers it important that someone independently reached these conclusions. Remember, Burrows was looking at UFOs without any awareness of crop circles, whereas Meaden researched crop circles and found that his data circumstantially supported a UFO field of which he did not know.

This link between UFOs and atmospheric conditions is something that has been looked at from time to time. There has been research showing possible correlations between UFO activity and sunspot maxima (when there is increased ionization in the atmosphere). Ufologists such as Delair and Vallée have examined the curious relationship between UFOs and clouds. Another interesting experiment was carried out in the USA by MUFON Central States Director Dan Wright, who attempted to find a pattern in the weather conditions when local UFO sightings occurred. For this he used 396 cases from the state of Michigan between 1947 and 1977, with precise date and time.[3]

Wright had co-operation from Mark Rodeghier (scientific co-ordinator of the J. Allen Hynek Center for UFO Studies) and Dr Fred Nurnberger, a climatologist from the state university. It should be added that the 396 cases were extracted from a base of a thousand reports to reduce the level of IFOs (identified flying objects) in the sample. Weather data came from ten major stations and 150 secondary reporting sources, so it can be termed 'localized' in every case.

Probably the most interesting result was the discovery that rain fell within twelve hours of more than forty per cent of all cases (up to 44.7 per cent in the period May to October). Indeed, as Wright himself pointed out, since people would tend to be indoors and less likely to see UFOs during wet weather, such discoveries are even more significant than they seem. The most common occurrence was for rain to occur *before* the sighting, so that UFOs tended to appear in the clearing conditions *after* a rain spell. This is consistent with examples we have seen in this book, where we noted a suggested link between UFOs and clearing weather depressions.

Energy

One other way in which weather has previously been associated with UFOs is through the strange meteorological phenomenon of ball lightning. In the next chapter we shall meet several cases reported as UFOs but which may well be some form of ball lightning. So what exactly is this and why should it be related to ufology?

In truth, scientists are still struggling to comprehend what is often seen as a floating mass of glowing energy. There is a tendency to assume that ball lightning occurs only during thunderstorms, and indeed for many years science rejected the occasional eyewitness accounts on the grounds that they were just misperceptions of bright lightning bolts. Perhaps, it was argued, the image persisted on the retina and made a phantom ball appear to dance around the sky.

Ralph Noyes, one of the modern ufologists who has turned the focus of his attention toward crop circles, has already entertained us with a novel in which he suggested that UFOs were an energy phenomenon.[4]

In one non-fiction article he discusses scientific research into ball lightning and notes that, since it became legitimized during the 1960s (due to one manifesting before scientists!), we have a dilemma. There are cases in which these floating energy balls have melted oven gloves, exploded a fly-swatter when one ball was mistaken for a fly and boiled off eighteen litres of water when a sample fell into a rain barrel.[5] He further cites scientists who found that in some cases huge energy levels were needed to explain the effects, whereas in others only trivial levels were involved. We know this since witnesses suffer effects but not the horrendous effects that would certainly have occurred from close proximity to the sort of energy levels we might otherwise presume. This discrepancy – or 'paradox', as Noyes calls it – is just what we find in UFO encounters. All scientific efforts to reproduce electrical malfunction fail, because truly enormous energy levels are required and there is good evidence (from other aspects of the case data) that these huge levels simply cannot have occurred – or the witness would have been fried![6]

It is also interesting to note that some of the physiological effects described by eyewitnesses of 'ball lightning' are similar to those in UFO 'close encounters'. One interesting example is the burning of a finger due to excessive heat within a wedding ring, which when reported in a UFO case led to speculation about eddy currents in the metal from 'UFO' radiation.

Paul Davies is a professor of theoretical physics at Newcastle University. His popular books on energy physics and quantum mechanics make him a familiar media commentator. He has some interest in UFOs, and he is another physicist who has recognized the importance of trying to understand ball lightning. He points out that, 'In spite of the name there is no clear link between ball lightning and ordinary lightning. True, most sightings of ball lightning occur during thundery weather, but not always in conjunction with a conventional lightning strike. And fair weather balls are by no means uncommon.'[7]

Davies discusses some of the many theories that have been proposed in recent years to explain ball lightning. These have a familiar ring to them, in that they range across a wide spectrum, including anti-matter particles, cosmic radiation reactions and controlled ionized plasmas. This last option is what makes ball lightning research so exciting, because physicists struggling to make nuclear fusion a reality (and so to realize the long-awaited dream of cheap and unlimited power) know that the key lies in finding a way to stabilize this notoriously unstable state of matter called a plasma. Ball lightning *may* be an example of such stability already at work within nature. Hence its understanding may prove vitally important.

The ball-lightning hypothesis has been used to explain UFOs by Philip Klass, an electronics graduate who is now an aviation and space journalist in Washington and a leading debunker of the UFO subject.

Klass is widely viewed in American ufology as Public Enemy

Number One. Jenny Randles has met him and disputes that judgement, although it is probably connected with his tendency to rebuke others and make strange gestures, such as offering large sums of money if anybody will prove to his satisfaction that UFOs exist. Although Klass's books on the subject have been an important critical contribution (something ufology attracts too infrequently – bar useless, sweeping dismissals), at times he presumes too much from too few examples.

In 1968 he published his first book, in which he suggested that the few unexplained UFO reports were the product of plasma balls or ball lightning.[8] Although he seems to have gone away from this position somewhat (charging evidence distortion and inevitably gaining the wrath of American ufology), history may show him to be at least partly correct.

We do believe that, when this phenomenon is eventually understood, it is virtually certain that some UFO reports will turn out to be forms of ball lightning. Whether this is in any way related to the Meaden Vortex theory is another matter. It is likely that there is a range of different natural phenomena occurring within our atmosphere for which the term 'UFO' has just become a convenient catch-all. What the research into ball lightning does show is that we have some way to go before we understand all the processes that are occurring within our own natural environment, and this, of course, makes it all the more evident that the ideas of Terence Meaden need consideration

Geology

There is another type of UAP (Unidentified Atmospheric Phenomenon) that has been proposed as a result of investigations into a further sidelight to ufology. French researchers, such as Ferdinand Lagarde, examined the massive wave of sightings in 1954 and discovered as long ago as 1968 that eighty per cent of them occurred in close proximity to a geological fault running underneath the Earth's surface.[9]

In the USA, *avant-garde* researcher John Keel was fuelling his ideas on 'ultra-terrestrials' with comments about energy forces and radiation fields and finding that major sightings sometimes had an odd link with earthquakes. Coincidence, of course – or was it?

Paul Devereux, a British 'earth mysteries' specialist, (editor of *The Ley Hunter* and one of the world's foremost experts in such folklore and supposed earth forces), got together with Andrew York and carried out a test study of UFO sightings in Leicestershire. They published several articles on this work in their magazine in 1975 and demonstrated (to *their* satisfaction, at least) that Lagarde was right. There was a clear relationship between the number of UFO lights dancing across the sky and the presence of geological faults. These are fractures between rocks, often at some depth, and they produce earth tremors when they slip and release the strain and tension built up over time.

Meanwhile a Canadian specialist in psychology and electrical effects on brain chemistry was an unlikely bedfellow. Dr Michael Persinger was interested in whether there might be a relationship between paranormal events (especially lights interpreted as ghosts or UFOs in different eras) and electrical fields which might interact with the brain of a witness to provoke bizarre hallucinations. He conducted a major computer study and published this in 1977 with a colleague, Gyslaine Lafreniere.[10]

This was a most important formulation of what has come to be called the 'tectonic strain theory' for UFO events, for these two Canadian scientists (who were not ufologists, it should be added) had found results similar to those noted by Lagarde and Devereux and had extended this data to develop a specific theory.

They were interested in the well-attested scientific fact that in the period leading up to some major earthquakes strange glows (similar in appearance to aurora) have occurred in the sky. The latter have even been photographed and (unlike UFOs) are not considered to be scientifically taboo, because they do not have bizarre interpretations foisted onto them. The physicists researching these glows had suggested that possibly they were the result of atmospheric ionization created by what is called 'the piezo-electric effect'. This principle is used in some types of battery or lighter systems, generating power by producing strain within a tiny quartz crystal; this causes the atoms to vibrate and squeeze out electrical energy that can trigger the ionization and provide the spark.[11]

Persinger and Lafreniere proposed that a column of invisible ionized air (which they termed a 'transient') might be created by forces within fault zones and float around the atmosphere for brief spells. In some circumstances it could glow through incandescence generated by ionization. If a witness came into close proximity of such a field, he or she could endure physiological effects and would describe these according to their varying distances from the source. Based on their knowledge of electric field effects on brain chemistry, Persinger and Lafreniere knew that these effects were remarkably like those found in UFO cases, including electrical tingling, eye-watering, skin-reddening, headaches and nausea, followed by loss of consciousness and hallucinations at the closest range.

Only a few ufologists were sufficiently free of the lure of the alien spaceship to see the importance of this research. Most dismissed it as another attempt by sceptics to debunk their pet subject into oblivion. But those who recognized the opportunity woke up to great new explorations – just as we now face a brave new dawn, thanks to Terence Meaden.

Paul Devereux was, of course, very alert to the implications of the continuing research of Persinger. He decided to compile all his data into a seminal 1982 book which tried to demonstrate the statistical reality of the geology link from a study of British UFO sightings and fault lines. He coined the term 'Earthlights' to replace Persinger's 'transients'.[12]

There were major criticisms within ufology of Devereux's 'earthlights', some well founded. For example, his statistical data base was weak; he did little to distinguish between the many IFOs and the unexplained cases, thus heavily biasing his sample, and there was little sign that he understood the clear relationship between focal-point ufologists, who attract cases to themselves like a magnet and so artificially enhance the apparent status of a location into a window area. This is just what we see with circles-researchers and the Wessex 'window', although, perhaps the windows attract the active ufologists to them.

Nonetheless, one fascinating result of Devereux's study was the discovery that the 'amber gambler' (nickname of an orange blob seen frequently in the Warminster area) centred on the *only* fault lines in Wiltshire – which passed almost straight through the town and its infamous hills. Although Devereux (even in his later work) has seemingly not taken the crop circles into account, we can smile at the fact that he found a predictable earthlights hot-spot at the very place at which the circles mystery soon came to establish itself!

Within a year, two further books appeared, independent of Devereux.

Yet another non-ufologist, the German biophysicist Dr Helmut

Tributsch, published a remarkable study of strange events associated with earth tremors. In this work, beautifully titled 'When the Snakes Awake',[13] he noted the way in which animals seem to sense the imminent arrival of an earthquake and behave oddly or evacuate the area; this is well supported now by evidence from all over the world.

What Tributsch suggested was that geophysical processes connected with the rocks and fault lines at times of earthquake released electrical charges and ionized gases into the atmosphere. He considered many mechanisms for the process, including piezo-electrical, but he rejected this for limiting reasons that Devereux and others were also beginning to appreciate. Tributsch finally settled on a more complex electro-chemical process.

Whilst he made little mention of strange light phenomena and seemed unaware of Persinger's ideas, Tributsch nevertheless introduced many features into the equation which he had no way of knowing were key aspects of the UFO data. These included gaseous clouds and odours (created by ionization of the various chemicals held in solution within ground rocks) and, of course, the question of the 'animal disturbance' effect which features in so many UFO and circles cases. Without mentioning UFOs, Tributsch showed how dogs, cats and other animals would be more aware of these emissions, due to sensitivity to electrostatic fields, stronger nasal abilities and proximity to the ground closer than that of human beings. Hence it is perfectly understandable why animals should react to an ionized vortex, transient or earthlight before any far less sensitive human might. Indeed animals are now used as earthquake alarms in some cultures!

The other book was written by Jenny Randles.[14] It began as an account of the Alan Godfrey abduction case from Todmorden, West Yorkshire, and expanded to include the extraordinary wealth of cases in the Pennine area. During her research the Persinger results were discovered, and it became increasingly clear that his ideas fitted perfectly with this 'case study' of one 'window'. There was even an earth tremor in April 1982 centred on the Craven Fault (passing right through the heart of a series of light phenomena). The final ten pages of Jenny's book were full of clues discovered from the dozens of first-hand cases she had cited. It is obvious in retrospect that they match the concept of an ionized form in the atmosphere tied in, perhaps, with the fault lines of the area.

Devereux had had little access to cases from northern Britain and in his book reported on a curious anomaly. There was one area in which the geological conditions were optimum and there should be a UFO window. But he had not found one there. He had no idea that Jenny was at that moment producing a book about this precise location (the Pennine foothills), recognizing it *as* a window from the data! Can this be coincidence? Surely not. It seems to show – yet again – that there *must* be substance in this claim of a direct causal relationship between atmospheric ionization, geological processes and UFOs.

Should meteorology be viewed as a separate issue or is it all part of one picture? At this stage we cannot be certain. There is scope for several different types of UAP within the overall UFO phenomenon. But they could be inter-related. Certainly it is worth noting that in their 1977 book Persinger and Lafreniere commented that their transients had a tendency to manifest near hills and that the passage of weather systems (for example, low-pressure masses) seemed to act as a trigger for the UAP to form. As these are so strongly in line with Dr Meaden's work, we must look at the options.

We await a new book from Persinger which we hope will not be too long in coming, but he has written widely in the UFO literature. Devereux has come up with a new title, far superior to his 1982 offering, being in our opinion one of the more important UFO titles published in recent years. He had a good deal of help in its production. Dr Paul McCartney (a geochemist) has contributed greatly to the theoretical search for the right electro-chemical trigger mechanism. And David Clarke and Andy Roberts add a chapter on the research into 'Project Pennine', picking up on and greatly expanding the fieldwork reported in Jenny's 1983 book. More importantly still, Devereux has been able to call on researchers worldwide to include status reports and many photographs proving that earthlights *are* indeed manifesting on a regular basis in window areas scattered towards all four corners of the planet.

Yet, perhaps even more dramatic still, he can report on (and include photographs of) research that has been conducted at the US Bureau of Mines in the appropriately named Boulder, Colorado (by Dr Brian Brady) and in London (by McCartney, Devereux and others). These have placed the same sort of rocks found at UFO windows under the same kind of strain induced by local fault lines and filmed exactly what results through high-speed cameras. The rock is gradually crushed, and mini-earthlights just like those reported in the sky are indeed produced.[15]

There is some way to go to bridge the gap between small and very short-lived flashes of light in the laboratory and those massive glowing shapes floating around the skies above window areas. Some responsible critics, such as specialist Chris Rutkowski, are proposing intelligent tests to answer remaining questions. However, the results to date from such a short period of research have been so spectacular and continue at such a pace that they easily dwarf any progress (if indeed there has been *any* progress!) claimed by those ufologists who are clinging on to the sinking ship the SS *Alien Delusion*.

Paul Devereux additionally proposes that witnesses might use extra-sensory perception to mould the shape of the ionized phenomenon into the likeness of a spaceship or alien. It would be foolish to deny this out of hand. Jenny had developed her own research into the Persinger and Devereux work by analysing reports of various claims about 'monsters', to see how they might fit the concept of an ionized field shaped by imagination.[16] However, it is premature, to say the least, to resort to the supernatural when we have come so far in our efforts to explain what is going on strictly within the confines of acceptable science. Such a concept is best kept on the back burner for the time being.

This relationship is perhaps pointing the way to yet another benefit that might emerge from ufology: a way in which to predict and possibly to prevent terribly destructive earthquakes.

It seems possible that the strain is 'leaking' slowly in some areas (and producing strange light phenomena), whereas in others it more often builds up and then releases in one major burst of earth-shaking power. If we understand the difference, we might find a way to turn earth tremors into spectacular lightshows – and to save lives!

Neurology

Michael Persinger has followed his own direction with his latest research. Having established that transients exist, he is now more concerned with demonstrating what they can do to percipients who get close to them. This has meant a concentration on ultimate 'close encounters' (in which alien contact is alleged) in preference to mere light phenomena. However, Persinger is convinced that they are connected in some way. He says of these 'visitor' experiences: 'We have strong, although inferential, evidence that [they] are associated with special kinds of electrochemical activity within the deep structures of the temporal lobes of the human brain. These portions of the brain are associated with the experience of meaningfulness, the sense of self and its relationship to space-time (which invariably invokes religious or cosmic associations), memory storage and retrieval, dreams, experiences of movement (like spinning or floating), smell, fear and images of internal organs.'[17] Persinger now believes that witnesses who report the closest encounters tend to be of a specific group, with advanced responses from their temporal-lobe regions. Much independent research within ufology has discovered trends that show that such people tend to be artistic and have good visual imagery and 'quiet' tendencies (which all fit the Persinger predictions).[18]

New clues are turning up all the time, such as the recent recognition that close-encounter witnesses tend to have excellent recollection of very early childhood (for example, describing life in their prams!). This is such a peculiar discovery, of no obvious relevance, that the fact that it is also one of the signs of enhanced temporal-lobe activity reported by Persinger may be important.

This all matches the Oz Factor state of consciousness in UFO encounters: a loss of contact with the real world, inward focusing, distortion of sense of time and place and other symptoms. And this is not restricted to UFO cases. It seems to be a part of other 'paranormal' experiences (such as ghost-sightings). We can examine such bizarre cases in terms of brain chemistry and interaction with electrical fields and come up with results that are strikingly similar to those discussed in this book.[19]

There is a gathering momentum within serious UFO circles that the areas just outlined are the way ahead, although Rutkowski amongst other critics still makes worthwhile points – such as asking why intense magnetic fields (for example, when travelling on the subway) do not cause hallucinations.[20]

Dr Kenneth Ring of the University of Connecticut has been one of the leading scientists studying the curious psychological phenomenon of the 'near death experience' (in which people who come close to death in accidents or surgery – and *without* the intervention of drugs – claim to experience oddly consistent visionary phenomena).[21] Now Ring has discovered a possible relationship between this unusual state of mind and alien contact experiences and has begun to probe ufology with the enthusiasm of a schoolboy discovering a new toy (a description that seems to typify many scientists who suddenly become ufologically enlightened!). From this has emerged what Ring calls an 'imaginal' theory, explaining UFO encounters as strange visionary events.[22]

Of course, all this revisionism is reaping its reward in terms of anger and frustration from the diehard ufologists. But such a level of intensity and emotional rebellion against the work does rather hint that at some inner level there might be a glimmer of awareness that this is indeed a serious challenge to the dominance of those much vaunted but highly elusive alien monsters.

To us, what is most important is that the groundwork for serious and truly scientific study of UFOs has been laid, and the ideas of Terence Meaden can now find their own level within it. Ultimately they will stand or fall upon their merits, but they are assured of some encouragement from researchers who have been thinking along similar lines for some while.

And if it is true that ufology might pave the way towards new energy forces, cracking the riddle of controlled nuclear fusion and possibly preventing earthquakes, then – aliens or no aliens – this subject has earned its place within our future, with strong scientific potential.

11   The Death of the UFO

For some years we have both followed the trail of exciting research that has been outlined in the previous chapters, believing that we were saving the UFO field from irrelevancy. More than once we have said that the crop circles are *not* caused by UFOs and that a large part of our zeal in fighting the media myth has been designed to preserve this segregation.

It seems that we must now admit a mistake. The work of those researchers into earth energies and, more recently, the masterful analysis by Terence Meaden persuade us that there *is* a link – and a vital one. The atmospheric forces creating the crop circles *can* also produce UFO reports.

Of course, as you have seen in this book, our defensive strategy was dictated by the need to argue that crop circles are *not* associated with UFOs in the popular sense (that is, as products of alien intelligence).

However, whilst many commentators, let alone ufologists, will perhaps agree with us that some of the thousands of UFO reports may possibly be caused by natural phenomena, few would even consider the idea that *every single one of them* might be. Once we sift through the unexplained UFOs and apply our new-found thinking, there will be no such UFOs left at all!

This is an extreme position to adopt. Let us see if it is justified.

We shall look at the spectrum of UFO evidence from the simplest cases to the most complex. If all such seemingly baffling reports do stand up to the Meaden Vortex theory and offer clear signs of a consistent pattern, we are well on the way to demonstrating that this *is* the answer.

Lights in the Sky

LOW-DEFINITION CASES

Despite the stories that you read in the tabloid press, the average UFO report is not a 'close encounter'. More than three-quarters of the sightings on the BUFORA data base (some 20,000 cases filed in the past thirty years) are nothing but lights in the sky. They nearly always prove to be explicable.

Well over nine out of ten are shown to be IFOs, and have nothing to do with novel phenomena. The diligent investigator will discover that they are aircraft lights, satellites, balloons or more bizarre possibilities (for instance, we have had owls glowing in the dark through ingested fungi and 'masquerading' as dazzling UFOs!). As time goes by, technology brings new options. For example, laser light shows reflecting off cloud miles from source are one current bane and the mid 1980s have introduced test flights of stealth aircraft, with sleek designs and quiet engines; serious UFO files have shown an increasing number of cases in which the evaluation eventually came down to 'probably' this secret technology. The same cases, viewed quite differently by the diehard school of ufology, may get published as 'probable spaceship'.

Sometimes that resolution is precisely what UFOs are! On New Year's Eve 1978 tens of thousands of people in northern Europe reported an object trailing across the sky. This *was* a spaceship – a Soviet one – re-entering the atmosphere in spectacular fashion. It was Cosmos 1068 burning up as its orbit decayed.[1]

Misidentifications can pose real dilemmas. Often there is no question that the witness *is* a rational, intelligent person, describing what he saw fairly well. But surprisingly large numbers of people have little idea what is visible in the heavens.

What sort of lights in the sky are left after weeding out the IFOs? The following cases offer clear evidence about novel atmospheric phenomena.

Yorkshire, 1980

Many stories emerge from those locations where UFOs are far more common than chance should dictate. We call them 'window areas'. The balls of light that dominate 'windows' (for example, the Marfa region of Texas, and the Hessdalen Valley in Scandinavia) are very unlikely candidates for intelligent craft.

One of the major 'hot spots' is the Ilkley Moor/Wharfedale region of Yorkshire. Here is a typical case from late November 1980.

The location was Otley Chevin and it was 3.30 a.m. A man was on his way to work (with the post office) when he saw a glowing egg shape heading south-west over the River Wharfe and drifting towards the moors. It was greyish-green inside but orange on the outside. It made crackling sounds 'as if it were surrounded by lightning'. The treetops over which it passed glowed orange, suggesting it was low down. The 'egg' disappeared upward, toward cloud. The man immediately reported it to Otley police, who advised that a patrol car had seen and followed the same puzzling light that morning.

This report came years late, when by pure chance the witness sat next to UFO investigator Nigel Mortimer at a lecture. Nigel had become interested in the subject on 23 November 1980, when he lived at Otley and (in a completely independent observation of perhaps the same thing) saw an egg shape at 1.10 a.m. Reports say that police near Harrogate had chased a light that day, increasing the chances that all these things refer to the same event. Yet another independent report is on file for 1 a.m. at Burley in Wharfedale, where a woman reported an oval with dark central patches.

These few days in November 1980 generated many other cases.

The flap culminated on 28 November (once again in the early pre-dawn hours) with an 'alien abduction' at Todmorden (see p. 214).

To deny that these cases offer hard evidence of something extraordinary, you would have to charge a great conspiracy between unrelated witnesses. The Wharfedale events alone show that something odd was occurring in the atmosphere. Indeed, there are frequent reports from these window areas of glows, strange 'lightning' and other evidence of atmospheric ionization around the time when UFOs are seen.[2]

There are excellent grounds for the belief that at certain periods (for example, 23–28 November 1980) atmospheric phenomena of perhaps several types are triggered into existence – and often congregate in those 'windows'. The evidence supports this, but not the contention that these reports refer to spaceships or intelligences. Skilled investigators who devote most of their time to turning UFOs into IFOs are satisfied that these are genuine 'unknowns'.

If this were the only evidence, it would be compelling, but, as you will see, it is by no means the only evidence.

In our opinion, the facts are clear. We need scientists who are specialists in atmospheric physics and meteorology to work with the information and seek out the common factors during these 'waves' or 'flaps'. We are convinced that such scientists will be able to discover the triggers which lead to the atmospheric ionization effects – producing UFOs, be they Devereux earthlights, Persinger transients or Meaden Vortices (or even all three).

To pretend that there is no scientific data within these cases is an error, just like the false assumptions rife within the UFO community and media that the stories reflect alien technology. They do not: they reflect scientific processes that are not yet fully understood.

The Yorks/Lancs Moors, 1988
We have cases that offer more details about the structure of these natural phenomena (which we prefer to call UAP, because 'Unidentified Atmospheric Phenomena' presumes less than the spaceship imagery which 'UFO' conjures up). In Hessdalen, Norway, excellent detailed coloured photographs have been taken by scientific research teams in sub-zero conditions, expecting to find UAP there, because they are so commonplace.[3] (see Plate 9) We also have some photographic evidence from a university expedition to the Brown Mountain area of Missouri,[4] and scattered photographs from the Pennine valleys of the Lancashire/ Yorkshire/Derbyshire area.[5]

Considering the ease of access to these British moorlands (several major universities within fifteen kilometres, reasonably hospitable climate even in winter, etc.), it is astonishing that no scientific monitoring of the extremely active Pennine window has yet occurred. This, we are certain, is only because science is scared off by the alien delusion that ufology represents. It ought to be relatively simple to find the correct atmospheric conditions and other factors which cause windows to trigger. A team from Manchester, Leeds or Sheffield University, for instance, could be ready to go out and monitor sites when meteorologists and atmospheric physicists advise them of developing conditions. We would happily pledge our assistance.

We do not mind making some perhaps reckless predictions about such an experiment (which would not be costly and would attract many student volunteers, given the nature of the work!). We believe that it would very quickly establish solid, scientific proof that strange processes occur in these locations – processes which can be scientifically recorded, observed and photographed.

A good case that offers some new insights comes from 4 February 1988, when a woman was driving across the eight kilometres of deserted moorland between the small towns of Bacup, Lancashire, and Todmorden, Yorkshire. (Both places are contenders for being the most UFO-haunted spot in Britain, with countless sightings.) At 8.10 p.m. the woman suddenly noticed an orange egg shape (sound familiar?) hovering over Tooter Hill. It was one-third the apparent size of the full moon and was carefully observed against roadside marker posts as it dimmed and descended behind the hill. The most interesting feature is the internal appearance of the egg, which the highly educated woman described as 'like a swirling liquid or fire embers with constantly changing patterns'. This fluidity – which may indicate rotation or even refer to a plasma state within the UAP – has been reported on other occasions by witnesses who got sufficiently close.[6]

Warwickshire, 1977
Here is another interesting feature which is also reported in several cases. It is one more clue about the ionization field that seems to surround these things.

30 December 1977 was cold, with near total cloud cover. At 4.30 p.m. four people at Exhall in Warwickshire saw a golden egg shape appear from the north and hover directly on top of some electricity pylons. As it hovered, it shimmered with a kind of fuzzy haze or aura. After a couple of minutes it shot away at great speed to the west, but – at the precise spot at which it had hovered above the pylons – the overcast sky formed an oval 'clearing' several times the diameter of the egg. It was as if the electrical charge of the phenomenon had ionized the cloud and caused its particles to dissipate by repulsion, leaving a 'hole' that took several minutes to become filled in again.[7]

There is a curious relationship between UFOs and clouds. Some UFOs emerge from out of strange masses in the air or disappear into them, never to return. To the ufologist determined to prove that UFOs are alien, this is an aspect difficult to comprehend. If we are accepting that UFOs are really atmospheric phenomena (UAP), we can readily appreciate why there should be a direct correlation with weather conditions and clouds. After all, most mundane vortices, such as tornadoes, emerge from out of strange dark clouds.

Singapore, 1953

Just one more case will suffice to make the link between UFOs and atmospheric events obvious. We discovered it when Jenny Randles had an article on UFOs published in the *AIR UK* in-flight magazine.

The witness had been with the RAF for twenty-seven years and in 1953 was based at RAF Changi in Singapore. He lived with his wife in a small bungalow at Katong.

One weekend, when another service couple were staying with them, the area was struck by terrific storm. This ceased very dramatically, as if they were in the eye of a hurricane. At that precise time an orange 'cricket ball'-sized sphere appeared nestling on the telephone wires behind the house. It was fuzzy-edged and made a loud hissing or fizzing sound. The object rolled gently along the wires and then curved off, floating through the sky and passing straight through the open louvre-shuttered windows. At this close proximity they could all see that it was really bluish white, with fluidic yellow patches inside (although they are not sure if it was really a different colour when inside the house, and if it was, whether this was due to their ability to see it more clearly there). The ball moved one metre off the ground at slow walking pace and traversed the kitchen. That it was generating electromagnetic or ionizing radiation of some sort is clear for several reasons: as it passed within three metres of the fridge, the motor began to shudder, accelerating and decelerating strangely; also, despite all the house lights being switched off, they glowed a peculiar dull orange whilst the ball was in the house; even the fluorescent strip tube in the kitchen lit up as the thing drifted by.

This UAP was inside for about twenty seconds and then flew in an arc backwards and went out through the same window, disappearing somewhere above the power lines. The four startled witnesses inspected the house but found no damage or scorching to windows or walls. Electrical equipment functioned normally.[8]

In simple terms this is what is called 'ball lightning'. But, as you saw in the last chapter, that is only just becoming legitimized. This is perhaps the one area where meteorology and ufology come into such obvious conjunction. Many people undergoing an experience such as this one at Katong would not know about ball lightning and might well report it in the context of a UFO. Atmospheric physicists miss out on useful data because of this.

The situation is even more problematic, in that the stranger the ball lightning event, the less likely it is to be reported to science, and the more likely that it will be regarded as a UFO by the witness. This biases the samples held by both groups of researchers. Ufologists get the extreme cases, whereas meteorologists may not realize that there *are* any extreme cases. Scientists form conclusions about 'what makes ball lightning' on incomplete data and so deny that cases which fall outside those parameters can be of any substance. Ufologists rarely see the less dramatic stories. Ufology may be full of 'super ball lightning' which science denies because cases were reported as UFOs which it cannot take seriously.

We even have a possible piece of movie film of this sort of UAP. It was taken by building surveyor Peter Day at Cuddington on the Oxfordshire/Buckinghamshire border on 11 January 1973 and contains twenty-three seconds of daylight footage of an orange egg moving low behind trees. There were independent eye-witnesses nearby, and the film has been extensively analyzed. It undoubtedly shows what was seen at the time within the sky.

But what *was* in the sky? There are complicating factors. A US Air Force F-111 jet crashed nearby forty minutes after the film was taken, after developing electrical faults at the moment the UFO film was shot. Do we see here a classic example of a UAP – perhaps a plasma vortex? Indeed, the closest witnesses did say that the object was dome-like and rotated. It was very close to the site of the 1989 Aylesbury quintuplet and to that of another case, in which a car was stalled by the presence of a UFO, so the area seems to be one of our 'windows'. Did the electrical effects of an ionized vortex trigger the plane crash? We do not know. But something odd took place – as the film conclusively proves.[9]

The suspicion that it was 'super ball lightning' emerged early in the investigation (with Kodak's laboratories in Hemel Hempstead expending great efforts on this). When Jenny Randles and a colleague presented the film to a gathering of top atmospheric physicists at a low-key special seminar in September 1978, the consensus opinion was that the phenomenon on the film *was* interesting, that it *was not* ball lightning and that the term UFO seemed apt. However, despite their being offered the film to take back to their labs for detailed analysis, none of the scientists would consider this. The taboo of ufology was too intense, and all seemed to fear the consequence of becoming closet ufologists!

MEDIUM-DEFINITION CASES

It may be easy enough to accept the concept of lights in the sky caused by atmospheric processes, but this solution seems more challenging in the face of 'classic' UFO designs – such as the disc or saucer.

However, this tradition is based upon a fundamental error. The first UFOs over the Cascade mountains of the USA were *not* shaped like saucers: only a journalist's misquote implied that they were. It is true that many witnesses report structured objects (often discs, domes or cigars) behind the phenomena that they observe, but, as many examples in Jenny Randles's earlier books demonstrate, this can also often be shown to be an error.

The cases with very definite structure represent only about a quarter of all sightings. Even then a very high percentage (over nine out of ten) turn out to be mistakes or misperceptions. Some of the common misperceived events do actually have structured shapes (for example, aircraft can look cigar-like when the wings are obscured by reflected sunlight, and weather balloons pear- or teardrop-shaped in the right circumstances). Usually there are not enough resources to check out every option (which takes time and money, when ufology is a hobby and has little of either). Sightings tend to be reported a few weeks or months (indeed, not infrequently years) later, so it can even be impossible to establish a cause. Official records of a myriad options may just not be available.

Additionally, witnesses tend to have the UFO myth so deeply engrained that simple lights are very commonly perceived by them as structured craft that never existed outside their imaginations. The perception system of witnesses uses the UFO stereotype to 'flesh out' lights on aircraft or stars and planets to 'see' an 'object' which is just not there.[10]

In the re-entry of Cosmos 1068, people often described a 'cigar' with windows, when only a train of burning debris was visible. Never having seen a space re-entry before, the witnesses evaluated the visual stimulus in terms of something familiar – an aircraft – and made its height, size and shape 'fit in' through subconscious misperception. Several fire brigades were called out to phantom 'air crashes', and even police and air-traffic controllers made the same mistake and 'saw' the non-existent cigar.

We have noted this process in operation with other large-scale sightings. For example, there has been a spate of in-flight refuelling exercises since the Falklands War of 1982 and the subsequent Libyan raid by USAF aircraft that was launched from Britain by President Reagan. Such operations involve giant tanker aircraft full of fuel and a retinue of smaller jets. The jets fly close to the tankers and are filled up by the use of a line and nozzle from one to the other. This is a precision operation and, because of the risk of collision, usually occurs out at sea and at great height. As a further precaution the aircraft are strung up with an unusual array of dazzling lights to make them impossible to miss.

'Reading in' shapes behind lights clearly appears to be a part of human nature and has nothing to do with intelligence or observational skill. Ancient man saw constellation patterns behind the random groupings of stars, and psychologists use the shapes we see in ink blots as a way to learn about the workings of our mind. In many cases in which we are not able to track back the sighting to its original stimulus the shape that a witness describes has to be treated with considerable caution. Whilst they may well have seen *something*, the 'thing' which they 'thought' they saw stands a fair chance of being far less structured than the one which they describe.

This explains why we have so many reports of structured craft but so few acceptable photographs of the same thing, and why the best photographs that have passed analytical tests turn out to be no more than blobs of unstructured light. This makes sense only if the unexplained UFOs *are* just blobs, whilst shape and artificial design are a product of human perception.

Bear in mind that, if we can see aircraft lights and re-entering space debris and 'read' a false shape behind them, we can do exactly the same with the atmospheric forces or UAP that we are proposing in this book.

However, we must take a look at the most reliable 'structured' cases to find out whether they fit the hypothesis of natural UAP.

South Wales, 1965, and Warwickshire, 1978

In Jenny's first book she described a case reported to her by a middle-aged couple from South Wales.[11] Further details are added by Arthur Shuttlewood in his account (also given to him by the witnesses).[12] Combined, the story described is most intriguing.

It appears to have been about 1965: a warm summer night. The location was a small village called Pyle near Bridgend. It was around 12.15 a.m. and the couple had just put the cat out into beautifully still and overcast conditions. The first odd thing noticed was the condition of the low horizon, which seemed to be covered in a white sparkling or shimmering mist. Then a red light appeared, streaking toward the mist, pulling up just alongside and below it, and 'twinkling' various colours. Next there was an enormous silent explosion, described as like a magnesium flare, though one of the witnesses first thought it was an atomic bomb going off.

Now, low on the horizon, there was a patch of dimming mist that pulsated and expanded/contracted in a rhythm. It split into two bits that were spiralling and rotating in a clockwise direction – 'like two very thick smoke rings' was the description. But it quickly solidified into a 'squashed bowler hat' and then a more classic domed, disc-like UFO. Another telling description of these changes was that they occurred as if the whole thing was shapeless clay on a 'potter's wheel' and was being moulded into a structure by a force exerted as the object rotated. Once it had solidified (still spinning), a series of glowing sparks (red, gold and blue) appeared under the rim of the object – 'like fireworks'. Finally the pulsating light went out, and the object desolidified back into mist which blended into the sky. Only the red light was left, and it moved fast into the sky. During the initial rotation and final disappearance, a noise like a roaring wind or jet was heard by the witnesses.

This case is fascinating for any number of reasons. One can think of no obvious solution in terms of misperception, yet the details match a Meaden Vortex remarkably well. The dark funnel of the vortex, the roaring wind sound, the rotation, solidification, glows produced by ionization and the sparks underneath: note just how many of these features crop up in cases throughout the rest of this chapter and elsewhere in this book. It does appear that a consistent phenomenon of some real type is being described.

This case was first reported long before Terence Meaden developed his ideas, and he appears not to have known about it. Possibly this is one of the earlier good observations of a Meaden Vortex at work. It occurred above a building site, so it is unlikely that a circle would have been left behind. But nobody thought to look for one anyway, because the circles phenomenon was simply not known to exist at the time.

Lest you think we are reading too much into a single case, after the warnings just given, consider the next account, which was reported completely independently of the Welsh encounter and investigated and recorded by the delightfully named UFO group HAPI (Hinckley Aerial Phenomena Investigations) in 1978, more than a year before the Randles/Warrington and Shuttlewood books were published (but well after the Welsh case was reported to those authors).[13]

This incident occurred at Nuneaton in Warwickshire, and we have the added advantage of the precise date and time – 29 May 1978 at 2 a.m. Compare the following details with the account from Pyle, and you will see why we have reason to be excited. Surely the same unusual atmospheric phenomenon is being described in both cases?

A secretary saw a gold 'flare' falling slowly out of the sky. This was joined by a bright light to the east which flew towards the golden ball and 'collided' silently. There was a huge explosion of white light which faded to leave a patch of grey mist. This mist, still low in the sky, began to drift to the north-east but solidified into a hat shape or domed disc which was now inside the grey patch. The whole thing was rotating. Now a curtain of bluish haze appeared underneath the UFO as the cloud drifted out of sight into the distance.

One could postulate needless conspiracies between witnesses to explain away these similarities, but easily the most economical solution is that they saw a real atmospheric event – one which sounds just like a Meaden Vortex. Both these cases occurred in the early hours on a high summer day – precisely when we know circle formation to be at its peak.

Soderbarke, Sweden, 1987
The relationship between UFOs and clouds is a persistent one.

The location of this event was Soderbarke in Sweden. The date 17 April 1987. It was 11 p.m. and a whole group of witnesses from two families were in a house with spectacular views over the South Barken waters. They observed an object like two plates one on top of the other, separated by a line of dark blotches suggestive of windows. The lower portion of the object glowed orange, and the entire thing was surrounded by mist. Indeed, it seemed to be solidifying out of this mist. As it moved low across the waters, it was 'swinging' and 'floating' and also 'wobbled or vibrated'. Eventually it seemed to be swallowed up back into the cloud, leaving just a vague glow for a couple of seconds, then nothing.[14]

Anglesey, 1978

One major question is whether we have any direct links between strange clouds, these odd glowing shapes and crop circles. Indeed we do, thanks to one of the most intensively investigated cases in recent years.

The scene was the mostly rural isle of Anglesey off the north-west coast of Wales. The events of 1 September 1978 centre around the village of Llanerchymedd and began at 5.30 p.m. when two local women claim that the sky seemed very odd. They describe the colour as a peculiar red, and the atmosphere as unusually still and heavy. A single round cloud was almost stationary and looked very black on the underside. Apart from this, the sky was uniform (with, it appears, total cover). This curiosity seemed at the time to have no relevance, and it is fortunate that a full investigation was conducted by Martin Keatman and Derek James, or this aspect might not have been recorded.

Many confusing sightings occurred in the village about two hours later, as darkness descended upon the island. A fair-sized panic ensued. It is likely that some of what transpired was exaggerated (and many of the closest witnesses were young children), but there is enough consistency (especially from adult witnesses) for it to be apparent that some interesting visual phenomena were happening. They appear to boil down to a bullet-shaped object (with the bullet point facing groundwards) surrounded by a red glow and descending slowly. One boy described seeing a 'silent explosion' and the bullet changing into a round patchy light with a darker centre. A woman described the phenomenon as a silvery-white oval that was rotating anti-clockwise.

The phone call which brought the police to the scene was said to have been dogged by unusual crackling and a heavy electrical humming on the line. A later military investigation of the site (although never admitted) seems to have taken place at 1 p.m. the next day, with helicopters circling the fields and a marker flare being dropped.

Some days later a detailed Keatman/James site-investigation revealed a curious set of traces in a barley field. To quote Keatman: 'It looked as though an object had gradually come down into the crop in a west to east direction, eventually coming to a halt and swirling the barley in a clockwise manner. The path was about thirty metres long, and the diameter of the swathed area was some five metres.'[15]

Some controversy developed over this case, with widespread national media publicity rapidly hyping tales of spacemen. Another group of investigators who worked with Keatman and James disputed (probably quite correctly) the literal interpretation of some events, but the details recorded above are those upon which the teams seem to agree.

This group, FUFOR (Federated UFO Research) were convinced that the traces were due to bad weather before their discovery. They sent sketches of the swirled circle of flattened barley to the Cheshire College of Agriculture, which gave a fascinating reply. (Remember, there was no crop circles mystery in 1978.) The College spokesman said:

> I think the reason for the flattened patch of corn would be due to one of two causes, or probably a combination of both. If the affected area was near the field boundary and there was a tree or some similar obstruction in the fence line, the swirling effect of the wind could be sufficient to produce the result you describe. If, on the other hand, the flattening was in the middle of the field, the most likely cause is a 'hotspot', resulting from some topographical factor. The hot air rises, producing a rush of cold air coming in at ground level, sufficient to lay the corn.[16]

We believe FUFOR were right in suggesting that a weather effect was the cause of this crop damage. But we are bound to wonder if it was a rather interesting weather effect – the sort which created the weird atmosphere on the night in question, the strange single cloud that drifted by and the rotating light phenomena perceived by witnesses as a UFO.

Hampshire, 1965, Zambia, 1967, and Cheshire, 1978
Just one further type of 'solid craft' will be described.

At 7 p.m. one evening in early September 1965 a husband and wife and their friend were in their car at Gillkicker Point, Gosport, Hampshire, admiring the view across the Solent toward the Isle of Wight. Suddenly something flew across the sea from the island, and one of the men got out for a closer look. The object was shaped like a bell, was glowing fluorescent green and rotated. Dark blotches round the edges (like windows) and three protrusions on the base were all visible, due to the tilt of the object. These protrusions were three round domes or hemispheres inset into a triangular pattern. Eventually the object vanished.[17]

This event occurred right in the heart of circles territory.

Another case, of seemingly identical nature, comes from Lusaka in Zambia. This was on 22 July 1967 at about 8.30 p.m. and was witnessed by dozens of people at an open-air cinema. A brilliant spotlight blocked the screen, but it was not a thoughtless motorist who was to blame. The glow was coming from a domed object in the sky. There were windows or patches of yellow light round the centre, and the thing made a noise like a 'swarm of bees but with a higher pitch' – loud enough to be heard even above the movie soundtrack. On the base of the dome were 'three ball-like objects'.[18]

Yet another story comes from a highly responsible businessman in Warrington, Cheshire. His wife was putting out the milk bottles at 10.45 p.m. on 28 October 1978 at their bungalow overlooking the Mersey. She saw a strange glow over a power station and electricity pylons and called her husband and two teenaged children. They all watched as the object began to pulsate and then flew right over their heads. It was a dome shape with a flattened base tilted at an angle and with 'three orange bumps inset into the dome in a triangular formation'. It made a faint humming sound.[19]

We could add many cases such as these.[20] Evidently some phenomenon that usually rotates, makes a humming noise, can emit powerful glows and tends to have a triangle of 'bumps' inset within the base is occurring in our atmosphere and cries out for an explanation.

Of course, many of these stories are presumed (by witnesses, media and ufologists) to represent 'craft'. But why? There may be a closer similarity to a multiple funnel tornado, and the three 'bumps' may even correlate with the triplet formation of circles.

Trindade Island, 1958

We even have some interesting photographic evidence concerning 'structured' craft, particularly the series taken aboard a Brazilian naval vessel taking part in the International Geophysical Year project on 16 January 1958. The survey ship was setting up a meteorological station on the uninhabited Trindade Island, several hundred kilometres out into the Atlantic Ocean, when the lens-shaped object flew by.[21] The pictures show a mass surrounded in a haze of cloud, smoke or debris (possibly atmospheric particles, dust or water vapour trapped in an electrostatic or ionizing field). There is also evidence of dark blotches inside the rotating form, and an electrically powered winch being used on the ship at the time failed during the passage of the object (Plate 14).

Again, ufologists tend to view this object as a solid craft and to speculate about its origin. We would argue that it is better to contemplate a rare but natural atmospheric phenomenon as the cause of the event.

We can readily envisage the Trindade Island photographs as potentially important visual evidence of a UAP – and perhaps of a Meaden Vortex.

Close Encounters

Millions of people are familiar with this term, thanks to Hollywood mogul Steven Spielberg. Indeed the 'close encounter' is today one of the most popular phrases in the English language, often applied to a whole host of circumstances which ufology never intended!

In fact, the original derivation of the wording in UFO terms comes from the late Dr J. Allen Hynek. In 1972 he described three categories of 'close encounter' (first, second and third kind) for his seminal book *The UFO Experience*, upon which Spielberg later based his movie *Close Encounters of the Third Kind*.[22]

In 1979 Peter Warrington and Jenny Randles (in consultation with the astronomer) regrouped and extended his classification scheme to add a 'fourth kind' encounter (now also commonly termed 'the abduction report'). [23] Close encounters are now distinguished from ordinary UFO sightings by virtue of the effects reportedly associated with the event. A 'first kind' encounter would include physiological or other effects reported by the witness for which there is no scientifically accessable evidence. A 'second kind' case would require semi-permanent effects – for example, marks on the skin, or a ground trace such as a crop circle. 'Close encounters of the third kind' remain as Hynek originally intended – as observations of reputed alien entities. The 'fourth kind' encounter is the step beyond that – those rare instances when witnesses allege that they go into the UFO, communicate with those entities and (very often) interact directly with them.

Alien contact is another matter. We look here only at close

encounters of the first and second kinds, which relate directly to the crop circles.

Ponder these questions:

Do these consistent reports clearly suggest that something interesting *is* being seen by apparently responsible witnesses?

Do the data also demonstrate that this phenomenon can generate energy in the form of radiation (both visual and electrical – and possibly of other types)?

Are there not clear indications that this seems to tie in with the ideas that Terence Meaden is proposing for a novel atmospheric vortex?

Should we now stop pretending that this evidence says anything – one way or the other – about the existence of life in outer space or of alien intelligences at loose upon the Earth, and realize that it represents a natural, physical process that offers beneficial opportunities to science?

Key West, Florida, USA, 1969

At 11.15 p.m. on 1 January 1969 two witnesses in a car at Key West, Florida (southernmost city in the United States), had a nasty shock.[24] A 'deep' (i.e. resonant) sound overhead was accompanied by a bizarre shower of needle-like hailstones that struck just one very localized spot. They tried to start the car engine and drive away, but it would not turn over. Suddenly a peculiar blast of warm air hit them, and there was a sensation of 'weightlessness' – as in an elevator, along with a feeling of what were termed tingling, electrical vibrations all over their body. Outside there was a silver glow in the sky directly overhead, and 'a tapering funnel-like stream of light' coming down from this. After a few moments the funnel vanished and the sensations disappeared.

This case was reported *as* a UFO and *to* ufologists. But on what grounds do we make such a judgement? This sounds suspiciously like a localized vortex akin to a tornado, accompanied by a short and unusual hailstorm and some peculiar electrical field effects.

USA, 1973 and 1983

One interesting question about the above case concerns the feeling of 'weightlessness' reported by the occupants. A possible explanation for this is that the vortex may have briefly sucked the car up into the air.

For instance, Jennie Zeidman of the Center for UFO Studies did a fine study of a report that a Bell UH-1H Huey helicopter was 'levitated' by a green beam of light.[25] This may be relevant; although we wonder what a close encounter with a Meaden Vortex would do to helicopter rotor blades!

The incident occurred at 11.02 p.m. on 18 October 1973 above Mansfield, Ohio (and was witnessed by at least one group of unconnected witnesses on the ground). At closest approach the object was seen as a greyish domed disc with green light pouring from the base. Fearing a near collision, the pilot dived to a dangerous low altitude of 500 metres after losing all VHF and UHF radio reception and seeing his magnetic compass spinning wildly at the rate of four revolutions per minute (something noted within circle sites by circles researchers and suggestive of electromagnetic radiation). The UFO seemingly 'pulled up' the four-man chopper to one kilometre before the pilot (later promoted to major) Lawrence Coyne was able to regain control.

Other cases show the power of atmospheric forces. For example, Catherine Burk was driving near her home at Bellwood, Pennsylvania on 15 October 1983 at approaching 9 p.m. It was dull and threatening rain. The following quotes come from MUFON investigator Stan Gordon, who investigated the case.[26]

Whilst travelling at 60 k.p.h. Mrs Burk '... became aware of a loud, whirling sound coming from her right side. She looked through the passenger window and observed a bright, silvery, saucer-shaped object that was flat on top, but having a protruding hemisphere on the middle of the bottom.' As the thing passed slowly over the car, the vehicle's side was lifted off the road a distance of several metres. The tilt rammed Mrs Burk against the side door as she desperately tried to get the steering and brakes to function (neither operated successfully; the headlights were also affected, flashing on and off). This levitation lasted only a few seconds, and her efforts to slide across and force the vehicle back onto the road met with failure, as the slope was too steep. 'The object made a slight turn forward and released its hold of the car. The car came down with a thud ...' The engine stalled for twenty minutes. Meanwhile the phenomenon vanished.

Mrs Burk subsequently had to wear a neck support. Some of her hair fell out (just as it would after exposure to radiotherapy). She suffered hearing-loss, severe headaches, itching blisters and eye disorders. All were linked to the incident, so far as she was concerned, and were not longstanding.

This witness filed an insurance claim for her medical bills. The insurance agency called on MUFON's help but could not rule that a UFO had caused the accident. One can imagine the precedent that would have set! In the end it was decreed that the incident was an 'act of God' – which, very probably, is quite a fair description!

Southern Australia, 1988
Probably the most famous incident that seems to fit alarmingly well into this disturbing pattern achieved massive (often ludicrous) global publicity, due largely to the coincidence that it took place in Australia amidst that nation's Bicentennial celebrations.[27]

It was around 4 a.m. on 20 January 1988, a time at which the coastal highway spanning the 2,000 kilometres between Perth and Adelaide was sparsely travelled on what was, of course, a high summer's day. There were two trucks heading east (in limited radio contact, although some miles apart) and a car sandwiched in between carrying Faye Knowles and her three sons (aged eighteen to twenty-four). For most of the time none of the vehicles was in sight of each other.

The Knowles suffered the brunt of the encounter (although one of the truck drivers also saw a strange light). Essentially the family described a yellowish-white mass, later sketched to look similar to a balloon or egg-in-an-eggcup (as some media reports referred to it). In fact, this is very much the sort of image you would expect of a cloud tapering down into a vortex tube. The strange object behaved in a peculiar fashion, heading towards them from the east, disappearing, reappearing behind them and finally causing near panic. The cat-and-mouse chase caused them briefly to turn the vehicle around in an effort to escape.

The 'close encounter' phase occurred without anything being visible. The witnesses were, however, convinced that the phenomenon was directly above them at this stage (Mrs Knowles put her hand out onto the car roof and felt some kind of strange sensation). During these moments of close approach they heard a humming sound, felt the car vibrating and then were all certain that it was actually picked up off the ground for a brief period. There was also a terrible smell and a fine greyish mist that entered the car through the open window. The Knowles further reported that their voices sounded strange when they spoke during this period of forced levitation. Eventually the car crashed back to earth, a tyre burst and they skidded to a halt in the bush beside the road. All the witnesses leapt out and hid until sure the thing had gone. Then they changed the tyre and hastily drove into the town of Mundrabilla as daylight broke.

Several secondary witnesses now gathered around and attested to the shock the family were suffering and noticed four shallow impressions (as if a downward force had pushed 'circular' dents into the metal). These were imbedded into the roof of the car, which was also covered in a fine dust and had a smell like bakelite (or perhaps electrical burning).

Extensive investigation of the case began quickly, involving Ray Brooke and others of the UFO Research South Australia team. They were actually called by the police when the Knowles stopped to report the incident. Unfortunately the media also got wind of the story, and one TV station intercepted the car on its way to meet the ufologists. The epic media circus was soon well and truly underway.

Several analyses of the dust were completed. Most (including those by the TV station and the police) found nothing odd, but one, from a group of ufologists, indicated high levels of unusual chemicals.

How does one evaluate this case? Of course, the popular press and many ufologists regard it as an encounter with a spaceship. Yet look at the facts. We have a shape like a glowing vortex, which moved just as a vortex would move if electrically attracted to a metal car body on a vast expanse of flat land (the 'UFO' was actually described as 'jumping about' from side to side in this motion). There was clear evidence of major air pressure of both a downward nature (creating the dents) and possibly an upward suction dragging the car into the air. Hints of major changes in air pressure causing speech anomalies. Plus signs of electrical or electrostatic charges (the smell and the fine dust particles, which may well have been attracted by the ionizing field of the glowing vortex or temporary magnetization of the car body). Even the smell is noted as part of vortices (for example, by Corliss).

One scientist, Peter Schwerdtferrger from Adelaide University, came up with the idea that this unusual incident might be a powerful 'dry thunderstorm' which the family merely chanced upon. Ufologists tended not to agree. However, because the UFO Research Australia team are a dedicated and objective group, they accumulated some interesting additional data from other witnesses who were out on the same road that night. One in particular is important because all that this car encountered (a little before the Knowles adventure and not too far away) was a sudden wall of great wind that hit them out of nowhere and disappeared just as rapidly.[27]

We believe there is considerable reason to speculate that this classic story of the modern UFO field may be an excellent example of what can happen when you are unfortunate enough to get too close to a Meaden Vortex.

Sweden, 1987

The Nullarbor Plains area of Australia has now been recognized as a UFO window. Indeed, there is even a road sign warning motorists to 'Beware UFOs' for the next few hundred kilometres! A further window is in southern Sweden, near Dalecarlia. The following close encounter is one of many from the area. Again it seems obvious what was responsible for the incident.[28]

At 3 a.m. on 31 December 1987 the cat and dog of a family at Sater were very restless, as if sensing something odd in the atmosphere. One woman (a retired nurse) got up and watched the dog outside, rigid, its jaws shaking. Going outside to investigate, she was confronted by an ice-blue sphere of an estimated six metre-diameter that hovered nearby at tree-top level. This sphere seemed to emerge out of a most peculiar mist that was greyish-orange and glowing and which fully surrounded the object. From the base, vivid blue-white flashes or sparks poured out that seemed to be grinding themselves into the earth and which were reminiscent of a small-scale and silent form of lightning. Not surprisingly the lady was distressed. Like the dog, she was rooted to the spot in fear and could not make her muscles work at all in order to cry out to her husband, only metres away. Her skin was creeping and her forehead pounding. All of which suggests that she was responding to the huge electrical field surrounding the object – and that both she and her pet endured muscle paralysis, which can result from this.

Meanwhile her husband could hear a faint humming sound from inside the house and hastened to see what was happening. He joined his wife as she was losing consciousness (saying that it felt as if her mind was being drained). The UFO vanished instantly – at the same moment as she recovered her senses with a sharp 'pin-prick' on her upper back. The first thing her husband noticed on arrival outside was that his wife, the dog and the cat all smelt powerfully of something like sulphur. This reminds us of many other cases in the subject's literature (such as the odd odour at Mundrabilla).

Half an hour later, after settling his wife, the man went out with the dog. He saw nothing but said that the air smelt very odd – 'like creosote'. This may have been the smell of ozone produced by the ionization of the local atmosphere.

The following morning the woman had a terrible migraine, and it lasted five days. A five-centimetre-long burn was found on the back of the jumper she had been wearing. All the threads had melted together.

The National Defence Institute carried out a scientific inquiry, as its personnel were convinced by the sincerity of this couple and had received other local reports of strange glows in the sky that night. They concluded that the jumper had been hit by 'a powerful burst of static electricity'.[28]

Pennsylvania, USA, 1988
Here is just one further case, from Harrisburg, Pennsylvania.[29] It was 5.25 a.m. (note the prevalence of this pre-dawn time factor in these cases) on 4 December 1988. A police officer was driving to work when he was dazzled by an egg-shaped mass of light directly above power lines in front of him. Such was the illumination that he swerved across the road; fortunately the highway was devoid of other traffic at the time. The glow ('like burning magnesium') was stationary but moving from side to side (possibly rotating). Then it shot away (leaving a trail of sparks in its wake). As it moved, it emitted a humming noise.

There were some interesting extra features to this story. A 'bluish mist' entered the police car during its proximity to the object. Later analysis showed the presence of potassium chloride (also found by one analysis of the Mundrabilla car ten months earlier!). The police officer described having felt a tingling sensation, like a mild electric shock, and a sensation of radiated warmth on his skin. Later he suffered a powerful headache, felt dizzy and sluggish for some time, had blurred vision for several hours and a sore feeling in his neck and spinal muscles and displayed to the first investigators on the scene a 'sunburn shadow', caused by his face having been 'burnt' but with the part shaded by his peaked cap not affected.

Moments after his own experience, the officer found a second car that had been even closer to the hovering UFO. He assured himself that the driver of this vehicle was all right, although the man sat there with moist eyes and a dazed look on his face. The engine felt cold (suggesting that the vehicle had been switched off for some minutes), and the inside smelt strange – 'like sulphur' (again). Unfortunately the policeman was so much disturbed by his own experience that he left without taking any details of this stranger or his vehicle.

In our view, it is not good science to ignore this overwhelming mass of detailed evidence. It implies, beyond any reasonable doubt, that some very real, possibly dangerous atmospheric phenomenon does exist.

Car-Stop Encounters

If the previous cases suggest a pattern, wait until you see the 'car-stop' or 'vehicle-interference' events! Terence Meaden recognized their significance from a superficial glance at the UFO data, discovering some in the Wessex area near where circles have appeared. In fact, there are now over 500 well-attested and carefully researched cases from around the world, and they provide the vital hard evidence which ill-informed commentators so often demand of ufology.

What makes these car-stop stories so fascinating is that they take us straight to the heart of the physical forces that are produced by these atmospheric phenomena. A few examples will make that clear, especially when you realize that these are plucked almost at random from the data base, which has already generated two major catalogues.[30]

France, 1954
In October 1954 there was one of the largest waves of UFO sightings the world has ever known. It focused on northern and central Europe. In just one twenty-four-hour spell the following independent cases occurred within France.[31]

On the night of 20 October, in the Lusigny Forest region, Roger Reveille spotted an oval that approached him through the wood, then shot upwards and vanished. Waves of heat poured out, powerful enough to cause the rain that was falling to turn instantly to steam! At the spot where the thing hovered, the grass was dry, although surrounded by sodden landscape.

At 6.30 p.m. that same day one M. Schoubrenner of Sarrebourg was in the Turquenstein area when an 'inverted cone' (a classic vortex funnel) appeared on the road ahead. His car engine died. He found his muscles turning rigid but he somehow applied the brakes and screeched to a halt. The base of the cone poured out a phosphorescent glow.

The next night, 21 October, M. Fillonneaue (a bricklayer) was stopped in his tracks by a 'large ball of fire' at Criteuil-la-Madeleine. He reported 'violent air displacements' in close proximity to the UFO, and the police investigation later found the car battery flat and the headlight bulbs burnt out as if through a power overload.

About the same time, at Pouzou, a man was driving with his 3-year-old child from their home at Cherbonniers when a glowing mass hovered over the road ahead, emitting light (red turning to orange) that was strong enough to dazzle them both. The man reported painful electric shocks that increased in intensity as the car moved towards the mass. Then the engine suddenly failed, the headlights went out and the child began to cry. Moments later the object shot into the sky, and the sensations ended. The car was operating normally again.

Southern USA, 1957
Such a concentration of so many events within such a short time-span is not unique. Of course, one might postulate an intensive alien invasion, but why invade through balls of light, glowing masses and tornado funnels which pour out electrical energy? Surely a far more likely possibility is that these 'flaps' are the result of localized atmospheric conditions just happening to be at an optimum level during the time in question?

For example, on the night of 2–3 November 1957 the area around Levelland, Texas, was subjected to an extraordinary series of car-stop episodes. At least nine independent reports are known for the 2½ hour period before and after midnight. There are other cases for the days either side of this in the south-western United States. In fact, thirty-six out of the fifty-eight known car-stops for the year 1957 come within the period 30 October to 9 November; almost all of them were from the USA, and most of those from the Texas/New Mexico region. This cannot just be a coincidence.

An interesting daylight sighting comes at 1.10 p.m. on 4

November that year from Orogrande, New Mexico. An electrical engineer was driving south on Highway 54 when first his radio, then his engine failed. Several other cars on the road appeared to have stopped. An oval shape came from the region of the nearby Sacramento Mountains and passed low over the road. As it did so, the engineer felt a wave of heat and an itching or prickling sensation on his exposed skin. The UFO disappeared upwards into clouds, which seemed to 'dissipate in the path of the object'. These features – which we have seen before in other cases – strongly imply ionization from whatever the 'UFO' was.[32]

Hampshire, 1967
Moving on a decade to another wave, you have already seen reference to one classic car-stop that occurred within the midst of circles territory – on the Avon–Sopley road near Bournemouth, 6 November 1967, p. 142. Here is another impressive and thoroughly investigated case. It took place on 26 October 1967 at 4.30 a.m. and involved an engineer and manager of a transport firm, W. Collett, who (it should be said) shunned the widespread media publicity for UFOs at the time and in contacting *FSR* was motivated only by his desire to put on record what took place.

He was driving a new Ford Transit minibus which had had its seating removed so that he could carry a load of metal castings to the West Midlands. He was on the A32, heading north and was a few minutes past the junction with the A30 at Hook when suddenly the entire electrical system of the vehicle failed. He lost engine, lights, radio – the lot. Presuming it was a loose connection, he got out to investigate but, despite an intensive inspection of the battery, spark plugs and distributer wires, there seemed nothing amiss. He did notice a dark mass in the sky above the road ahead but was rather preoccupied with other matters and simply got back into the bus and tried again. It still failed, but after pondering his predicament for a few moments he tried again and it started normally. The weather was cold, clear and frosty, so he assumed it was just a minor self-correcting problem and so continued with his trip.

But only a few hundred metres down the road there was a second all-systems shutdown. This time when Mr Collett got out of the cab he noticed something strange about the atmosphere. There was a pressure on his eardrums, not unlike the one most people feel inside an aircraft due to cabin pressurization effects. Recalling an old remedy, he held his nose and blew air out, which helped to relieve the strain. There was something else peculiar – a smell. This was described as like arcing electrical equipment – indeed, he likened it to bakelite (which we saw used as a comparison in an earlier case). Mr Collett opened the bonnet, established that the smell was not from here and yet again found nothing amiss with the engine.

The dark object was still immediately ahead of him, and now he paid more attention. It was described as 'like a squat ice-cream cone' (once again a classic vortex funnel shines through the spaceship presumptions of ufology). There was a rim separating the domed top from the tapering cone at the base. After a few moments the dark mass drifted away over some trees.

Returning to his bus, Mr Collett found that the power operated normally, and he had no further troubles despite driving several hundred kilometres on his journey to his destination and back. However, he did suffer some problems co-ordinating his muscles.

The case was reported directly to Charles Bowen, then editor of *Flying Saucer Review*. Mr Collett had tracked the magazine down as being 'expert' on whatever it was that he saw, but he insisted he did not believe in aliens. To their credit, *FSR* did an excellent job of investigating this report, including a medical follow-up by Dr Bernard Finch, who completed his report within two weeks of the incident.[33]

Finch noted some interesting clues. He said that when Mr Collett had stepped out of the cab on the second occasion (at closest approach to the UFO), he had had what he described as 'a feeling of oppression, the kind of sensation we all get before a thunderstorm'. Other effects of pressure changes and exposure to an electrostatic field were also referenced, such as subsequently having a 'tingling numbness and crawling feelings' in the nerve endings at the tips of his fingers, which Dr Finch argued was nerve regeneration. Also a severe toothache the witness was suffering from at the time of the incident vanished – possibly an indication of one beneficial side-effect from potential minor nerve damage.

Whilst assuming that a 'flying saucer' was responsible, Dr Finch pondered the interesting question of what would have occurred had this witness come even closer to the presumed radiation field associated with this UFO. He speculates that it might have rendered Mr Collett unconscious. In a moment you will see a case in which this is exactly what did happen.

Of course, we have absolutely no need to interpret this incident as evidence of an intelligently controlled craft. With the help of Dr Meaden's research and years of hindsight, it does very much look as if the phenomenon encountered by Mr Collett on the road to Reading was an ionized vortex.

Cheshire/Derbyshire, 1968 and 1974

The tenuous link here in terms of county (Hampshire) relates both 1967 British car-stop cases discussed in this book with the modern crop circles. But this idea can be cemented much further by the next, rather significant report.[34] Whilst as a car-stop it is fairly minor in nature, it did have an excellent investigation by BUFORA researcher Roy Dutton, a mechanical engineer. And its precise location is, as you will see, of immense interest.

The date was 4 March 1968 and a Mr Burnell was driving his new Triumph Spitfire sports car at about 9 p.m. on what was a clear, dry night. He was on a quiet rural lane at Higher Chisworth on the Cheshire/Derbyshire border.

A small golden ball of light appeared in the south (from the New Mills direction) and sped across the valley northwards, towards the Longendale area. As it passed close by, several effects struck the car at once. His radio became silent, the headlights failed, the engine cut out and the car jerked to a halt. Only seconds later, with the object now gone, the headlights returned to full power all by themselves, and Mr Burnell had no difficulty in restarting the engine. But the radio still refused to operate. Despite attempts to repair this by his brother-in-law (who was a television service man), it proved impossible, and the four-month-old set had to be replaced.

The car was kept two more years and never gave trouble again. The radio was available for study by Roy Dutton, and it was discovered that a failure of two key transistors was the only fault; indeed, once they had been replaced (even though this was ten years later), the radio operated perfectly. It seems that the cause of such a burn-out could only have been a power surge back in 1968.

Mr Burnell had been driving to cottages on the slopes of a prominent hill just under 300 metres high. This is, in fact, the very hill in whose lee the hay rise and circle event beside Marple Ridge (see p. 109) was to take place twenty years later! These events are only three kilometres apart. The entire area has been littered with strange sightings. Earthlights researchers Devereux, Clarke and Roberts note numerous incidents from the Longendale area in their work – strange lights and legends of glowing 'ghosts'. A local bend is even named the Devil's Elbow because so many weird things have been happening there throughout the centuries.[35]

Just to the south-west of here (about three kilometres from Higher Chisworth) is Werneth Low, another prominent hill. Just before Christmas 1974 an interesting UFO event was reported from here, when at 7.30 a.m. a vertical 'cloud cigar', with one flattened end and a tapering base, floated above the peak. This changed shape (from round to oval to cigar and back to oval again) before disappearing and discharged several small spheres from the blunt end – 'like soap bubbles being blown'. The witness elaborated on this description, saying that they seemed to cling briefly to the end, then rush away southwards (toward the Marple–Higher Chisworth area, in fact).[36]

Brazil and Japan, 1973
Given how few car-stops there are (relatively speaking), this direct link with circles in two of them is very impressive evidence of a causal relationship. The international distribution of these cases is equally well founded.

For instance, at 3 a.m. on 22 May 1973 Oniloem Papero was driving between Itajobi and Catandura in Brazil when his radio was drowned by static and the engine began to fail. A dark grey shape emitting blue beams and making a buzzing sound hovered above the road ahead. Papero noticed a loss of air (as if it was being sucked out of the car), and even after opening the door he found it hard to breathe. He was also hit by a wave of heat. The frightened chap decided to run away as fast as he could but felt a force pulling him back towards the dark mass – as if it were tugging him into it. A thin beam or tube of light was emerging from the underside of the UFO, and Papero rapidly lost consciousness. He reports a couple of other bizarre features (including that the car became transparent, so he could see right into it) but this is likely to have been an hallucination or dream that occurred during this period of unconsciousness.

This witness was found an hour later by some passers-by, and he and the car did recover. However, his hair had reputedly changed colour from brown to black – although when it regrew it did so in its normal shade.[37]

The tube (or vortex funnel) was reported even more precisely in a case just a few weeks later (unknown date in July 1973) at Tomakomai, on Hokkaido Island, Japan. The witness was a 20-year-old security guard on night patrol at a deserted coastal lumber yard.[38]

He was sitting in his car listening to the radio after completing his rounds. Suddenly a light appeared and, as he told investigator Jun-Ichi Takanashi, '... began to expand and contract alternately with extreme rapidity'. Then it '... began to descend with a spiral motion' and gave out intermittent flashes of greenish light in the form of rays or bolts. Next it descended over the sea and from the underside let down a '... glass-like transparent tube ... [and] when the front edge of the tube touched the surface that part of the tube began to glow and appeared to be sucking up water'. A sound (described as like an insect) accompanied the lowering of the funnel into the water, but soon ended. The orange-coloured light then shot back across the sky directly over the lumber yard. When it was above the witness, he had various odd sensations, such as 'an excruciating pain' in his head. The object was now seen to be oval, with a rim of dark blotches or shadows round the centre. After leaving the water it had become more white than orange. Eventually it disappeared by flying into a dark mass behind him. Several similar lights (about five in all) were coming from different directions and entering what sounds like another 'cloud cigar'.

When the experience ended, the witness noticed that his radio was emitting strange noises and was not working properly, and he felt numb (semi-paralysed and tingling?) and had a terrible headache. He was unable to sleep and was very glad to be relieved at dawn.

UFO interpretations were placed on this story, but it represents a fine description of an ionized vortex behaving like a waterspout when over the sea. Even the colours (orange when water vapour was ionized, white when not) are predictable. The way in which five objects entered a dark mass is very akin to the Werneth Low story recounted above and yet again furthers the connection between these glowing atmospheric effects and clouds.

Lancashire, 1977
There are many classic cases which demonstrate these points. For instance, the Nelson, Lancashire, sighting of 9 March 1977 is typical in that it fulfils most of the criteria beside Pendle Hill.[39]

Tasmania, 1987 and 1974

We could go on repeating further remarkably similar reports, but the same clues are already obvious. We will conclude with one recent case to demonstrate that these close encounters continue into modern times. This was investigated by Keith Roberts, a stalwart of the Australian UFO Centre.

At 9.30 p.m. on 14 December 1987, near Launceston in Tasmania, a grey egg or oval swooped down and 'landed' on the road ahead of a Mercedes car. Both engine and lights failed instantly. The brakes were slammed on and the vehicle screeched to a halt in front of the mass. Light was pouring from the base, but it was so intense that it hurt the eyes to look at it for more than a second or two.

The one man in the car jumped out and fled behind a tree, where he promptly began to vomit. (The nausea persisted even into the following day.) From behind the tree the terrified observer watched his car being dragged towards the UFO some ten metres along the road, as if being tugged by a giant magnet. It left rubber tread and scuff marks on the surface of the highway.

A Landcruiser truck now appeared coming down the road towards the scene. Its lights failed in proximity to the UFO but its engine did not. This truck was diesel-operated, and the case is one of several on record in which standard engine systems (such as on most cars) *have* lost all power but those which operate without the need for an electrical spark (such as diesel trucks) have not been affected even when just as close (or closer) to the UFO. But these diesel-engined vehicles *have* lost systems (for example, lights) which require a battery. For the witnesses in every single one of these cases to have invented the same fact is hardly tenable. This seems a vital clue about the electrical forces that are associated with car-stops.

The UFO in this case took off with a 'whirring' sound, and the car-driver and truck-driver swopped notes on what they had seen. The car was covered in specks of bitumen from the road surface (which seemed to have partially melted); it also suffered serious electrical faults which had to be rectified in the wake of the incident.

Investigators failed to trace the exact spot on the road, because there were several places in the area where bitumen seemed to have melted and been repaired by the council. Does that suggest that this harrowing close encounter is not without precedent?

Quite possibly so. Indeed, we have at least one other case from the area (dated 16 September 1974) when a woman with two child passengers lost power and headlights on that highway as a 'deafening, vibrating noise enveloped the car', filled it with a choking electrical smell and gave powerful tingling electric shocks to the occupants. Once again we see the same trend repeated.[40]

If these stories did not have the supernatural trappings of ufology, such consistency and solid scientific nature would surely have brought intensive exploration from physicists and electrical researchers. We *need* that to happen, because it should be obvious after reading these reports that some very powerful atmospheric forces are involved, dragging cars along roads, sucking up air etc., just as one would expect from a vortex similar to an ionized tornado.

It is time we retired those creaky, unreliable (and mythical) alien spaceships.

Encounters of the Third and Fourth Kind

Even the closest encounters take on new meaning when you evaluate them in the context of the Meaden Vortex. Almost every case we looked at in the UFO records seemed to offer new clues that fitted like missing pieces of a wonderful jigsaw puzzle.

In our opinion, the connections and patterns are far too overwhelming to be ignored. Indeed, ufologists have stumbled in the dark for over forty years trying to fathom out the mystery – and in the main they have failed. We think the reason is now quite obvious: they lacked a theory that unified the mass of data. Terence Meaden may well have inadvertently provided it.

Ufology has sought to impose its own interpretations onto the evidence, and these were generally linked to an intelligence or spaceships. This was simply not a very productive line of reasoning, because any difficulties that the data threw up could be obscured by the claim, 'We don't understand alien logic.' This escape-clause allowed the mystery to prosper whilst the answers stayed well out of reach.

Meaden's dramatic theoretical scenario has opened doors that were formerly slammed shut. Those of us ready to progress can apply *his* thinking to *our* data, and it works like a magic spell, transforming our evidence. What was once confusing becomes clear. What used to leave us scratching our heads trying to fathom out alien motives for sucking water up into tubes or dragging cars along roads and filling them with funny smells now suddenly takes on the nature of fascinating clues about the scientific origin of these atmospheric processes.

But is there nothing the Meaden Vortex cannot handle? Is it not true that there are some reports from reliable and apparently sincere witnesses who have reported meeting aliens and even allegedly been abducted by them?

It is true, but they are as rare as car-stops. Studies by psychologists and psychiatrists reveal an unambiguous result. This is not a fairy tale cooked up by wide-eyed believers in alien contact. They are not stories from fantasy merchants. The incidents seem 'real' and come from well-balanced individuals. We cannot dismiss them for the sake of a quiet life.

Nevertheless, accepting that sincere, credible people report events that *seem* real is a long, long way from accepting that what they claim is 'the literal truth'. As we saw, while American ufologists tend to be happy with a face-value impression of this strange evidence, most other researchers are not. In fact, there is (at least for us) an overwhelming majority of evidence which demonstrates several crucial facts about these alien encounters.

First, they are consistent only in so far as the basic format of the experience is concerned. Beyond that they follow cultural trends. The aliens differ across society – British witnesses see tall, polite Nordic beings, whereas Americans report small, grey-faced and rather cold scientists. In other words, the form the alien takes matches the spirit or character of a nation in which it is seen.

Secondly, the stories also display absurdity levels which cannot be acceptable. The aliens say they come from ridiculous places, such as a planet on the far side of the sun or from some galaxy whose name is straight out of a Buck Rogers comic book. They are inconsistent in why they come and what they do.

A third major clue is what we call 'cultural tracking'. The science inside the UFO during an abduction, or the spiel offered to witnesses during contact, is always at about the current level of technology, never beyond it. As we now have nearly half a century of tales, we can see this trend easily. The stories from decades ago do not feature technology we have invented since then, such as digital number displays, lasers and microchip computers: instead they have an alien technology almost ancient by comparison. The current cases do include these features, but nothing *beyond* 1990s'

Earth technology. It does not take much thought to understand how this one simple fact, almost on its own, destroys the naïve myth of aliens riding super-advanced spaceships with science far beyond our ken.

Fourthly, as if all this were not enough, the reports are clearly subjective in nature. The more bizarre they are and the closer they get, the more they seem to be single-witness incidents. Multi-witness cases usually involve families. In other (non-alien) sightings the witness-per-case ratio rises to 2.6. Furthermore, alien contacts have dream-like features, such as floating sensations, time-jumps, missing memories and impossible discontinuities in their sequence of events. They do not flow like real life.

Fifthly, nor do we have *any* sort of hard physical evidence, such as alien debris, or *anything* provably alien at all, not even photographs of the inside of a UFO, the alien pilots or somebody being taken into a UFO as witnessed by an outsider. We *do* have some hard evidence and photographs of other UFO categories – even first or second kind close encounters to a limited extent, so this lack is a very serious issue. There are also several cases in which witnesses were seen by third parties during the time when they were supposedly with the aliens in a spaceship. These third parties are insistent that the witnesses were *not* in a UFO but stayed where they had been at the onset of the experience, although they did seem to be in a strange state of consciousness (variously described as akin to a trance or deep sleep).

Finally, there is accumulating evidence that witnesses to these alien contacts share characteristics. They tend to be artistically creative, with very powerful abilities of visual imagery. In other words, what seems to separate the ones who 'merely' have a close encounter from those who have full-blown abductions is that most abductees have highly advanced visual creativity.

For us these points are absolutely damning against the concept of alien intelligences riding spaceships and interacting with human beings. They only seem to make sense through the concept of a physical stimulus that – in certain circumstances and with specific types of witness – can trigger an altered state of consciousness. The initial phase of the experience can be shared by anyone, because it involves physically real atmospheric phenomena. It is *seen* as a glowing UFO. The 'alien contact' phase is an adjunct and occurs only in limited and special conditions to a restricted number of people whose encounter then continues beyond the limits of a 'normal' case and follows culturally determined lines.

If we are right, this altered state of consciousness is where these creatively visual people undergo a vivid experience which does indeed seem completely real. They are quite honest in their reporting of these events. The witnesses have just seen a bizarre atmospheric force which they have almost certainly interpreted as a UFO. In today's Space Age, that has inevitable connotations, so it is easy to see what pattern a dream-like or hallucinatory sequel will entail. It will follow the 'alien' myth.

We have met one car-stop case in which the witness *was* rendered unconscious when he came too close to a vortex. He recalls brief snatches of 'memory' from what seems to have been an hour of unconsciousness. These included weird features, and this seems to have been a 'partial' abduction.

There are other cases with such strange overtones. They attract attention toward the abduction phenomenon, even though in statistical terms alien contacts represent less than 0.5 per cent of the entire UFO spectrum. Many of these stories emerge through the dubious use of regression hypnosis, employed to try to fill out this 'missing memory'.

Had the witness to that Brazilian car-stop been subjected to hypnosis in order to 'find out' what 'happened' during the 'missing hour', we need no supernatural powers to suggest what the result would have been. A garbled version of the alien delusion would have emerged, no doubt with some individual features and a number of consistent themes but the recognizable myth nonetheless. The impression of seeing the car turn transparent would probably have become an integral part of the developing storyline, somehow tied in with the 'aliens' having been responsible for this. In fact, this witness was discovered by passers-by lying unconscious on the ground – and that is almost certainly the *only* 'real' thing that happened to him after his close encounter with a very physical atmospheric vortex. Hypnosis would have been more likely to confuse the issue by stimulating false data rather than help elucidate what took place.

Looking at the literature of the alien contact experience in the light of these comments can be very rewarding.[41] Let us examine a few case histories of this variety to see how well the evidence shapes up to its greatest challenge. We are tempted to ask: if the Meaden Vortex can explain even these remarkable stories, what obstacles are left standing in its path?

South Wales, 1972

A typical basic-level alien contact fell into Paul Fuller's lap when he was lecturing about crop circles at an Open University seminar in South Wales. The witness, a taxi-driver in his late thirties, appeared to believe that he was the only person in the world who had ever undergone an experience like it, although that is far from the truth. He had not previously discussed it with anyone, which is surprisingly common. We believe that as many as nine out of ten cases of this type go unreported.

On a cool, dry night in October 1972 at approximately 11.30 p.m. the witness was driving along the A48 from Port Talbot to Swansea after visiting his girlfriend. After crossing the Ferry Bridge he realized that the car was being paced by something – described as a dark, flattened saucer with a rim of reddish light on the base. It then passed directly over the top of him, and he slowed down and parked in a lay-by overlooking the (now-dismantled) steelworks. After a moment or two he got out of the car (which remained unaffected). He stared up at the object, which hovered a short distance away in the south-west. He began to feel strange at this point. The witness describes these feelings as a sense of air pressure from above, pushing down onto him (the same impression as offered by the eyewitnesses to the Marple hay fall and numerous car-stop cases), a rhythmic pulsation (which again suggests a rotating air disturbance) and the extremely common close-encounter symptom of the hair on his arms and head standing up as if responding to a mild electrostatic charge.

However, this case goes beyond the levels of the straightforward because of something else that he says was visible. Just above the glowing rim and jostling about were 'three dark grey shadows'. Shadows or blotches (often seen to be rotating) are another frequent description by witnesses to these phenomena. Often they are interpreted as windows. In this case the witness felt they were entities (although he admits he could see no details). He began to develop the impression that they were about to capture him, but he was clearly animating what were in fact just blotchy shadows.

The next thing he knew was that the UFO took off into the sky and was gone. He reported some of the typical Oz Factor (isolation) features during this close-encounter phase.

There are quite a few cases in which the entities are only dimly perceived and may be misperceptions of something else. If this was a form of UAP, the witness could have seen mist or particles clinging to the surface through the forces at work and mistaken these for alien beings. The possible vortex photographed above Trindade Island (see Plate 17) has what may well be viewed as 'aliens' on the rim, if you use your imagination.

Is it not probable that the physiological and electrical 'car-stop' effects reported in such cases indicate that a powerful *natural* phenomenon was encountered, and that the 'time lapse' (and anything that emerges from our dubious efforts to unravel it) is a psychological construct of the dream state that followed? Treating them as alien kidnaps is a mistake, leading witness, investigator and society into a self-deceptive cul-de-sac.

Essex, 1974

The first true British 'close encounter of the fourth kind' that was investigated through regression hypnosis has become a landmark in the field but now takes on new possibilities if we think along these lines.[42]

A man, woman and three children were together in a car at Aveley in Essex. This in itself makes the case almost unique, as that number of witnesses to a close encounter of the fourth kind is very uncommon. However, this is not as valuable as it seems on first glance.

The car drove into a patch of green mist that appeared straddling the road ahead. The radio set started to crackle and splutter, and the driver yanked out the wires to prevent a fire. Then there was a 'jump' in memory. Arriving home, the family discovered that over 1½ hours were 'missing' from recall, and they started to have nightmares along the lines of strange alien faces. An odd blue light had been fleetingly witnessed just before they drove into the mist – hence the UFO interpretation of events.

Both adults were hypnotically regressed much later (the children were too young). These hypnosis 'memories' diverged for much of the way during 'recall' of the missing time. The adults were 'separated' by the 'aliens' etc. The dream faces became the central players in an abduction drama, in which there were medical examinations, trips round the UFO and alien messages conveyed. Science-fiction plot lines ruled: a sort of mixture from TV serials and other UFO abduction stories that had been in the media. However, there were also some impossible (dream-like) elements to the stories that were recounted by these witnesses. They included the car's stalling and then being 'beamed up' right through the walls of the UFO, where it changed colour and where the witnesses saw themselves inside the car *at the same time* as they were on a balcony in the UFO.

There is no doubt that these people were completely sincere. They were also highly intelligent. Jenny attended one 1979 hypnosis session at their home in Essex and was thoroughly impressed by them both. She left quite happy that something had occurred – but not convinced that it was something physically *real*.

In fact, although the incident had happened in October 1974, it was not investigated until four years later (a typical delay in such cases). To interpret the abduction account in terms of an alien kidnap, when it is so different from the conscious recall, seems needlessly extreme. Why not work on the premise that the family encountered some sort of atmospheric vortex and suffered a period of unconsciousness after driving off the road? Later they subconsciously filled in the gaps in their memory, as those dreams understandably came to plague them over the subsequent years. In this way we see the hypnosis as a way to 'flesh out' the plot already sketched in outline by years of dream images.

Of course, the story also paralleled some of the UFO and science fiction data with which the family must have had contact (everyone does in today's Western society). Even if they did not consciously recall any of this, the motif is engrained within our culture, and the human mind is adept at retaining every scrap of information. So this was available for use as an image source during both the triggered loss of consciousness, thanks to the UAP, and the special state of hypnotic regression that was later imposed.

The key witness was very artistic and visually creative (with ESP traits also). Is this why the case became a close encounter of the fourth kind and did not remain an extreme example of the car-stop variety?

Remember that all that this family experienced in *reality* (so far as they and we can state) was a blue light, a strange green mist, some minor electrical disturbance and an unaccountable short loss of memory, later fleshed out by an abduction tale.

Brazil, 1979
Here is another fully developed encounter, one which shows the differences between conscious memory and what later emerges to take on the guise of the so-called 'full story'.[43]

It occurred on 15 October 1979 at Ponta Negra in Brazil and was investigated extremely well by Irene Granchi and Bob Pratt of MUFON. The chief witness was 'Luli Oswald', stage name of a leading Brazilian concert pianist, who has the classic hallmarks of being involved in ESP and 'psychic healing' (indicating the sort of traits that are becoming well established for abductees).

On the night in question she was driving a 25-year-old student down the coast to collect something he had accidentally left there earlier in the day. The weather was dull, although earlier rain had ceased. Their outward journey included conversation about UFOs and the sighting of a light out to sea. It was about 11.30 p.m.

Here is what they consciously recall having seen. A light rose up from the sea, pulling with it a towering column of water. Beside the car and above a hill was now a dark cigar (with orange patches), out of which emerged three balls of light that rolled down towards them. The car suffered electrical impedence and began to falter. Then there is an apparent loss of consciousness, and their next memory is of being still inside the car, a little further down the road, without any recall of how they got there. They then stopped for some coffee but found that the time was now 2 a.m. – implying that over two hours had disappeared from their minds in one 'jump'.

Investigation proceeded a few days later – after the concert pianist had been recommended to a ufologist by her priest! One side of the car was found to be heavily magnetized. Her eyes burned badly for a few days after the incident, and she also had a burning sensation when she urinated. All of this suggests that some form of electromagnetic radiation was emitted from the UFO during the close encounter. However, because nobody thought to consider this a case of some strange atmospheric event, the assumption of most ufologists was inevitable: hypnosis was required to see what the aliens were up to. Indeed, Luli was soon hypnotized by Dr Silvio Lago (the young man never was).

What new 'memory' came out to plug the gap? Basically the same sort of thing as in the Aveley case, although the entities were quite different. Those at Aveley were typical of European encounters – tall, thin and humanistic; Luli's were classics of the South American tradition – cold and ugly dwarfs. She described the car's being pulled up into the air by a beam of light and rematerializing inside the UFO. There are unaccounted 'scene-jumps' in her recall. The aliens performed medical probes and sample-taking on the now naked woman but rejected her after a gynaecological examination. Not much information was passed to her (unlike at Aveley where there was more information exchange and sight-seeing than there was witness examination). She also reported that the entities claimed to come from a 'small galaxy near Neptune'. Being an intelligent woman, she well understood how astronomically absurd that statement is – but, just as we are forced to reveal the nonsense said and done in our dreams if we report them accurately, Luli could only honestly tell what *seemed* to have occurred.

Presumably you can see how the case has a solid, consciously recalled core which is totally consistent with an atmospheric phenomenon. All the bizarre and scientifically illogical aspects of the alien abduction phase are later additions that gather like moss around that core. To the ufologist cases such as this are wrongly presumed to be on one evidential level.

Yorkshire, 1980

Our final case is often termed the most significant abduction in Britain, and it even made a recent American list as one of the most detailed and evidential cases in history. It has a key factor that is rarely considered.[44]

The incident involves West Yorkshire police officer Alan Godfrey, who was on night duty in the small Pennine town of Todmorden (one of our previously mentioned UFO windows – and where crop circles have been seen). The date was 28 November 1980 (again, in a period earlier cited as one of intense atmospheric activity filled with cases), and it was 5.05 a.m. The weather that night had been miserable, with plenty of rain, but this had now ceased as a clearing frontal system swept over.

Godfrey was looking for some cows which had been disturbing a housing estate. He drove down Burnley Road out of the town and spotted an object spanning the road ahead. It was like a glowing, spinning top separated by a line of dark blotches (which, as usual with witnesses, he naturally described as windows). The base was rotating. He could see that the trees at the side of the road immediately beside the thing were moving about quite markedly, though the wind was calm elsewhere. He tried his radio to call base, but both UHF and VHF radio channels were indecipherable. There was now a memory lapse, later found to be of ten minutes' duration. His next recall was of being further down the road staring into dark and empty sky. The UFO had gone.

PC Godfrey doubled back, met a colleague and inspected the site where the 'spinning top' had hovered. The road surface at this point was dry – in a swirled, circular pattern, just like the crop circles in fields! One can just imagine what might have resulted had this hovering object been above a cereal field instead of a wet highway. But it should be recalled that at that time the only crop circles known had virtually no publicity outside the south-west.

As you will no doubt appreciate, what the policeman actually saw fits the idea of a Meaden Vortex extraordinarily well: a fuzzy 'spinning top' generating wind forces at a time when the meteorological conditions were optimum and with even a classic 'crop' circle left on the wet road! Had the case concluded at this point, we might now regard it as an unusual and invaluable eyewitness account of circle formation.

Alan Godfrey reported his sighting when he learnt that some officers from an adjacent force had seen a bluish glow in the sky nearby at around the same time. A UFO investigation headed by Harry Harris, Mike Sacks and Norman Collinson quickly began. Eventually, after several months and initial reluctance, Godfrey met doctors and underwent regression hypnosis experiments. From these sessions we see PC Godfrey describing a new 'memory' to fill the gap.

This memory is like all other abductions both before and since. Part of it is consistent with the pattern and part scientifically absurd. His car engine cut out. He floated into a strange room and suffered head and body pains which he interpreted as a medical examination. There were little robots and a tall, bearded man who said (by telepathy) that his name was Yosef. And there was even a big black dog on board! Despite the hypnosis sessions, there are still large gaps and many scene-jumps in the story, as we have noticed in other abduction cases.

It is important to add that Godfrey himself *never* expressed conviction about the literal reality of his hypnosis testimony. He was commendably honest, describing it to Jenny Randles in 1982 as being realistic but dream-like. In February 1988, when he appeared on a live TV show with her, the by-then retired policeman went further and noted that he had read several UFO books between his experience and the start of the hypnosis sessions. Whilst he was positive that he had seen something real above the road, he seems willing to accept the suggestion that the 'on-board' (i.e. alien) memory was an unconscious confabulation during hypnosis – a sort of dream to satisfy everyone hooked by the case and to ensure his own peace of mind.

We think this typically sincere and no-nonsense discussion by this impressive percipient is one of the most significant statements made by a UFO eyewitness in the entire history of the phenomenon.

If we accept what he suggests, it effectively shows that what Alan Godfrey met by chance on Burnley Road could very well have been a completely real, physical phenomenon of strange proportions – a Meaden Vortex, and that the rest of the story should be evaluated on an entirely different level of reality and credibility. It may well have been a 'story' inadvertently created by his mind (during the 'time lapse' – if this ever truly existed – or during the hypnosis used to plug the real, or imagined, gap).

Of course, if this happened with one of the best-attested and most respected 'alien contacts' in this subject's literature, resulting in a full-blown abduction, what price the alien nature of *any* remaining close encounter?

Even the strangest case in the UFO archives seems to have been explained and offers some of the strongest evidence that it was a vortex!

The Meaden Vortex Theory in Action

Let us look at one last case to see just how well the theory discussed in this book can account for what has become a classic close encounter. It was investigated by two of Australia's best ufologists, Bill Chalker and Keith Basterfield.

The location was eight kilometres from Rosedale, Victoria. The scene a large ranch-style property of which the witness, George Blackwell, was the caretaker. It was 1 a.m. on 30 September 1980.

Blackwell was first disturbed by noises amidst the cattle, then a strange screeching and whistling sound. There was obvious panic amongst the livestock, and he went out to investigate. It was clear and mild and still quite moonlit, so it was easy to see what was occurring.

The UFO which was observed was described as 'domed', 'with a white top', and 'orange and blue lights on its surface'. Its diameter was later fairly accurately gauged as eight metres. The thing flew past a hay shed and toward a concrete water-tank that was exposed to the air and housed some 10,000 gallons. The motion was quite slow, and when it reached the tank the dome seemed to climb onto it and hover in one position for about a minute. It then rose up again and 'landed' some distance beyond the tank.

By now the caretaker was concerned, and he went indoors, quickly changed, got out his motorcycle and within five minutes was riding the half-kilometre towards the object as it still hovered and whistled on the ground. He got to within about fifteen metres of it (without noting any effects on the motorbike) and at close proximity experienced a curious sensation – feeling 'like a plate of jelly'. At this closer position Mr Blackwell had a better view of the object. He saw that there was a white dome atop an orange, glowing base and that around the bottom there were circular 'windows' or 'lights'. The whole thing was rotating anti-clockwise.

After it had remained on the ground another couple of minutes, there was an increase in the whistle to 'an awful scream', and the witness had to cover his ears to protect himself from the pain. Then, 'Something like a black tube appeared around the base of the object and this seemed to inflate to tremendous size.' There was a huge bang and George was nearly flattened by a severe blast of hot air. The thing was now rising slowly, his motorcycle headlights showing that the tube seemed more deflated towards the centre of the base and that six 'spokes' emerged from the same central position. After it had risen to about four metres in the air, the sound stopped, but the object was trailing away, a mass of debris being deposited to the ground in its wake. This material comprised stones, weed and cow dung. The rain of debris ended and the object rose higher and higher and disappeared silently into the eastern distance.

George Blackwell returned home quite stunned by what had transpired. He noticed that the clock in the house read 1.50 a.m. when he first looked, but his watch read 1.10 a.m. It was only then that he realized that his watch had stopped. He took it off and placed it on the table; it started again, but every time he tried to wear it during the next couple of days it stopped working. Possibly this indicates that he was 'charged up' with sufficient electrical energy to interfere with the delicate mechanism of the timepiece, but this gradually dissipated.

The caretaker was unable to sleep and suffered physiological effects in the form of headaches and nausea. Soon after dawn he returned to the site. He had seen some odd marks on the ground in the darkness, and these now clearly stood out as a typical crop ring – about forty centimetres wide and eight metres in diameter. It was flattened in an anti-clockwise direction. Yellow flowering grass was removed from the inner circle but there were six 'spokes' coming from the centre, where the grass was virtually undamaged in swathes. This is an identical effect to that noted in some British crop circles. The debris trail leading away to the east was also clearly evident. It was also later discovered that all the water left in the concrete tank had vanished (as if sucked up or evaporated during the close encounter).

Inevitably one can interpret this as an intelligently controlled craft which visited the property and took away samples. However, there is virtually no reason why such a concept can be justified, except by wishful thinking.

We might have tried to contemplate a natural phenomenon that could have been responsible, but before Terence Meaden started to research crop circles we had no real framework in which to do so. Now we have a ready-made answer, and look how this story takes on dramatic new insights!

Suddenly we see how the whistling, screeching noise fits in perfectly with other reports of vortices in the meteorological literature, and how the witness even felt a huge blast of air that nearly knocked him flat. This reminds us of other cases, such as the Apperley Dene, Northumbria, encounter. The debris trail is another feature which makes perfect sense in the light of that interpretation – with the vortex sucking up material as it rose away. Again that was an aspect of Apperley Dene, but it was even more noticeable in the Marple hay fall.

Now we can analyse the UFO and recognize that a rotating, spinning top (as described) is very similar to that in so many other reports. The windows or blotches on the side are common aspects. We can see how the Rosedale sighting is very much like the Alan Godfrey UFO seen at Todmorden, for example. It is very easy to interpret what George Blackwell saw as a rotating vortex with almost no need to stretch any of the facts that he referred to. He even gave us a perfect description of a vortex funnel (the 'tube') emerging from the underside of the object – something we have seen in several other UFO close encounters.

The water connection is also interesting. We have seen how, when a vortex is in proximity to water, it often glows orange. This matches the Meaden predictions due to the properties of physical ionization of water vapour. In the Todmorden case, water off a road surface was swirled dry; there have been similar accounts elsewhere. At Rosedale it may be that evaporation or suction accounted for the disappearance of the water in the tank.

Presumably there was not a particularly strong electrical or ionizing radiation field associated with this UFO – at least in the latter stages. We can assume that from the lack of any electrical impedence on the motor cycle when within fifteen metres of the vortex. We have seen that in other cases this does occur, with clear evidence that some physical force (probably acting on the ionic flow within electrical circuits) creates serious consequences for any equipment nearby.

However, there was some field associated here – if we judge from the sensations and subsequent illness reported by the witness, perhaps from the reaction of animals (which might have responded to increased sensitivity to ionization or chemicals thus released into the atmosphere) and also, possibly from the suggested effects on the watch.

Indeed, we can even speculate as to what would have occurred had the witness ever thought that his watch showing 1.10, whilst the house clock reported forty minutes later, was due to some sort of 'missing time' period, rather than electrical impedence. Excited ufologists, or those more willing than Basterfield and Chalker, might then have arranged for him to be hypnotized to 'find out' what 'really' happened in the minutes he cannot account for. That did occur in very similar circumstances with the Alan Godfrey saga, and we saw how even the witness to that case could not be satisfied about the reality level of his 'alien kidnap' testimony via hypnosis – only his conscious recall of something that was decidedly real.

We feel entirely justified in predicting that, under different circumstances and with pressure from the media or ETH theorists, it is more than possible that George Blackwell would have 'remembered' an 'alien abduction' under hypnosis and that this would have followed the stereotypical lines of the alien myth. In this way an impressive encounter with a strange physical phenomenon would have been turned into something that it never was. Would there then have been any way back towards the truth? Who could have sorted out what was real or imaginary, or physical or delusionary, especially when the witness himself would almost certainly have been incapable of making this distinction?

And so to the question of the circles. Here a quite complex

circle type (a ring with internal spokes) was left in the wake of the encounter. In isolation – without the sighting of the physical cause – it would have been another mystery to add to our ever-growing catalogue. As it stands, it becomes a further beautiful example of an eyewitness description of crop-circle formation.

As we have seen throughout this book, we now have these in such abundance that there is no longer any reasonable doubt what is going on.

We cannot accept that the Rosedale 'UFO close encounter' represents anything other than a fine eyewitness account of someone accidentally coming into close proximity with a strange natural atmospheric phenomenon. This force caused physical effects and left a ringed circle behind. As with all the other cases where there have been eyewitnesses, it seems totally at odds with traces left by a visiting 'spaceship', requires absolutely no need to invent hypothetical intelligences to explain it away and is, in our view, a hundred per cent consistent with the idea of a Meaden Vortex.

We are satisfied that this case is like countless others which presently sit within the data files of UFO groups throughout the world. They are ignored by science as mumbo-jumbo. They are hailed by ufology as prime examples of the alien delusion. But they are neither.

What we have here is a scientific phenomenon which diligent research has successfully uncovered, and it deserves recognition and immediate absorption within our physical textbooks, meteorological lore and children's encyclopaedias.

The longer we continue to deify what is purely natural and to dismiss a phenomenon right there in front of our noses, the more we choose the path of self-deception in preference to the one that leads to knowledge and enlightenment, the further we descend into this alien delusion, the more time it will take to learn the inner workings of what is surely – beyond any question – just a fascinating natural phenomenon.

We believe that cases such as this, when analysed through the new dawn brought by Dr Meaden's research, *must* sound the death-knell for those extraterrestrial spaceships and the quaint (but now completely unnecessary) 'alien intelligences'. Instead they can be seen to herald a new understanding of the wonderful and dramatic forces that flow around each one of us all the time – forces that are not in outer space but right here within our own environment.

Appendix 1: Commentary by Meteorologists

It is often argued by critics that Terence Meaden stands alone with his theory. Other professionals utterly reject it. Andrews and Delgado have even been quoted as suggesting that the Met Office in Bracknell burst into laughter at the very thought of weather processes creating crop circles.

Yet Meaden is a respected atmospheric physicist, and he has colleagues in TORRO (the Tornado and Storm Research Organization) who appear to support his views. One of these, Dr Derek Elsom of Oxford Polytechnic, has even organized the world's first scientific conference on the crop circles at that venue in June 1990, and specialists from all over the world will present papers.

We decided to include just a sample of some of the scientific comments that have been accumulated since Dr Meaden recently 'went public'. Many we obtained for this book. We were surprised that, with one exception, the support for the novel concept of an ionized vortex was apparently so strong.

But first here is some evidence that not all farmers reject the weather based or natural phenomena solutions for these marks on their land.

FARMERS' COMMENTS

Peter Hopper, agricultural editor of the *Eastern Evening News* (Norwich), 4 March 1989, 'Riddle of the corn rings unravelled by the wind':

> A number of people have seriously believed [that] the phenomenon is the result of UFOs taking off and landing. Such illusions are now being mercilessly destroyed ... A variation on the plain circle is the circle with a ring around it. However, the most impressive of the crop circle systems formed by atmospheric vortices concerns quintuplet sets ...'

Cliff Garner of Husbands Bosworth, Leicestershire (*Harborough Mail*, 20 July 1989):

> I am as mystified as everyone else, but I think all this about the Martians having landed is a standing joke. If I had to advance a theory it would be some kind of wind current with an eddying effect, although why it should have occurred where it did I don't know. The way in which the perfect circle was formed suggests this cause to me but it is really only a guess.

Gloucestershire Echo, 3 August 1989:

Three circles have mysteriously appeared in a field on the outskirts of a quiet Gloucestershire village. The large shapes suddenly appeared overnight in a cornfield on the edge of Woolstone, near Bishop's Cleeve. Baffled residents, some of whom lived within yards of the field, heard and saw nothing to give them any clues to what caused them ... Villager Anne Rawlinson's husband Michael checked his barograph and found it had registered a significant drop in air pressure at around 6 a.m. Said Anne: 'We don't think it was a visit from Martians but then again we can't say what it was.' 'A natural phenomenon – some sort of whirlwind – is our best bet but whatever it was it's very odd to say the least'.

Tim Jackson, deputy head, Department of Agriculture, at a college in Hampshire, in a letter to Paul Fuller dated 1 February 1990:

I am sceptical of descending vortices exploration, at least on its own, perhaps with a little help from well intentioned believers some natural vortex might explain in part. My reasoning is that natural systems are chaotic and would never lead to such regular demarcation of damaged to undamaged areas of crop. The UFO theory is simply ludicrous. The magnetic effects have more possibility as a non-chaotic phenomena, perhaps again combined with hoaxers?

COMMENTARY BY SCIENTISTS

Dr John Snow, Associate Professor of Meteorology, Purdue University, Department of Earth & Atmospheric Sciences, Indiana, USA. Letter dated 27 March 1989, to Paul Fuller:

(1) The phenomenon could well be a hoax. However, I feel the number of circles observed, the large area over which they have been found, and the apparently long period over which they have been observed (8 or more years) make this an unlikely explanation. The apparent ease in which the few known hoaxes were identified also argues against the vast majority of circles being 'manufactured' by some group.

(2) As there is little likelihood that the circles are hoaxes, we must consider them to be evidence of some natural phenomenon. Given what is known about flow around obstacles and the frequent occurrence of circles in apparent association with hills and other topographic features, I support the hypothesis that the circles are produced by some form of vortex resulting from flow over/around a terrain feature. The limited number of eye witness accounts support this hypothesis. It would be very helpful if the circles phenomenon were clearly documented elsewhere in the world. [NB: We hope this book helps to achieve that.]

(3) The details of the process(es) by which the circles are formed, particularly in the cases with the more complex patterns, are very worrisome to me. The points made by Dr Mason (see below) are valid criticisms that need to be answered. I suspect that the response to his criticisms is that to produce the clean cut circles, the atmospheric structure in the lowest 100 meters or so must be 'just right', with a proper layering of stable and unstable air.

(4) My laboratory work with vortices shows that many different flow configurations are possible, yet my 'back-of-the-envelope' scratchings indicate that only simple circular patterns should be formed, albeit of varying diameters.

I do not see how the flow fields known to me can produce the complicated patterns documented by Meaden and others. I suspect that the properties of the crop play an important role in determining what we finally see.

In summary, my current thinking is that some form of vortex phenomenon is at work here, but many (perhaps most?) of the details remain obscure. Continued documentation and systematic field investigations appear warranted. I am waiting to see the response to Meaden's recent article in *Weather*. However, I am coming to believe that sensationalism works against any serious scientific investigation taking place. This is unfortunate since there are several leading researchers in the UK who are experts in the areas of flow around terrain features who might otherwise be sufficiently intrigued to carry out the requisite field studies.

Dr Paul Mason, Head of the Physical Research Section at the Meteorological Office, Bracknell, Berkshire. From a letter to Paul Fuller dated 26 September 1986:

I am a research worker concerned with flow and turbulence in the atmospheric boundary layer: the lowest kilometre or so of the atmosphere. I have also been concerned with vortex generation in flows past surface mounted bodies ... It would be foolish to be too dogmatic about whether or not wind could cause circles but I have a few thoughts ...

I could not rule out (or give much support to) the idea of a very short lived [tornado] being fairly stationary and giving some rough circle of damage.

I am also aware in connection with flows past steep hills (slopes greater than 30 degrees) that the hills can generate trailing vortices and these can give vortex damage on parts of the hill lee slope ... Although there are no theories, it is possible that the orographic flow could interact with the tornado generation to give a preferred and perhaps localised tornado.

I thus feel that rough circles of the type that some observations may refer to could (but may not be, and you note some difficulties) be caused by a localised tornado ... I cannot believe the wind in tornadic structures could be so structured as to give the exact 'ring' (found in some formations). It was just because of this that I offered the view that winds certainly did not cause the effect.

From a letter from Paul Mason dated 24 March 1987 to Jenny Randles responding to an invitation to take part in the free scientific debate on circle formation that BUFORA staged in central London later that year:

Although I remain interested in these circles, and as you note may get involved with the media again ... I am afraid that I find the combination of a BUFORA meeting and the press too risky for a proper resolution to the problem. I must however say that I am impressed with the objective and sincere concern that you and Paul Fuller are giving these phenomena ...

At the moment I am happy to accept that some of these circles may indeed be caused by short lived whirlwinds. In hilly terrain there are also strong reasons to expect such whirlwinds to form in preferred locations. Having said that I do not believe that the circles with outer rings, or very regular satellites, are likely to be of meteorological origin. My reasons are just that we don't have any theories ... and we do have a number of good reasons to expect more chaos than these patterns suggest.

From a letter from Paul Mason to Paul Fuller dated 21 February 1989:

> With regard to Dr Meaden's Vortex Theory I am afraid that as far as the circles are concerned I don't think it is at all relevant ... All observations of such, and other meteorological vortices, are highly turbulent and irregular. I just cannot conceive how any meteorological vortex could have produced the highly ordered patterns seen in the cornfields.
>
> In summary, I do *not* support the meteorological explanation at all. I am sure that my views will delight the ufologists but in spite of some difficulties I think the most probable explanation is the ingenuity of some dedicated hoaxers.

Larry Mulholland, *American Weather Observer*, Vol. 6, No. 10 (October 1989):

> Plasma vortices are spinning parcels of plasma which may be responsible for the mysterious field and rings [*sic*] found in snow, sand and other surface materials all over the world ... I have personally seen such field rings near Davenport, Iowa following an intense thunderstorm. While I was not witness at the actual time of its occurrence, the ring was not produced by a microburst and was not a hoax perpetrated by any Davenporter. The corn was layer-over from a central point with stalks radiating outward in all directions; too strange for any conventional explanation. Was it a plasma vortex?

Dr Tokio Kikuchi, Kochi University, Japan (Dr Kikuchi holds a PhD in Geophysics and teaches physics and fluid dynamics). Translation from Japanese text of the preprints of the Meteorological Society of Japan, October 1989:

> One of the reasons [for the] recent publicity is brought about by UFO maniacs. They consider [the circles to be the] footprints of UFOs. It is out of the question to make such hypotheses, but it is also a fact that our knowledge of sciences cannot explain this phenomenon at present. Since it is probable that some kind of atmospheric vortex is involved, we must study this phenomenon from the point of view of boundary-layer meteorology.

Letter from Dr Kikuchi to Paul Fuller dated 13 October 1989:

> I must say that I [do] not have enough information whether [Dr Meaden's theory] is valid or not ... Of course, this does not mean that Dr Meaden's theory is hopeless. On the contrary, it is highly probable that some kind of atmospheric vortex is relevant [to] this phenomenon. This probability is much higher than ... 'the ozone crisis' or an 'intelligently controlled UFO' ... There are many kinds of atmospheric vortices in various scales and it may not be impossible that a new kind [has been] discovered in England. A recent example is the 'downburst' which we discovered in 1974 by Professor T.T. Fujita of Chicago University. A vortex ring approaching the ground plays an important role in the phenomenon. My present point of view, as a scientist, is that 'whirlwind' should not be ruled out until more scientific data come out.'

Trevor Appleton, weatherman for TV South West, quoted in the Plymouth-based *Evening Herald*, 12 August 1989:

The 'mystery' of the two unexplained circles which appeared in a South Hams field and led to speculation about UFOs has been cleared up by TV weatherman Trevor Appleton ... Mr Appleton, a meteorological consultant, has expressed surprise that the UFO theory was expounded. The explanation generally accepted by meteorologists, he says, is that the circles are caused by mini-whirlwinds.

'The damage occurs when a descending vortex – or whirlwind – strikes the crop from above,' he said. 'The crop is flattened to the ground and simultaneously constrained to follow an outward spiral course from the centre until the flattened area terminates at a sharp perimetry beyond [which] the crop is unharmed.'

Mr Appleton has confirmed to us that these preliminary quotes are attributable to him, although he has not studied the data in any depth.

Professor Y.H. Ohtuski, Waseda University, Japan. Letter to Paul Fuller dated 31 October 1989:

I can agree [with] the [Dr] Meaden's model of the plasma vortex for the circles effect *because we cannot attribute it to any other physical forces*. It is a nonsense to consider intelligent UFO forces.

David Reynolds, researcher into atmospheric vortices, University of Lancaster, and also resident of a 180-acre arable and dairy farm. Letter to Jenny Randles dated 18 November 1989:

It seems that many who dismiss Meaden's theory do so because they only consider it with a fleeting glance; [but] many of the doubts which the sceptics raise *are* answered ... The most unfortunate aspect of the circles effect is the way in which some supposed scientists are pushing totally unsubstantiated claims as to the origins of the circles, in the process blinding the layman by deliberately ignoring Meaden's theory ... I am surprised that Dr Paul Mason, head of the physical research section of the Meteorological Office, seems able to confuse tornadoes, eddy whirlwinds and Meaden's circle creating vortex.

Meaden has clearly pointed out that tornadoes are not the vortices responsible, but a previously unrecognized trailing or eddy vortex that descends like a tornado ... despite the (apparent) increasing complexity of the circles, the scientific facts that have been emerging increasingly support the ionized vortex theory. There are good eye witness reports of circles forming, and of vortices occuring close to places where circles were later found. However, one of the most important advances after establishing the cause of the circles has been the direct correlation of the passage of sea-breeze and weak fronts with circle formation

After scientifically and objectively considering all the theories of circle formation, circle descriptions and associated evidence that all researchers present, I can conclude beyond all reasonable scientific doubt that the circles are caused by ionized vortices.

Professor Heinz Wolff, science consultant to the joint Anglo-Soviet space mission 'JUNO', commenting on the circles during a BBC Bristol local documentary which used some of our early data for this book and which was by far the best TV feature on the phenomenon to date. Responding to a question about Colin Andrews' suggestion that the circles could be the result of an 'outside intelligence':

> It is barely credible. I said I was prepared to be amazed. However, being a scientist I would go first for those things which I could explain using the laws of nature and only at the very last resort grasp at the supernatural or the outside intelligence ...

Responding to a question about Meaden's theory:

> It appeals to the scientist in me and I could imagine that there is something rather like micro weather, and I could even imagine the lack of sympathy of meteorologists who really deal with micro weather therefore perhaps they haven't examined the tiny things; and there are effects with very sharp edges like Ball Lightning, [and] I could imagine that there are other effects which are perhaps allied with it which could make the circles.

When asked to choose between several competing theories:

> I think ... I would still plump for meteorology, weather, some kind of little whirlwind with rather sharp edges, perhaps accompanied by electrical phenomena which descends from the sky.

B.J. Burton, a meteorologist at the Met Office in Bracknell, reviewing Meaden's 1989 book *The Circles Effect and Its Mysteries* for the February 1990 edition of the *Journal of Meteorology*:

> In chapter 3 the author shows that topography seems to play an important part in the location of crop circles. In this context I am minded of some informative explanations on the formation of vortices and waves in the lower atmosphere related to quite modest slopes, when the lower atmosphere is stably stratified, which seems to be a common prerequisite for the crop circle vortices ... My own experience as a meteorologist would support the view that night-time cooling can often lead to the establishment of very strong vertical wind shear in the lower layers of the atmosphere. This coupled with high static stability would create conditions favourable for the formation of waves over even modest hills ...
>   In the final chapter, Dr Meaden discusses alternative explanations for the formation of crop circles ... In the space of some four pages, the author is able to show that these have been 'loosely-phrased suggestions and wild guesses'. My own view, after reading the book, is that the circles effect must have some physical explanation, and that most likely there is some hitherto unrecognised atmospheric phenomenon, which could quite possibly be of the plasma vortex type as envisaged by Dr Meaden ... One is left with the feeling that some vital discovery may be just around the corner.

POSTSCRIPT

1990 is already seeing more debate within the scientific community. Tokio Kikuchi and John Snow have combined forces to produce a paper for the mainstream of the meteorological press entitled 'Speculations on the origin of circular crop damage'. They kindly made an advance copy available to the authors of this book. In this paper they discuss the work of T.T. Fujita, an American researcher who has studied ground traces left by what is called a 'microburst' (for example, from a tornado vortex). These scientists say: 'The discovery of the circles effect and its possible explanation by a swirling vortex ring/microburst provides a new research topic in boundary-layer meteorology ... We suggest that there is a need for quantitative field observations to place the circles effect on a truly scientific ground.'

We agree completely. It is pleasing to be able to end on such an upbeat note – with calls for future research (which may at last legitimize some aspects of ufology and hand over our data to the professionals). Even critics seem to accept this need, as shown by John Simpson of Cambridge University, who reviewed Terence Meaden's work for the meteorological house journal *Weather*. Whilst not being convinced about all aspects of the plasma vortex theory, Simpson said: '... we must hope for some more authenticated measurements in the future ... We should all bear in mind the [quotations from Meaden] ... Science advances by the unexpected happening ... Chance favours the mind that is prepared.'

During 1990 we canvassed the opinions of twenty-nine professional meteorologists and atmospheric physicists. How did the Meaden theory fare? In the latest tally, eleven positively support it, twelve are willing to consider it and only two believe it is untenable.

Appendix 2: The Earliest Known Circle

Prior to summer 1989, the earliest known circles in Meaden's collection included a single one found in a field of beans or oats in Kent (in 1918) and a single circle near Aberystwyth in mid Wales (in 1936).

Of course, if the circles are created by some 'natural' process, accounts of identical markings should be discovered dating back through many centuries. Prior to 1989 this lack of historical data was a major difficulty for those promoting a 'natural' explanation to the mystery. The only solution seemed to be that some factor had recently changed to trigger crop circles by this process.

However, after receiving BUFORA's 1989 status report *Controversy of the Circles*, penned by the present authors, Betty Puttick of St Albans in Hertfordshire wrote to Jenny Randles (11 August 1989) to alert us to the case of the 'Mowing Devil' of 1678. In our opinion, this story must rank as one of the most important discoveries in the entire circles debate (see Plate 15).

THE MOWING DEVIL: OR, STRANGE NEWS OUT OF HARTFORD-SHIRE
Being a True Relation of a Farmer, who Bargaining with a Poor Mower, about the Cutting down Three Half Acres of Oats: upon the Mower's asking too much, the Farmer swore *That the Devil should Mow it rather than He*. And so it fell out, that very Night, the Crop of Oat shew'd as if it had been all of a Flame; but the next Morning appear'd so neatly mow'd by the Devil or some Infernal Spirit, that no Mortal Man was able to do the like.

Also, How the said Oats ly now in the field, and the Owner has not Power to fetch them away.
Licensed, August 22nd 1678

So reads the introduction to the original woodcut reproduced in W.B. Gerish's collected pamphlets *Hertfordshire Folk Lore* (written early in this present century). This was republished in (Mrs Puttick's edition in) 1970 by S.R. Publishers of Wakefield.

In the body of the text there is a flowery account of how a farmer refused to pay what a labourer requested, and then eyewitnesses saw his field lit by a strange fire and before next morning discovered his crop neatly flattened in several precisely defined areas that appear for all the world to be the phenomenon under present discussion.

Jenny obtained assistance from Jennifer Westwood of the British

228

Folklore Society and established that this was indeed a genuine item recognized in their literature. A liaison was struck up, because it was felt possible that other folk-tales might hide material that was relevant to the Meaden Vortex or crop circles.

Indeed, as this remains a likely possibility, we would encourage readers to study the folklore sections of their own county libraries and report to us any findings that might conceivably indicate vortex effects from the distant past.

In the few weeks in which we were discreetly keeping this matter to ourselves whilst checking into its background, another paranormal researcher, Bob Skinner, independently stumbled across the same story whilst looking at old books in Farnham market. He obtained a paper by Lewis Evans, 'Witchcraft in Hertfordshire', which was reproduced in *Bygonne Hertfordshire*, edited by William Andrews. The importance of Skinner's discovery was that Lewis Evans' account was written in 1898 and predated all known examples of cropfield circles, thus excluding any possibility that the woodcut could be a modern fake planted amidst the current controversy.

Of course, this did not exclude the possibility that the *original* woodcut could be a fake perpetrated in 1678 for some unknown reason, or that it was nothing more than a fictitious tale. But if this were so, our hoaxer would have made some astounding guesses about the nature of modern crop circles in his yarn. Consider for example:

1. We know from the woodcut text that the event was supposed to have occurred in an unknown part of Hertfordshire during August 1678 and that the affected field was sown with oats. This fits in very well with the timing of modern crop circles, many of which appear during August, and of course many of our modern circles are being discovered in oat fields.

2. The woodcut claims that the oats were 'so neatly mow'd by the devil or some infernal spirit, that no mortal man was able to do the like'. This suggests strongly that the affected crop was laid down in a particularly neat manner, similar to that currently being observed. This possibility is further enhanced by the schematic illustration on the cover of the woodcut which shows a single circle with what appears to be some kind of spiral pattern and possibly an outer ring.

3. This illustration depicts the devil (complete with horns!) laying down the crop inside the circle. The text claims that '... if the Devil had a mind to shew his dexterity in the art of Husbandry, and scorn'd to move them after the usual manner, he cut them down in round circles, and plac't every straw with the exactness that it would have taken up above an Age for any Man to perform what he did that one night.' Clearly the laying-down of the crop in this manner suggests some kind of banding affect, although no mention is made of layering or a distinctive spiral centre. Furthermore, note that it would take 'an Age' for any man to perform what the devil did on that night. If we assume that the devil was considered to be similar in size to humans, the 1678 circle would certainly be of dimensions similar to those of many of our modern crop circles, based on the original woodcut illustration.

4. The text clearly refers to *'circles'* (plural). This seems to prove that multiple circle patterns appeared in a Hertfordshire field more than 300 years ago.

The 'Mowing Devil' case strongly suggests that crop circles have a long-established history. Nobody *saw* the devil create the circle in 1678, apparently just some strange light effects above the field – and in daylight the circles were suddenly present, exactly what seems to be happening all over the world three centuries later.

Today we are interpreting these same circumstances as evidence of an 'unknown intelligence'. In that distant era of magic and superstition the 'aliens' were replaced in the popular imagination by the 'devil'. In common with other anomalous events, the woodcut not only placed the tale in a religious context but may have confabulated the account in order to teach mortal man some spiritual lessons.

The woodcut also makes it clear that the event occurred less than three weeks before publication and that the whole county was agog with the news. Of course, in the seventeenth century there were no aeroplanes or balloons, so crop circles would have been discovered only from the ground or nearby hills. There was also no instant media to rapidly spread the news, and so it is quite possible that earlier reports were simply not remembered.

If crop circles have been appearing for more than three centuries, it seems difficult to reconcile that fact with the claim that they are being created as 'warnings' by an 'intelligence'. On the other hand, it is substantial evidence in support of the claim we have made throughout this book that crop circles are the product of a natural process that is a part of nature and has *always* occurred but which has only recently become recognized as a mystery and given needless supernatural connotations.

Appendix 3: The 1990 Season

As we go to press the 1990 crop circle season is underway. Because of the publicity of 1989 and a continual effort by the BBC TV show Daytime Live thousands of people all over Britain have been looking out for new circles. This is the most intensive scrutiny ever given to the subject.

Inevitably, this has brought remarkable results. Circles appeared earlier than ever before – in the first few days of May – and by the end of that month fifty new examples were already on record.

These include the largest circle yet found – sixty metres in diameter – and more 'new' types. The most spectacular is a triple-ringed circle with four satellites in quintuplet formation. There has also been discovered a curious dumb-bell shape where a bar connects two circles side by side in one field.

Most cases have this time centred on Wiltshire, with a few in Hampshire. But reports of circles further afield are coming in as expected. Jenny Randles investigated one reported circle in winter wheat which was visible from the very busy M62 motorway near Burtonwood in Cheshire. Discussions with the farmers revealed this was not a crop circle (at least in any conventional sense) and may have another type of explanation. All the crop in the centre had totally vanished, leaving weeds surrounded by normal ripening wheat.

Our catalogue of overseas cases has also increased dramatically with many new spectacular examples from the USA and Australia coming under investigation during 1989–90. It is now quite certain that this is a global phenomenon whose true extent has simply been overlooked in the past.

However, we do believe that the new varieties and artificial nature of some of the May 1990 circles strongly supports our contention that the basic vortex-produced phenomenon is being severely contaminated by widespread hoaxing, especially in Wessex. Just as we predicted, new patterns and an escalation in the total number of circles is occurring alongside the increased opportunities for media attention.

We do not believe that this is just coincidence: the media must now face up to its responsibility and help to destroy the myth of alien circles.

Appendix 4: A Crop Circle Code

Crop circles are wonderful things to look at and it is always tempting to go right inside if you chance upon a fine example out in the field.

However, this book is not written to encourage either vandalism or thoughtlessness. Please remember that circles very often appear on private land and that the crop in which they form is the product of a considerable investment of time and money by the farmer in question.

We would urge you to keep a watch out for new circles and report them to us, care of Robert Hale Limited, Clerkenwell House, 45–7 Clerkenwell Green, London EC1R 0HT.

We would also suggest that you try to find a high vantage-point to get some photographs of the site as soon as possible. But please follow the crop circle code:

1. Never enter a field to get a closer view without first finding out who owns it and getting their full permission.
2. Always check with the landowner as soon as possible, because they may want to know of the circle or they may have a simple explanation for it.
3. If you do have permission to enter a field containing a circle never do so recklessly. Follow the tramlines through the crop and do not wander around the centre of the circle itself, causing needless damage to the evidence. Take photographs and measurements if you can, but be very careful.

Remember that crop circles are a natural part of our landscape and should be treated with the same respect that you would expect any visitor to accord to your private property.

Glossary

BUFORA	British UFO Research Association
CISU	Italian Centre for UFO Study
CPR	Circles Phenomenon Research (group)
CUFOS	Center for UFO Studies (USA)
DSTI	Department of Scientific and Technical Intelligence
FUFOR	Federated UFO Research
FSR	*Flying Saucer Review* (magazine)
HAPI	Hinckley Aerial Phenomena Investigations
IFO	Identified Flying Object
MoD	Ministry of Defence
MUFON	Mutual UFO Network (USA)
SIUFOP	Society for the Investigation of UFO Phenomena
TORRO	Tornado and Storm Research Organization
UAP	Unidentified Atmospheric Phenomena
UFO	Unidentified Flying Object

Afterword

The circles effect is the most astonishing observational discovery in the geophysical science to have come to the attention of scientists and the public in recent years. It is all the more remarkable because it is a phenomenon which takes place 'in our own backyard' – that is to say, in the fields of Britain's green and pleasant land, with a distinct and peculiar propensity for the wavy landscape of Wessex – and yet it has been overlooked for so long.

Not only are the circles delightful to gaze upon and challenging to think about, but the spinning balls of air and light which accompany them are an additional wonder of the atmosphere in their own right. Research proceeds apace, and fresh discoveries are appearing in quick succession. We may be sure that for years to come the circles and their creator-vortices will provide a testing and exciting forum of debate for atmospheric experimentalists and theoreticians alike. And all the while the pioneer researchers are being watched by an inquisitive public thirsty for news as the story unfolds.

Already we know enough to declare that the results of these findings are having far-reaching consequences in areas of research well beyond the one in which it began. One of these is the UFO problem for it turns out that within the UFO movement a genuine physical effect, chiefly in the form of low-level lights and ground traces, has been the object of scrutiny for a long time. This is the vortex phenomenon which at night can be seen by the action of its electromagnetic properties.

UFO research is an area mostly ignored by busy scientists because ufology unwillingly bears the stamp of being the domain of cranks, mystics, dreamers and ET hopefuls, with the result that the patient work of seriously motivated researchers within the movement gets to be insufficiently well projected. Instead, the good work is all too often swamped by the publicity so readily provided by the media to the eccentrics, the charlatans, the hoaxers and the sci-fi writers whose primary aim is to seek a limited renown, high book sales, or both.

But there *are* serious workers, and Jenny Randles and Paul Fuller are such individuals. They approach the UFO problem intelligently, in the searching way that detectives would. Their aim is to get at the truth by applying real science and the latest theories instead of flirting with the pseudo-scientific extravaganzas of the mythmakers. The result is an understanding of a greater number of mysteries from the collections of the world's UFO societies than would have been envisaged even a year ago, a task which has been aided by the publication of the book *The Circles Effect and Its Mysteries*. Whereas the unscrupulous heap one mystery upon another in order to confuse the credulous and distance themselves and the reader from the solution for the sake of high-volume sales, Jenny Randles and Paul Fuller pursue answers the rational way, and it is this which makes the book commendable. Although I cannot say that I agree with everything in it, it is nonetheless an honest attempt to deal with the truth of the alien dream – an effort which culminates by exposing the reality of the delusion.

It is reassuring to know that the solution to the circles effect, via the electrified vortex, is at the same time the answer to so many other long-standing puzzles. What is more, I can confidently predict that the circles have many surprises yet in store for us.

Dr Terence Meaden
Wiltshire, February 1990

References

If you wish to contact the authors to report any circles or to offer your comments, please write to *CIRCLES*, care of Robert Hale Limited, Clerkenwell House, 45–7 Clerkenwell Green, London EC1R 0HT. (An SAE is appreciated if you would like a reply).

The following books are alluded too frequently in our text and are available for your consideration, offering very different perspectives:

Andrews, C., and Delgado, P., *Circular Evidence* (Bloomsbury, 1989)

Meaden, G.T., *The Circles Effect and Its Mysteries* (Artetch/TORRO, 1989)

Fuller, P., and Randles, J., *Controversy of the Circles* (BUFORA, 1989)

The following magazines are also cited in various references, and full details of their availability are as follows:

Fate, 170 Future Way, Marion, Ohio 43305, USA

Fortean Times, 96 Mansfield Road, London NW3 2HX

Flying Saucer Review (FSR), Snodland, Kent ME6 5HJ

International UFO Reporter (IUR), 2457 W. Peterson, Chicago, Illinois 60659, USA

Journal of Meteorology, 54 Frome Road, Bradford-on-Avon, BA15 1LD

Magonia, 5 James Terrace, London SW14 8HB

MUFON Journal, 103 Oldtowne Road, Seguin, Texas 78155, USA

Northern UFO News, 37 Heathbank Road, Stockport SK3 0UP

UFO Brigantia, 84 Elland Road, Brighouse HD6 2QR

UFO Times, 103 Hove Avenue, London E17 7NG

A unique joint subscription at reduced price is offered by *UFO Brigantia* and *Northern UFO News* (via either address).

Probe Report and *The Unexplained* are no longer in print. Copies of *Probe* may be available via the BUFORA address below, and most of the material in the part-work *The Unexplained* has been republished (often more than once) in assorted Orbis hardcover and softcover books concerning the paranormal which are widely available.

Organizations that you may wish to contact for further information are:

TORRO (Tornado and Storm Research Organisation, address as for *Journal of Meteorology*.

The J. Allen Hynek Center for UFO Studies, address as for IUR (publisher of the traces catalogue by Ted Phillips and report on the Ohio helicopter case by Jennie Zeidmann)

MUFON (Mutual UFO Network – address as for the *MUFON* Journal.

In Australia you will find of great value the files and publications of UFORA (UFO Research Australia), PO Box 229, Prospect, Western Australia 5082.

BUFORA (British UFO Research Association)
Both authors are senior members of this organization, which investigates and researches UFOs in a serious manner and maintains extensive data files. BUFORA has many specialist publications in addition to *Mystery of the Circles* (1986) and *Controversy of the Circles* (1989). Several (for example, the vehicle interference report, *Fire in the Sky* and the annual survey of world ufology, *UFO World '89* etc.) are featured in the references below. BUFORA also publishes *UFO Times*. Details of the group are available (please send a large SAE for info pack) from 16 South Way, Burgess Hill, RH15 9ST.
For a complete up-do-date report on circles and other UFO activity, phone BUFORA's 'UFO call' service, operated in conjunction with British Telecom (at 25p per minute off peak anywhere in the UK): 0898 – 12 18 86.

REFERENCES FROM TEXT
All books and magazines have been published in the UK, except where another country of origin is given.
FSR   *Flying Saucer Review*
IUR   *International UFO Reporter*
J Met   *Journal of Meteorology*

Introduction: An Alien Delusion
1. Andrews, C., and Delgado, P., *Circular Evidence* (Bloomsbury, 1989), p. 189
2. Ibid., p. 172
3. Ibid., p. 168
4. *FSR*, Vol. 32, No.6 (November 1987)

1   The Arrival of the Circles
1. Andrews and Delgado, op.cit., pp. 20–21
2. See books by Janet and Colin Bord on British monuments and landscape.
3. Shuttlewood, A., *The Warminster Mystery* (Spearman, 1967)
4. *Probe Report*, Vol.1, No.2 (1980)
5. *J Met*, Vol.6, No.57 (March 1981)
6. *Probe Report*, Vol.2, No.3 (1981)
7. *FSR*, Vol.27, No.5 (1982)
8. Ibid., Vol.27, No.6 (1982)
9. *J Met*, Vol.8, No.75 (January 1983)
10. *Probe Report*, Vol.3, No.2 (1982)
11. *FSR*, Vol.29, No.1 (1983)
12. *Northern UFO News*, No.103 (1983)

2   The Intergalactic Cavalry
1. Randles, J. and Warrington, P., *Science and the UFOs* (Blackwell, 1986), pp.61–6

2. Paper by Jean Velasco in MUFON conference proceedings, 1987
3. Keyhoe, D., *Flying Saucers are Real* (Fawcett, US, 1950)
4. See for instance Adamski, G., *Inside the Spaceships* (Abelard-Schuman, 1955)
5. Randles, J., *Abduction* (Hale, 1988; Headline, 1989; Inner Light, US, 1989)
   6. Hopkins, B., *Missing Time* (Merak, US, 1982); *Intruders* (Random House, US, 1987; Corgi, UK, 1988)
7. Klass, P., *UFO Abductions: A Dangerous Game* (Prometheus Books, US, 1988)
8. *FSR*, Vol.33, No.2 (1988)
9. *UFO Brigantia*, November 1989
10. For detailed discussion of this topic see Randles, J., *UFO Reality* (Hale, 1983)

3 The Nature of the Circles
1. Andrews, C., and Delgado, P., op. cit., p.125
2. Ibid., pp. 172–3

4 The Contenders
1. For a complete discussion of this related topic we recommend D.N. Riley, *Aerial Archaeology in Britain* (Shire Archaeology, 1982)
2. *Today*, 6 July 1989
3. *FSR*, Vol.34, No.2 (June 1989)
4. Ibid., Vol.32, No.1 (1987)

5 The Hoax Theory
1. See report by D. Simpson in *Magonia*, March 1976
2. *FSR*, Vol.16, No.4 (1970)
3. Ibid., Vol.16, No.6 (1970)

6 'Unknown Forces'
1. Andrews, C., and Delgado, P., op. cit., p.166
2. Good, Timothy, *The UFO Report 1990* (Sidgwick & Jackson, 1989)
3. Andrews, C., and Delgado, P., op. cit., p.167
4. Ibid., p.155
5. Ibid., p.156
6. Ibid., p.169
7. Ibid., p.167
8. Ibid., p.92
9. Ibid., p.92
10. Ibid., p.104
11. *FSR*, Vol.33, No.2 (June 1988)
12. Ibid., Vol.33, No.3 (September 1988), pp.7–13
13. Andrews, C., and Delgado, P., op. cit., p.188; Kinder, Gary, *Light Years* (Atlantic Monthly Press, 1987)
14. Brookesmith, Peter, *The Alien World* (Orbis, 1984), pp.41–53
15. Andrews, C., and Delgado, P., op. cit., p.35
16. Ibid., p.164 for example
17. Ibid., p.140

18. Ibid., p.168
19. Andrews, C., and Delgado, P., op. cit., pp.73 and 82 and Plate 39

7   *The Plasma-Vortex Theory*
1. *J Met*, Vol.10, No.97 (March 1985)
2. *Now!*, 29 August 1980
3. Meaden, Terence, *The Circles Effect and its Mysteries*, pp.27–8
4. *J Met*, Vol.10, No.97 (1990)
5. Ibid., Vol.13, No.132 (October 1988)
6. Wingfield, G., in *UFO Report 1990*, ed. Good, T. (Sidwick & Jackson, 1989), p.58
7. *J Met*, Vol.14, No.144 (December 1989)
8. *The Unexplained*, No.132 (1983)
9. Rowe, M., 'Britain's greatest tornadoes and tornado outbreaks', *J Met*, Vol.10, No.100 (June 1985)
10. Letter to Dr Terence Meaden, 29 August 1988
11. Further letter to Dr Terence Meaden, 3 November 1988
12. *J Met*, Vol.15, No.146 (1990)
13. Corliss, W., *Tornadoes, Dark Days, Anomalous Precipitation and Related Weather Phenomena* (Sourcebook Project, US, 1983), p.173
14. Holford, I., *Guinness Book of Weather Facts and Feats* (1977), p.193
15. Photograph in *J Met*, Vol.13, No.132 (October 1988)
16. Corliss, op. cit., p.169
17. Ibid., p.167
18. Ibid., p.155
19. Meaden, T., op. cit., p.48
20. Corliss, op. cit., p.170

8   *Assessing the Vortex Theory*
1. Andrews and Delgado, op. cit., p.125
2. *Ley Hunter*, 109, 1989
3. Cook, N.J., Coulson, B.H., and McKay, H., 'Wind conditions around the rock of Gibraltar', *Journal of Industrial Aerodynamics*, Vol.2 No.4 (1978)
4. Genkins, G.I., Mason, P.J., Moores, W.H.M and Sykes, R.I., 'Measurements of the flow structure around Ailsa Craig; a steep three-dimensional isolated hill', *Quarterly Journal of Royal Meteorological Society*, Vol.107 (1981)
5. Andrews and Delgado, op. cit., p.172
6. Ibid., p.173
7. *Weather*, Vol.44 (January 1989), pp.2–10
8. *UFO Report 1990*, op. cit., p.59
9. Meaden, T., op. cit., pp. 15–16
10. Andrews and Delgado, op. cit., p.55
11. Fuller, P., 'The secret of the circles', *Exploring the Supernatural* (April and May 1987)

9   *A Vortex Case Book*
1. *Evening News*, London, 18 July 1967
2. Randles, J., and Warrington, P., op. cit., pp.105–8

3. *Northern UFO News*, No.113 (1985)
4. *Northern UFO News*, No.112 (1985)
5. *Sunday Express*, London, 8 July 1984
6. Morell, R., 'Study of angel hair', *UFO Research Review* (Nottingham)
7. Michel, A., *The Truth about Flying Saucers* (Hale, 1957)
8. Many such reports can be found in the pages of *Fortean Times*
9. Report by M. Sampson and BASE in *Northern UFO News*, No.129 (1988)
10. Shoemaker, M., 'The Truth about the magnetic cloud', *Fortean Times*, No.48 (1987)
11. Randles, J., *The Oz Factor, The Unexplained*, No.156 (1983)
12. Randles, J., 'Through the glass darkly', *The Unexplained*, No.82 (1982)
13. Randles, J., *Abduction* (see Chapter 6, No.11), pp.99, 104
14. *Northern UFO News*, No.31 (1976)
15. *FSR* Vol.21, No.5 (1976)
16. Randles, J., and Warrington, P., op. cit., pp.117–27
17. *FSR*, Vol.23, No.4 (1977); Vol.23, No.6 (1978; Vol.26, No.2 (1980)
18. *BUFORA Journal*, Vol.6, No.4 (1977)
19. Ibid., Vol.24, No.2 (1978)
20. Report from R. Hall, *BUFORA Journal*, Vol.6, No.6 (1978)
21. Andrews and Delgado, op. cit., p.133
22. *J Met*, Vol.14, No.143 (November 1989)
23. See full account in the now declassified 'Project Blue Book' files in the national archives in Washington DC, summarized by J. Ruppelt in *The Report on UFOs* (Ace Books, US, 1956). For more information see *The UFO Encylopedia*, ed. Story, R. (NEL, 1978)
24. Michel, A., *Flying Saucers and the Straight Line Mystery* (Criterion Books, US, 1958)
25. Philips, T., J. Allen Hynek Center Traces Catalogue (CUFOS files)
26. Ibid., (NICAP files)
27. Ibid., (Fate files)
28. Ibid., (Brian Cannon and H.H. McKay files)
29. *FSR*, Vol.16, No.1 (1970)
30. Personal investigation by T. Philips of CUFOS
31. Roberts, W.K., in *FSR Case Histories 7* (1971)
32. Philips, T., op. cit., (CUFOS files)
33. Ibid.

10   What UFOs Really Are

1. Burrows, G., 'Notes on UFOs', *BUFORA Journal*, Vol.4, No.3 (1974)
2. Burrows, G., 'UFOs and NIFOs', *BUFORA Journal*, Vol.4, No.7 (1975)
3. Wright, D., 'UFO events and the Michigan weather', *MUFON Journal*, No.228 (April 1987)
4. Noyes, R., *A Secret Property* (Quartet Books, 1985)
5. Noyes cites M.D., Altschuler, E. Huldner and L.L. House, 'Is ball lightning a nuclear phenomenon?' *Nature*, No.228 (1970)

6. Noyes, R. 'Paradoxical energy levels', *MUFON Journal*, No.242 (June 1988)
7. Davies. P., 'Great balls of fire', *New Scientist*, 24–31 December 1987
8. Klass, P., *UFOs Identified* (Random House, US, 1968)
9. *FSR*, Vol.14, No.4 (1968)
10. Persinger, M. and Lafreniere, G., *Space-Time Transients and Unusual Events* (Nelson-Hall, US, 1977)
11. Finkelstein, D. and Powell, J., 'Earthquake lightning', *Nature*, No.228 (1970)
12. Devereux, P., *Earthlights* (Turnstone Press, 1982)
13. Tributsch, H., *When the Snakes Awake* (MIT Press, 1982)
14. Randles, J., *The Pennine UFO Mystery* (Grafton, 1983)
15. Devereux, P., *The Earthlights Revelation* (Blandford, 1989)
16. Randles, J., *Mind Monsters* (Aquarian Press, 1990)
17. Persinger, M., 'Neuropsychological aspects of the visitor experience', *MUFON Journal*, No.247 (November 1988)
18. A detailed summary of this research is carried in J. Randles' *Abduction*, op. cit.
19. Randles, J., *Sixth Sense* (Hale, UK, 1987; Salem House, US, 1987)
20. Orbiter (43 Harrison Street, Reading, USA, MA 01867, November 1989)
21. Ring, K., *Life at Death* (Coward, McCann & Geoghagen, US, 1980)
22. Ring, K., 'Toward an imaginal interpretation of "UFO abductions"', *MUFON Journal*, No.253 (May 1989)

11 The Death of the UFO

1. Randles, J., *UFO Reality*, op. cit., pp.44–9
2. Many cases and ionization-effect reports from the area in J. Randles, *Pennine UFO Mystery*, op. cit.
3. Project Hessdalen (Box 14, Duken, Norway N-3133)
4. Rutledge, H., *Project Identification* (Prentice-Hall, US, 1981)
5. Devereux, P., *The Earthlights Revelation*, op. cit.
6. *Northern UFO News*, No.137 (1989)
7. Report by K. Phillips, *Northern UFO News*, No.51 (1978)
8. *Northern UFO News*, No.124 (1987)
9. Randles, J., *Fire in the Sky* (BUFORA, 1989)
10. Randles, J., *UFO Reality*, op. cit., pp.39–42
11. Randles, J., and Warrington, P., *UFOs: A British Viewpoint* (Hale, 1979), p.208
12. Shuttlewood, A., *UFO Magic in Motion* (Sphere, 1979), pp.40–43
13. Report by J. Taylor and HAPI in *Northern UFO News*, No.53 (1978)
14. Report by Vasterbergslagens UFO in *UFO World '89* ed. J. Randles (BUFORA)
15. Keatman's version can be found in *FSR*, Vol.25, No.5 (1980)
16. The FUFOR version is in *BUFORA Journal*, Vol.8, No.5 (1979)
17. *BUFORA Journal*, Vol.4, No.1 (1973)
18. Ibid., Vol.3, No.12 (1973)
19. *IUR*, Vol.11, No.6 (1986)
20. More cases and clues can be found in J. Randles, *Mind Monsters*, op. cit.

21. See J. Randles and P. Warrington, *Science and the UFOs* (cover) and J. Randles, *UFO Conspiracy*, op. cit.
22. Hynek, J. Allen, *The UFO Experience* (Henry Regnery, US, 1972; Corgi, UK, 1973)
23. Randles, J., and Warrington, P., *UFOs: A British Viewpoint*, op. cit.
24. BUFORA vehicle-interference case catalogue, No.222 (UFOIC files)
25. Zeidmann, J., *The Ohio Helicopter Case History* (CUFOS, 1981). See also J. Randles, *UFO Conspiracy*, op. cit., pp.102–5
26. Gordon, S., in *MUFON Journal*, No.200 (December 1984)
27. Extensive files on this case courtesy of UFORA (especially Basterfield, K., Godic, V. and P., and W. Chalker)
28. Case file courtesy of B. Salgstron
29. Report by S. Gordon and L. Varnicle of PASU in *MUFON Journal*, No.253 (May 1989)
30. Catalogue edited by M. Rodeghier available from J. Allen Hynek Center for UFO Studies (CUFOS), and another, edited by G. Falla from BUFORA. They contain much that complements one another.
31. Cases compiled by J. Vallee for his study of the wave. See a report in *The Humanoids*, ed. C. Bowen (Henry Regnery, US, 1974; Futura, UK, 1975)
32. BUFORA catalogue, op. cit., Case 249 (C. and L. Lorenzen files)
33. *FSR*, Vol.13, No.6 (1968)
34. Detailed report from T.R. Dutton in BUFORA catalogue, op. cit.
35. Devereux, P., *The Earthlights Revelation*, op. cit., pp.87–116 (Section written by Clarke, D., and Roberts, A.)
36. Randles, J., and Warrington, P., *UFOs: A British Viewpoint*, op. cit., p.78
37. BUFORA catalogue, op. cit., Case 154 (APRO files)
38. *FSR*, Vol.22, No.1, (1976)
39. Ibid., Vol.23, No.2 (1977)
40. Ibid., Vol.21, No.5 (1975)
41. For a UK perspective see J. Randles, *Abduction*, op. cit., and a US overview, *Intruders*, op. cit.
42. Report by A. Collins and B. King in *FSR*, Vol.23, No.6, and Vol.24, No.1 (1978)
43. Again J. Randles, *Abduction*, op. cit., has many similar cases worldwide
44. For an updated report on this case see Chapter 5 of P. Hough and J. Randles, *Death by Supernatural Causes?* (Grafton, 1988)

Index